GW01607257

Janez Bogataj

Handicrafts
of Slovenia

International Exhibition
Catalogue

Janez Bogataj

Handicrafts of Slovenia

International Exhibition

Catalogue

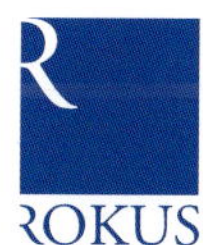

JANEZ BOGATAJ

Handicrafts

OF SLOVENIA

International Exhibition
Catalogue

Text
PROF. DR. JANEZ BOGATAJ
•
Translation
WAYNE TUTTLE
EVA KRIŽNAR
•
Design
ŽARE KERIN, KOMPAS DESIGN, D. D.
•
Photography
JANEZ PUKŠIČ
•
Editor
KATARINA KLEINDIENST
•
Litography
DANILO FRLEŽ, STUDIO ROKUS
•
Typeset
INTER MARKETING, D. O. O.
•
Printed by
GORENJSKI TISK, D. D.
•
First edition
1000 COPIES, LJUBLJANA, FEBRUARY 2000
•

Sponsored by the Ministry of Culture of the Republic of Slovenia

Http://www.mojstrovine.com

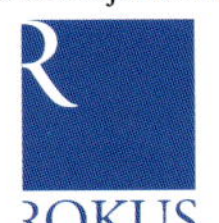

ROKUS
Rokus Publishing House Ltd.
Studenec 2 a, Grad Fužine, 1260 Ljubljana
Phone: +386 61 140 97 99, Fax: +386 61 140 02 77
Http://www.rokus.com, e-mail: rokus@rokus.com

CIP – Kataložni zapis o publikaciji
Narodna in univerzitetna knjižnica, Ljubljana

745/749(497.4)“19”
929:745/749(497.4)(058.7)
050.87(497.4):745/749

BOGATAJ, Janez, 1947 –
Handicrafts of Slovenia : international exhibition : catalogue / [text] Janez Bogataj ; [photography Janez Pukšič ; translation Wayne Tuttle, Eva Križnar]. – 1st ed. – Ljubljana : Rokus, 2000

Prevod dela : Mojstrovine Slovenije : mednarodna razstava

ISBN 961-209-151-X

105953280

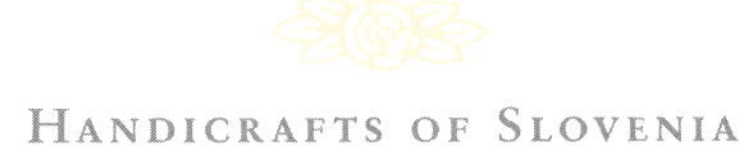

Handicrafts of Slovenia – at the junction of Europe's Alpine, Pannonian, and Mediterranean worlds

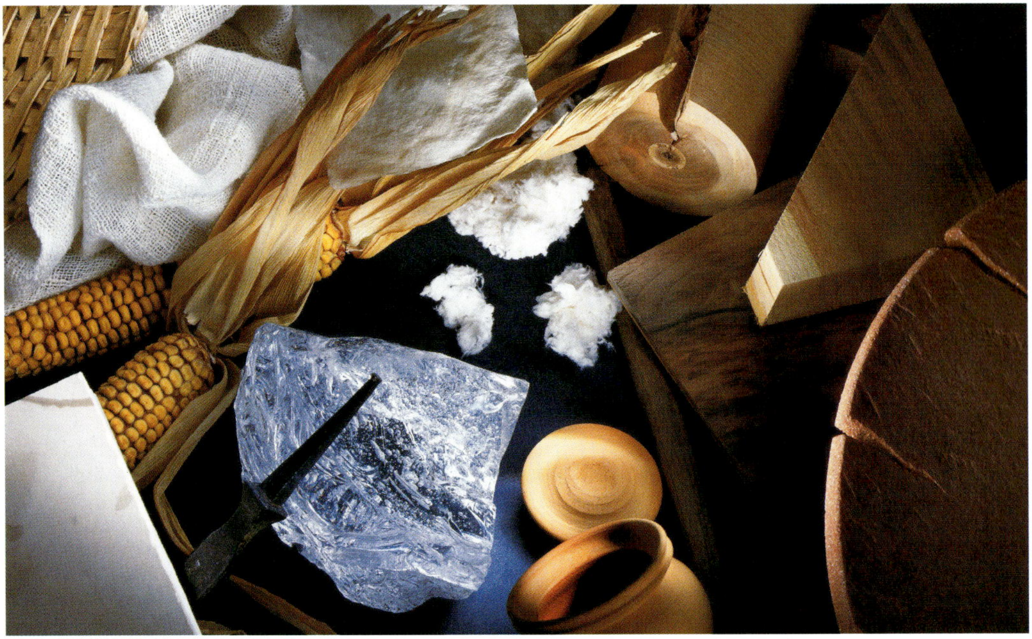

Slovenia is among the countries that contributed significantly to changes in the world at the end of the 20th century. With independence from the multicultural and most certainly very diverse Yugoslav federation, Slovenia's centuries- or even millennium-old bond with Central or more precisely Southeastern Europe is again coming to the fore. This bond was formed through various components of everyday life and holiday customs, diverse types of economic endeavour, and contacts on the material, social, and spiritual levels. Slovenia's territory and population developed within a variety of social systems, and its identity developed as a synthesis of very diverse cultures and lifestyles. During the period of Slovene enlightenment, the poet and journalist Valentin Vodnik (1758–1819) described Slovenia–then, of course, a part of the Hapsburg Austrian Empire–as a "RING OF EUROPE." With this interesting metaphor, which today could easily have all the qualities of an advertising slogan, he pointed out the fundamental characteristic of our identity, as much from the perspective of our heritage as from the perspective of our modern way of life or lifestyle. Our identity lies in basic features that originate in the very geographical position of Slovenia, which like a ring completely encircles the junction of Europe's Alpine, Pannonian, and Mediterranean worlds. This ring encompasses not only a unique and extremely diverse natural environment but also very diverse European cultures and lifestyles as well as new influences from the Balkans experienced over more than seventy years of formal contact in the framework of the former Yugoslavia.

Of course, the structure of the culture and lifestyles of the population within this "Ring of Europe" is not simply the sum of the three large European cultural and geographical worlds that meet in Slovenia but rather their unique synthesis. This synthesis created not only variety and diversity but above all a creative richness demonstrated on various levels and in various relationships, as much from the viewpoint of historical development as from the modern point of view. This richness and diversity is illustrated by the modern masterpieces of Slovene craftsmen, representatives of those activities we call "handicrafts" or "applied arts." Although today these activities have a modern creative image and framework, they nevertheless derive in large measure from the more or less distant roots of our heritage and continue their historical mission, primarily the objectification of contacts between people, that is, the bonds of communication based on creativity in the framework of individual fields and activities. Herein lies the basis of their present and future mission.

Humankind entered the new millennium well aware of the rapid leaps in technological and universal development. The temporal dimension of our everyday life and holiday customs, our way of life in general, has succumbed to this reality as well. Although essentially positive in meaning, the word "development," which implies progress, has acquired increasingly negative connotations in the modern world. In the majority of cases, every development is initially genuinely useful and progressive, but the wake spreading like a fan from its cutting edge can bring numerous negative phenomena, activities, influences, and revelations. The triangular symbiosis between man, culture, and the environment, the human involvement in the relationship between the natural and cultural environments, is thus often destroyed.

On the other hand, gaining increasing significance today is a parallel process of development through which man and nature cooperate productively and benefit mutually. Through such cooperation, new masterpieces appear that can be a link with historical memory, with our heritage, but can also be completely new forms of creativity. Even in the latter case, however, we cannot ignore the links to our heritage that may be expressed in newly-considered forms and

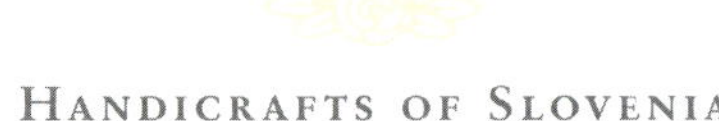

meanings and in the development of expertise in the original materials, techniques, and work rhythms validated countless times in the past. Thus we have before us genuinely challenging examples of technique, content, function, esthetics, and more. They represent an inexhaustible source on which to build and above all to search for new creative paths and solutions. We are speaking of modern creativity but with an historical dimension.

This interweaving of heritage and modern creativity is also one of the fundamental conditions for preserving the identity of individual places, countries, and environments. With the start of the new millennium, both Europe and the world as a whole face the issue of preserving cultural differences on national, regional, and local levels, that is, how to preserve individual identities. Preservation alone, however, is not enough or is at most a partial solution. We must think and work primarily toward the creation of such elements and cultural forms that in their symbiosis of functionality and esthetics will ensure the survival of permanent typical features, characteristics, specialties, and differences of individual environments and the world as a whole. This is one of the fundamental messages inherent in the modern creative handicraft endeavours in Slovenia presented by this touring exhibition.

The touring **HANDICRAFTS OF SLOVENIA** exhibition is part of a comprehensive project begun by the publisher Založba Rokus in 1999 with the simultaneous publication of an extensive monograph on Slovene handicrafts in Slovene, English, French, Italian, and German. The exhibition is therefore a visual presentation of the book's important message. The television series published on videocassettes in parallel with the book and the exhibition has a similar function. Slovenia and its masters of handicraft creativity not only wish to participate in fostering greater knowledge and promotion of this young European country and its rich thousand-year-old heritage but also to present a colourful palette of the most diverse cultural, technological, creative, and communication elements that can enrich common world endeavours toward higher quality human life.

A small gem of folk philosophy, an old Slovene proverb says, **"IT IS NOT THE FLOUR BUT THE HAND THAT MAKES THE BREAD."** Naturally, this beautiful thought has a deeper metaphorical meaning, pointing out that even in the most modern developed world, the human hand is still a significant alternative to machines and robots manufacturing items in great numbers through mass production. The hand allows man to continue the oldest and most elemental contact with materials, that is, with the natural environment of which he is a part. Thus it brings a new dimension of quality into his life, not only through the use of basic materials but also through the special messages conveyed and inherent in handicrafts that enrich our everyday economic, social, and spiritual endeavours.

Handicrafts of Slovenia

The rich diversity of contemporary Slovene handicrafts is the consequence of historical development and particularly of Slovenia's location at the junction of Europe's Alpine, Pannonian, and Mediterranean worlds. Their great variety and simultaneously recognizable individuality are also linked to the wide range of basic materials available, one of the fundamental conditions for the appearance, development, existence, and change of individual branches of handicrafts.

For centuries, the basic material for handicrafts in Slovenia's alpine world has been wood. Stone is native to the Mediterranean or Primorska region of Slovenia and offers its most discernible creative manuscript. This is especially true of the unique area called Kras, known for its unique natural phenomena and the origin of the word "karst," which denotes the natural wonders found here in all the major world languages. Slovenia's Pannonian region employed still other natural materials such as wheat straw, cornhusks, natural flax fibers, and quality clays, the basis of pottery and ceramic products. Along with these materials typical of inherited and modern forms of creativity in all the regions of this "RING OF EUROPE," Slovenia and its master craftsmen offer many other masterpieces made from reed and wicker, beeswax, wrought iron and other metals, glass, handmade paper, tanned leather, and numerous other natural materials.

The exhibition presents Slovene handicraft masterpieces according to the individual materials used. Slovenia's foremost artisans were selected according to professional criteria as the best of the best. The majority continue a long tradition of handicraft skills, renewing or building on historical memory. While some handicrafts reach back to prehistoric times, others are a consequence or a reflection of mercantile endeavours in the framework of the Austro-Hungarian monarchy. In this period, true handicraft regions developed as opposed to individual production, areas and places known for their specific activities and branches that we can trace to the present day. A third group includes typical representatives of the newest creative searches or the continuation of a heritage model in their technology, if only in the conceptual, content, or functional sense.

With its many-faceted alternativeness, the handicraft heritage and its contemporary forms provocatively remind us of values that frequently lie unnoticed on our doorsteps. We pass them with eyes closed and do not see them, let alone taking time to discover and learn about them and enrich ourselves with the recognition that they can completely change everything that shapes the quality of our modern life, in Slovenia or anywhere else in the world.

Prof. Janez Bogataj, Ph.D.

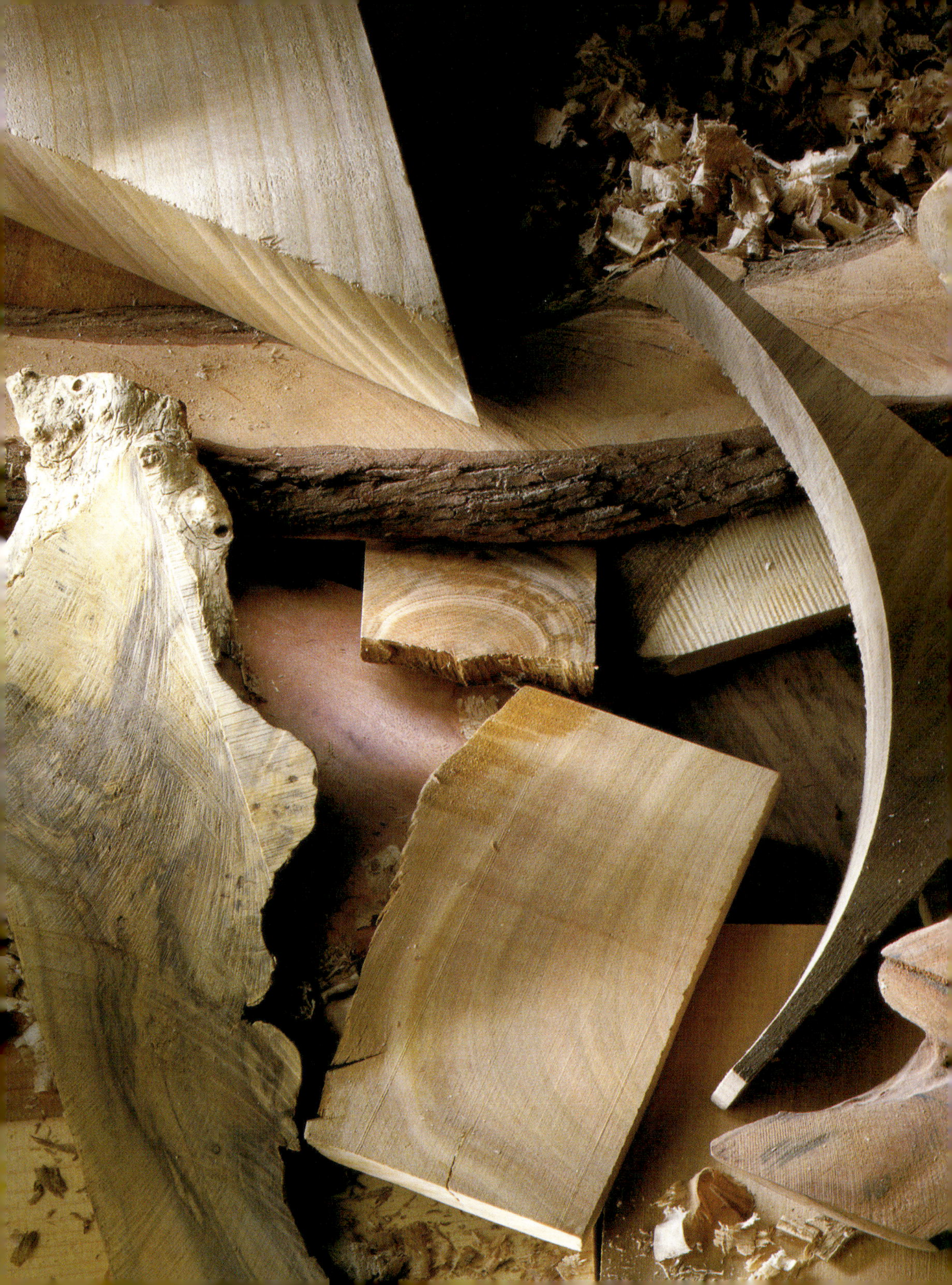

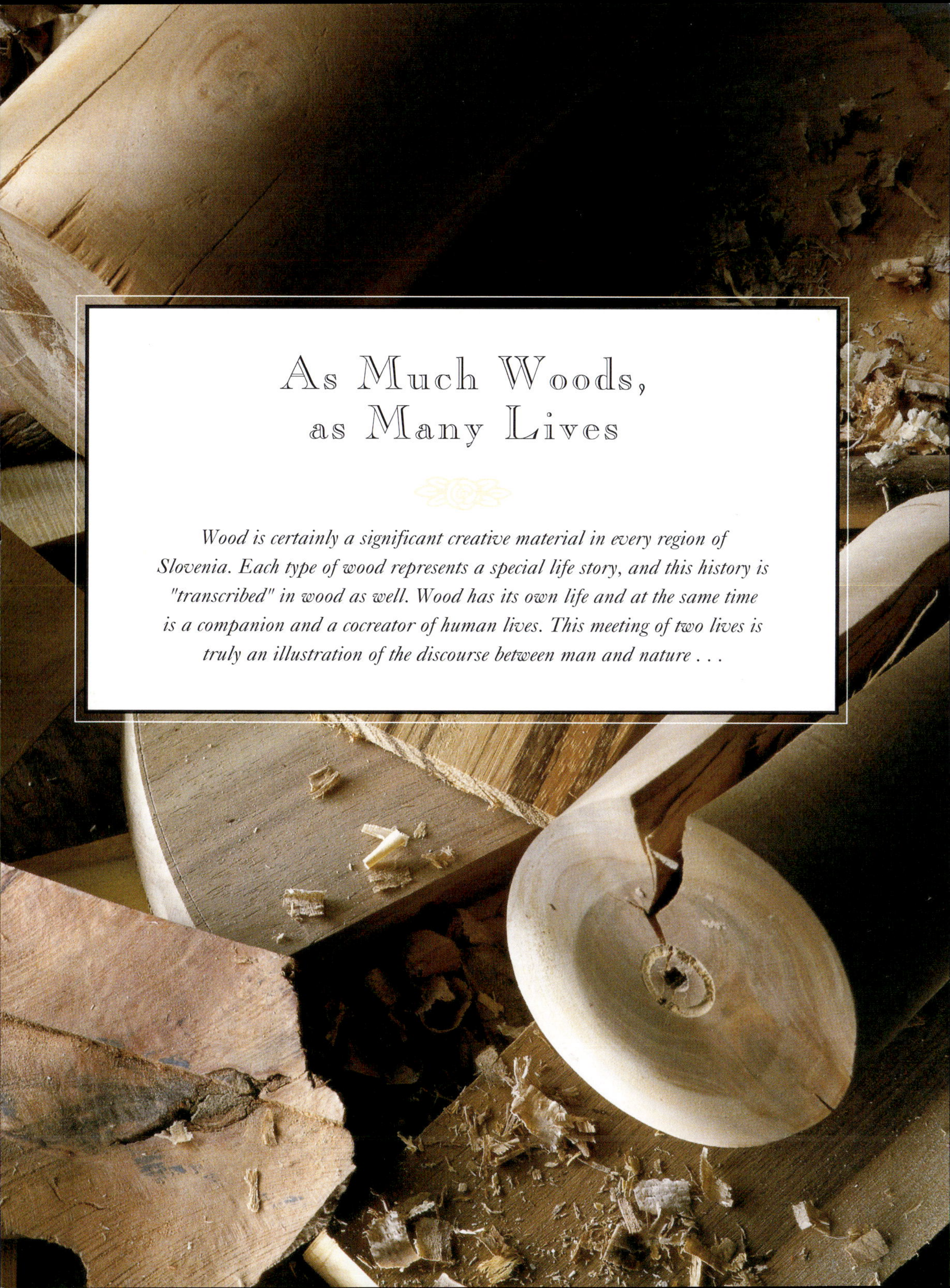

As Much Woods, as Many Lives

Wood is certainly a significant creative material in every region of Slovenia. Each type of wood represents a special life story, and this history is "transcribed" in wood as well. Wood has its own life and at the same time is a companion and a cocreator of human lives. This meeting of two lives is truly an illustration of the discourse between man and nature . . .

Slovenes have a unique relationship with wood. Nowadays, this relationship may even be intensifying, since for us wood holds a special value that is reflected in numerous details in our work and home environments. However, we must not see this positive relationship toward wood as simply a reaction to the aggressiveness of modern life with all its plastic and automation. Slovenes formed a positive relationship with wood over centuries, developing numerous technological skills and knowledge as well as a whole range of diverse handicrafts that employ wood as their primary expressive and creative material. The manual production of wooden objects for everyday use and household tools has a rich tradition in Slovenia, several centuries old. The Slovene term "*suha roba*" (literally, "dry goods") covers the various working methods and the products historically made and still being made today from dried wood. The residents of central and southeastern Slovenia (Ribnica Valley, Kočevsko, Notranjska) have been engaged in the production of woodenware for centuries. As early as 1492, they obtained the emperor's permission to peddle their homemade wooden products throughout the Austrian Empire. With this decree, the emperor gave the local people a basic means to earn money, that is, to survive and therefore remain in this region of Slovenia. Even in later periods of development and under subsequent social systems, the people used the permission historically granted by the emperor to assure themselves a regular primary or supplementary source of income. The most typical and numerous products of all periods until the present have been wooden spoons and ladles. These are followed by turned wooden plates, various wooden vessels, kitchen utensils, various tools and parts of tools, interior furnishings, etc. A whole range of occupations and types of *suha roba* have been preserved to the present as the specialties of individual families and their workshops. These provide either the primary income of the household or have developed as a source of supplementary income along with farming or as additional handicraft work along with a profession. In addition to their manufacture, the sale of *suha roba* products also developed through the centuries. The people of the Ribnica Valley in particular were known as peddlers in many Central European countries, recognizable by the bundles of the most varied wooden products that they carried on their backs from place to place.

Of course, modern *suha roba* activities cannot be regarded solely as inexhaustible fountains of creativity. Many makers of wooden items simply fill orders. The demands of modern life make changes in the range of products required, but this presents no major obstacle to suha roba manufacturers since they have enough "historical" experience. Nevertheless, the range of items in demand changes more quickly in the modern world, and the variety of items is much greater than in the past when such changes were linked to universal changes in the rhythm of life. Among the many makers of *suha roba* there are, of course, some outstanding individuals who with their techniques, design, and esthetic talents produce exceptional products, either as a continuation of historical memory whereby "historical" items acquire new functional meanings or as a search for completely new design solutions. This duality of creativity in wood and from wood is not just typical of the traditional *suha roba* regions but rather of all regions in Slovenia where individuals seek creative challenges in the precious natural material represented by various types of wood.

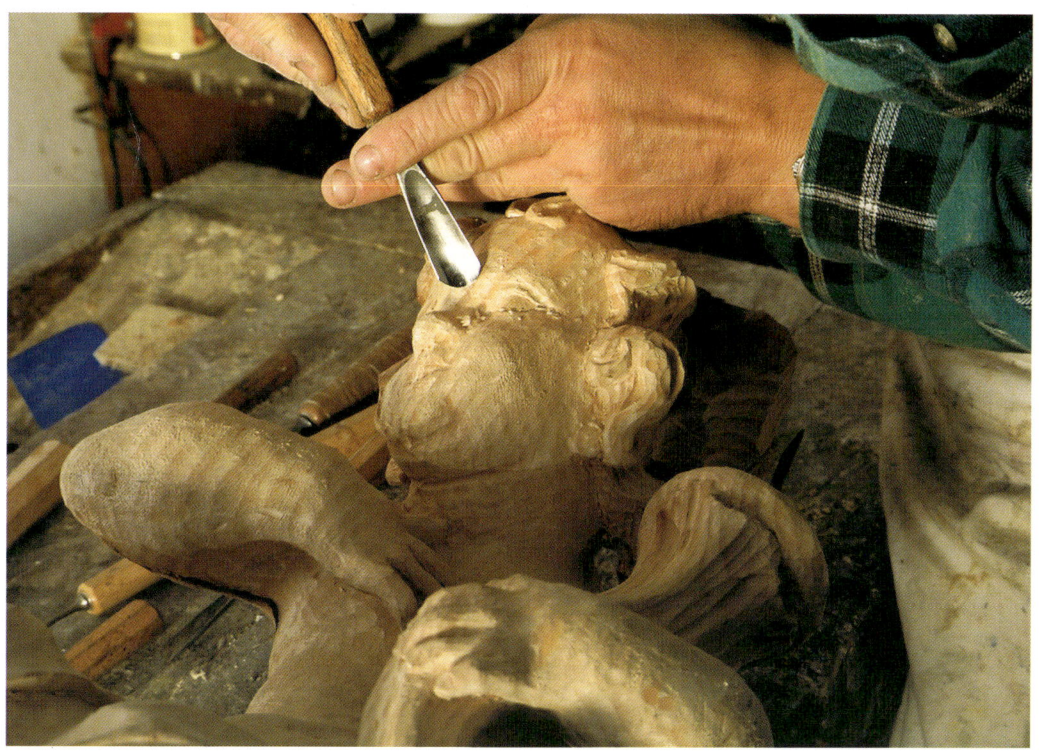

Matija Kobola – knife, chisel, and axe ►

In Šalska vas in Kočevsko works a master who continues the old tradition of *suha roba,* in the technological sense as well. With axe, chisel, and knife, he makes or, to put it more accurately, hews and chisels spoons, ladles, and the wooden vessels or *nečke* that were once used for cleaning grain, kneading dough, and carrying or storing things. They were also often used as baths or cradles for babies.

Anton Marolt and his butter molds ▼

Along with wooden spoons, carved molds for shaping and decorating butter also belong among the traditional *suha roba* products. While today their function is mostly decorative, such molds were in everyday use until World War II. These wooden molds were not only used in individual households but were also an important sales item in domestic and foreign markets. The production of molds was often the domain of local self-taught carvers, while *suha roba* manufacturers produced them in larger numbers.

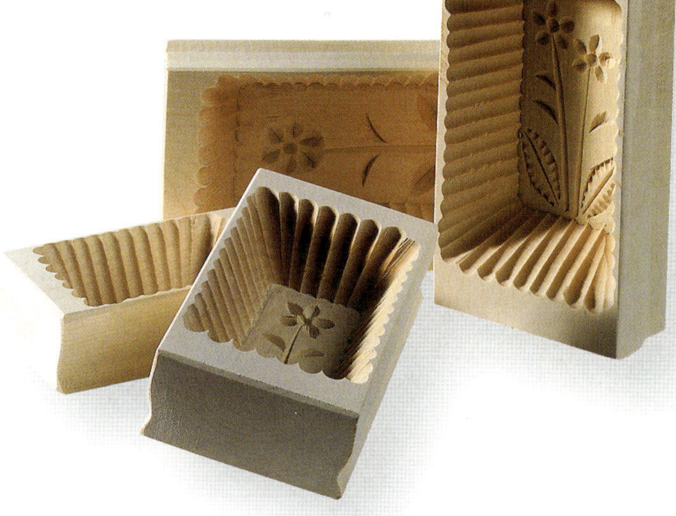

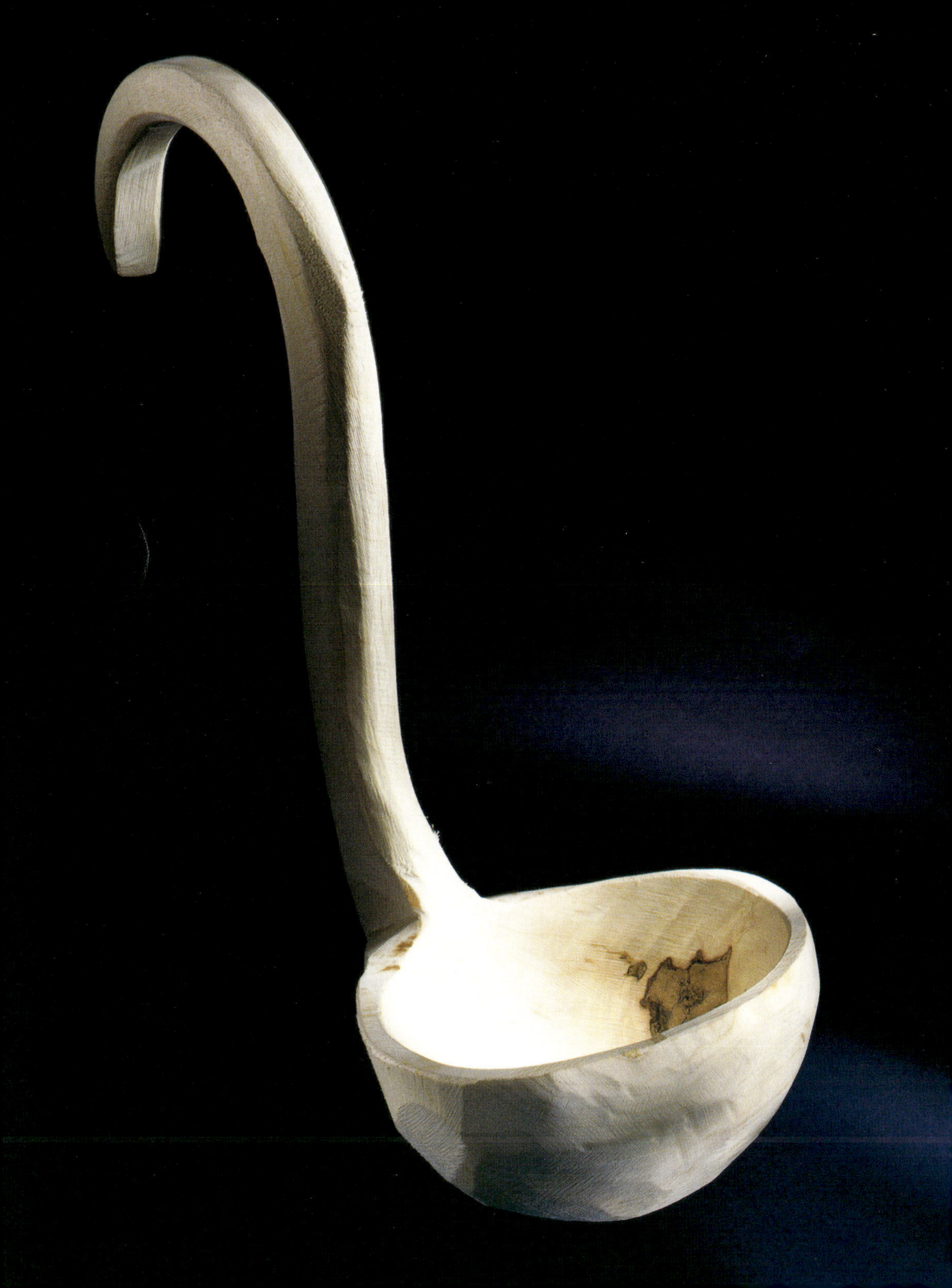

Is there any sausage left in the box? ►

In the mountain village of Gorjuše, **Ivan Jeklar** produces wooden boxes with rimmed lids made of pine and larch as they have been fashioned for centuries. The sides of the boxes and the rims of the lids are overlapped and stitched together with thin strips of fresh pine root, and this natural seam is the most beautiful ornamentation on each box. The boxes were and still are universally useful. In the past, workers used them to store sausages and minced lard when they went to work in the forests. They were often used to hold sewing kits, herbs and spices, seeds, documents, and men's shaving kits.

First the father, then the son . . . and now a master workshop ▼

In the 1980's, **Jernej Kosmač** was among the first in Slovenia to begin systematically producing replicas of items from our cultural heritage, particularly items made from wood. Thus, numerous objects in museums and private collections were given new life, acquiring not only decorative but also new uses and even educational and symbolic significance. Work in the home handicraft workshop attracted Jernej's son **Matej** as well, and together they now produce a whole range of the most varied products. Among the most popular are undoubtedly their wooden pocket sundials once used by herdsmen in the mountains and the replicas of cobbler's lamps that direct light to a certain point on the work table using glass balls filled with water.

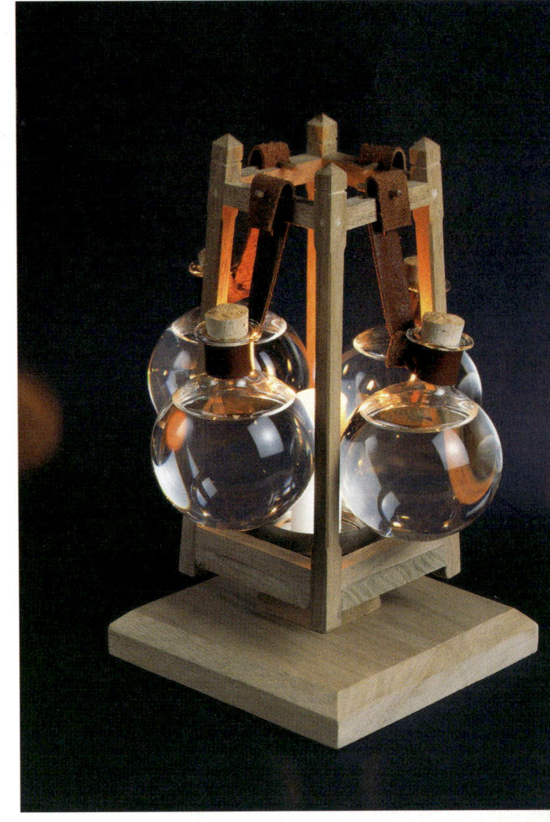

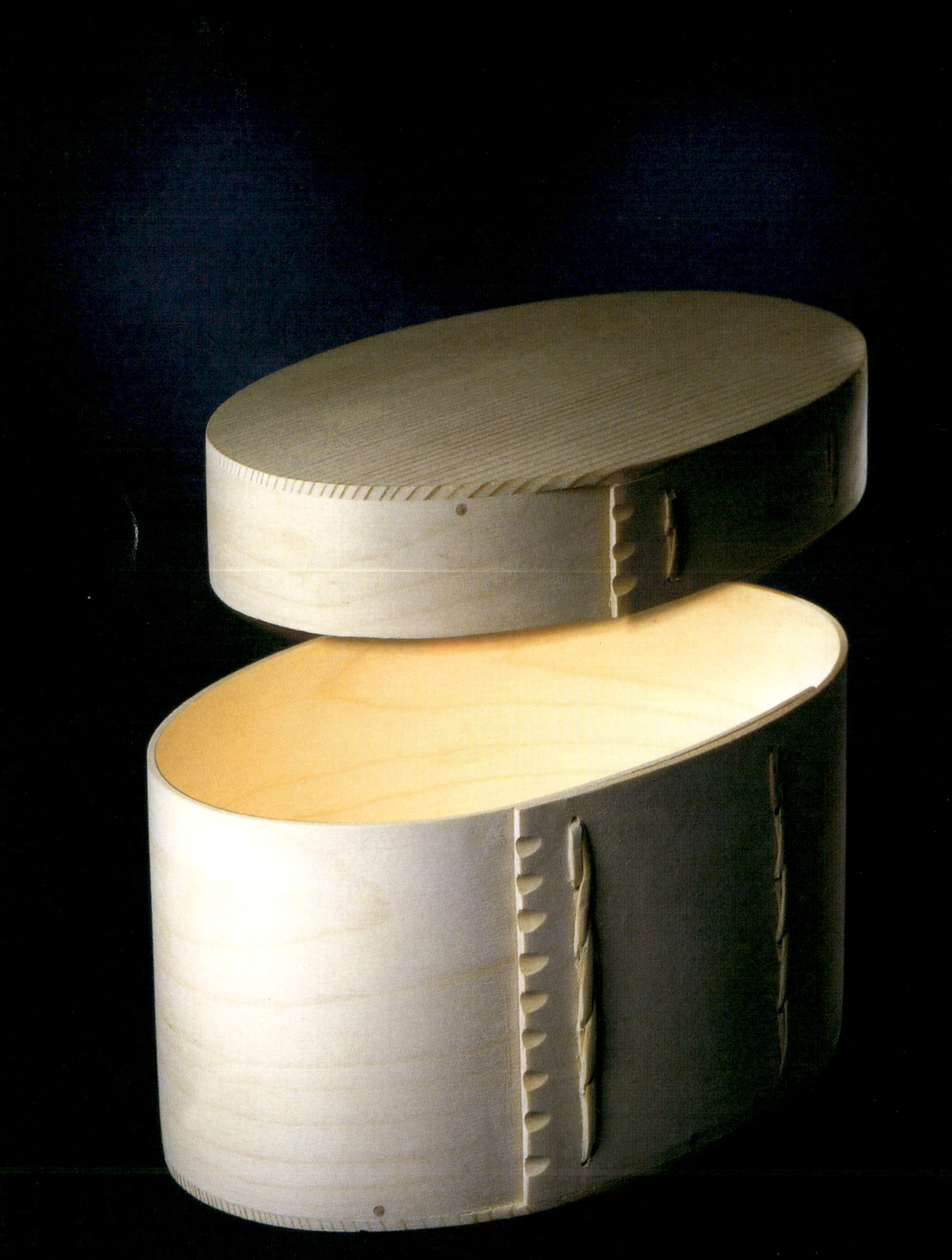

Alpine clogs of Dejan Ogrin ►

Herding dairy cattle in the Slovene alpine world marked the culture and the way of life in a very unique way. Today, this historical memory is preserved mainly in museums. In their mountain hamlets, herdsmen made various items from wood, including footwear–clogs. The production of clogs was revived by the young master Dejan Ogrin, who makes replicas of traditional wooden clogs in Bohinjska Bistrica. The lower part is made of poplar while the upper section is woven from larch or pine. His clogs are not only a popular tourist souvenir but also useful and healthy footwear.

At Marjan Semolič's, whips still crack ▼

The production of whips braided from split wooden strips of the nettle tree (*Celtis australis*) that grows on the fringes of fields and vineyards in the karst region of Kras has almost disappeared. This essential piece of equipment was linked to the use of horses and cattle in farming and transport. Today, Semolič is the last whip producer in Brestovica, where there were many such masters until the end of World War II. Producing a single whip takes almost a month, and each whip passes through the master's hands at least fifty times.

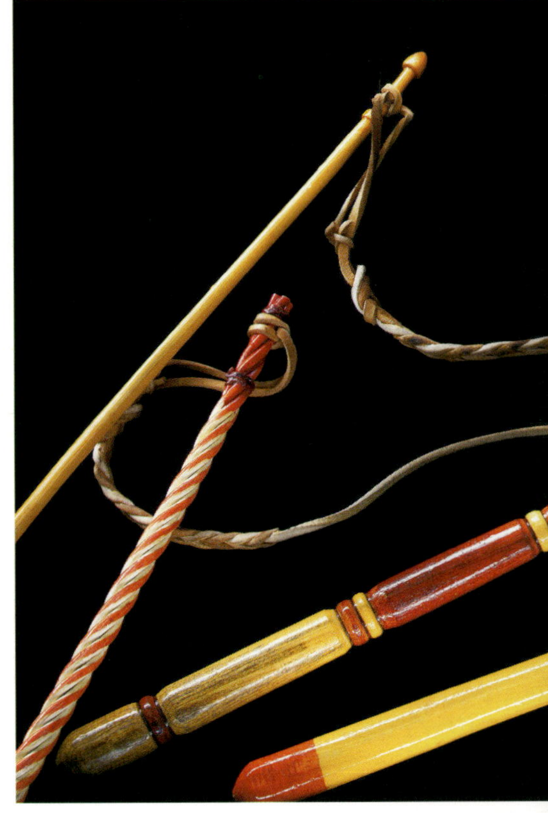

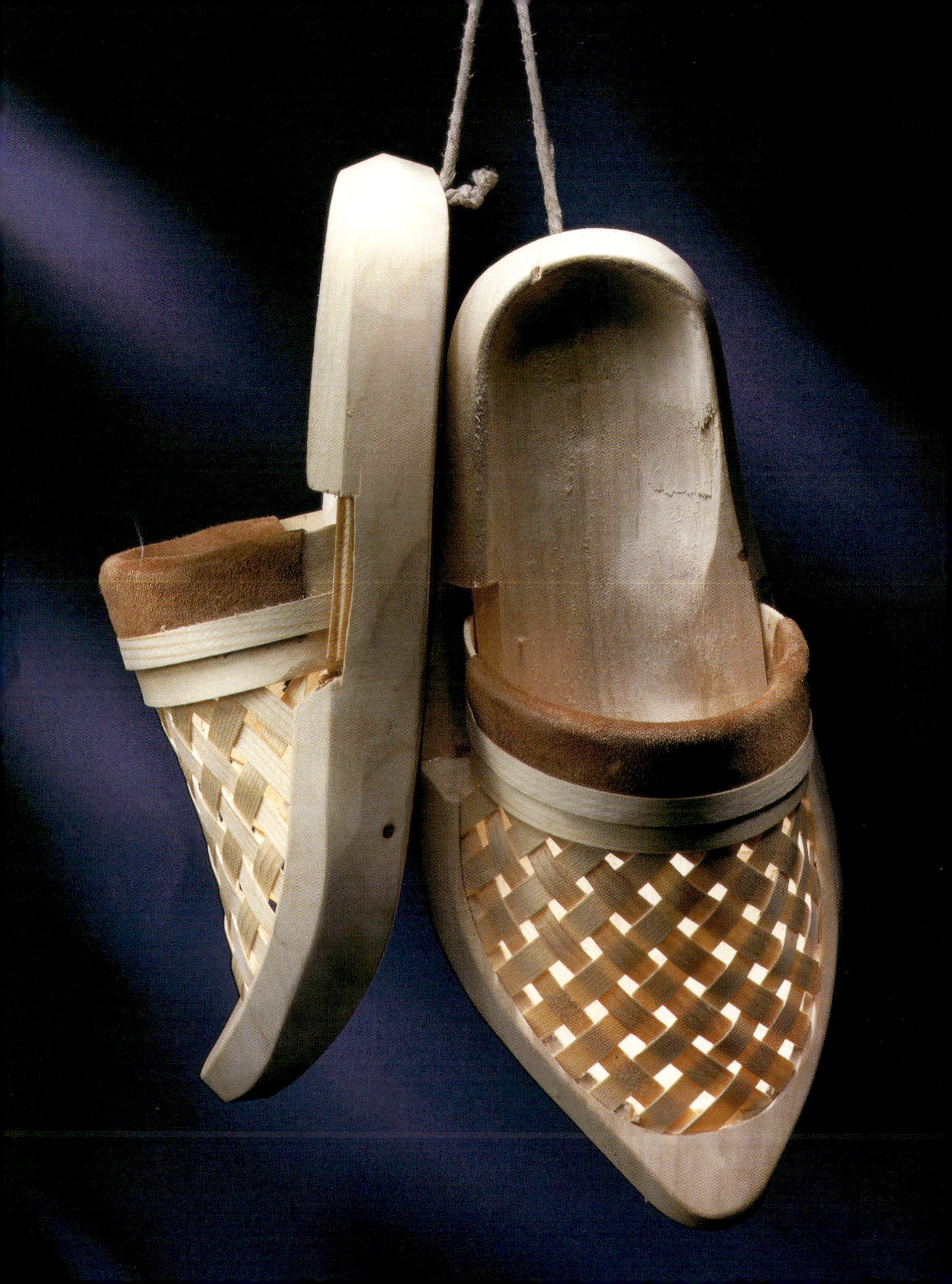

Alojz Lotrič – the last pipe maker in Gorjuše ►

Nowadays, the tobacco pipes known as *gorjuške fajfe* are only decorative. They are a continuation of the historical memory of a carving and designing handicraft activity pursued especially during the winter months in this mountain region probably from the 18th century onwards. In the first decades of the 20th century, more than 3500 pipes were carved and decorated with inlaid mother of pearl (intarsia) every year. They meant an important additional source of income for many of their makers and were sold in distant markets from Alexandria to England.

Linked spoons – a symbol of marriage ▼

Janez Golob from Zagorje ob Savi offers us a unique handicraft skill. From a single piece of linden wood, he carves a wooden chain with links of various lengths. At each end, he carves a wooden spoon so that the chain connects two spoons. Thus, the basic skill of carving a wooden chain produces an item with symbolic meaning: entering a marriage a couple is joined on all levels, including eating. Naturally, this product is no modern invention but rather a continuation of a part of our heritage, a traditional symbolic gift to a bride and bridegroom.

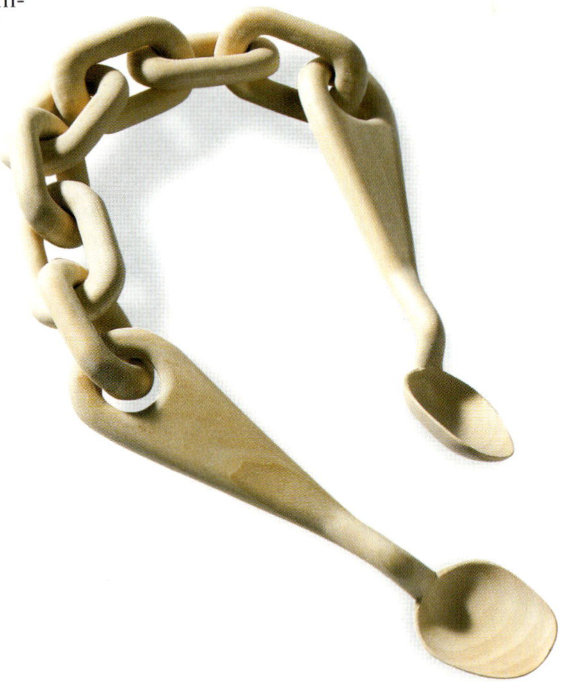

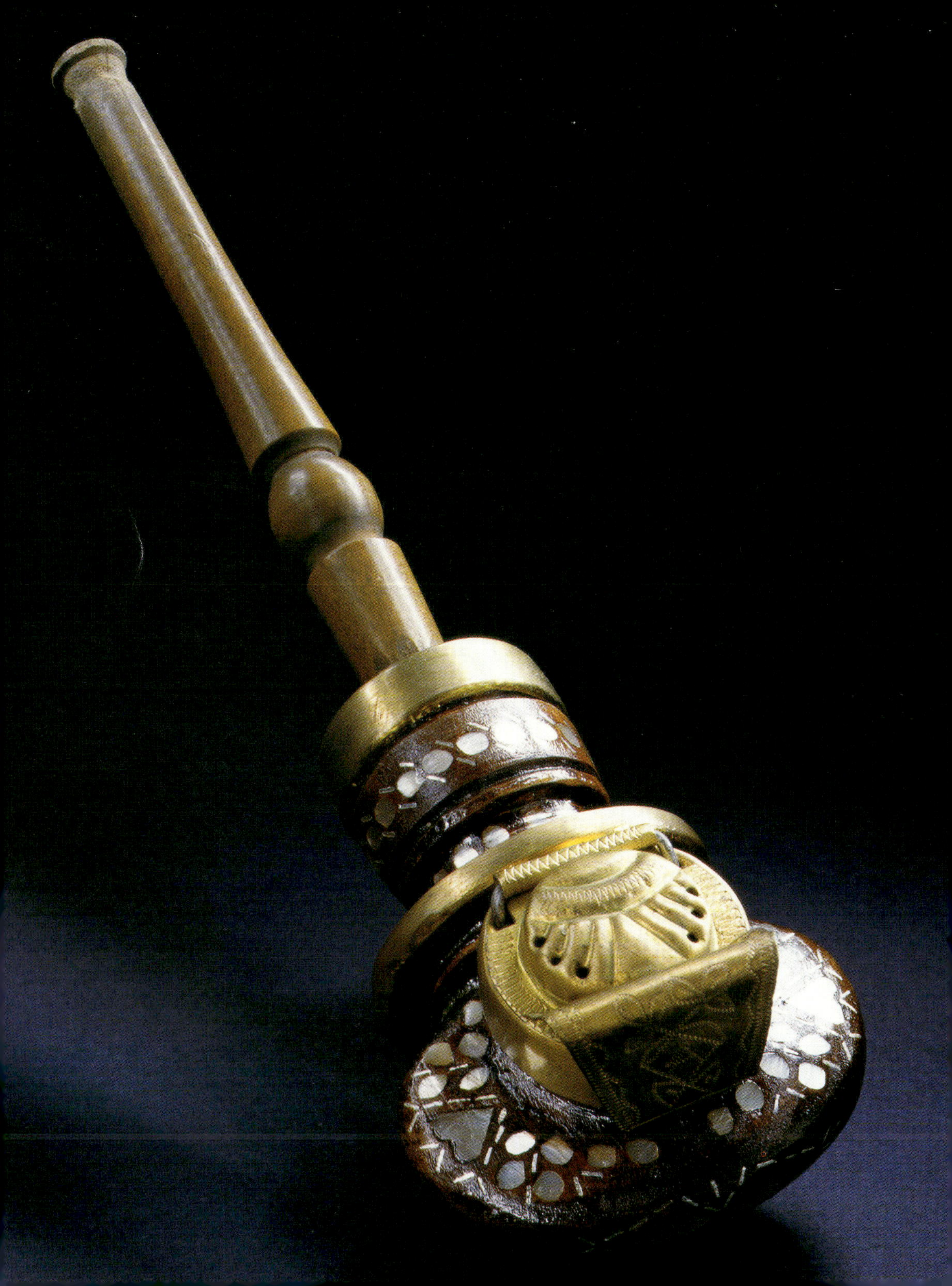

Petra Plestenjak-Podlogar carves molds for honey gingerbread ►

The first carved wooden molds for shaping gingerbread appeared in Europe in 15th century. Individual areas, especially cities and towns, developed various local recipes as well as characteristic shapes, motifs, and decorations. Molds were made in carving workshops and by self-taught individuals. Škofja Loka was the foremost of Slovene towns known for the manufacture of such molds and gingerbread items traditionally made with honey called *mali kruhek* ("little bread"). Decorated gingerbread figures were the most frequent gifts for expressing love and also had special meanings on certain holidays. Modern wooden molds are no longer intended just for making gingerbread cakes but can also be used for decoration.

The first home intercom . . . ▼

Another object belonging to the heritage of Slovenia's alpine region is the carved wooden dove, a depiction of the Holy Spirit, which in the country was usually hung above the table in the main living area. It hung on a string connected to the front door, and when the door opened, the dove moved and so announced a visitor's arrival. Carving such doves, especially the fan-like wooden lamellas of the wings and tail, takes genuine skill. With his unique artistic images, **Andrej Ozebek** from Mošnje pri Podvinu in Gorenjska is outstanding among the makers of such doves. His doves are an excellent souvenir of Slovenia's alpine world.

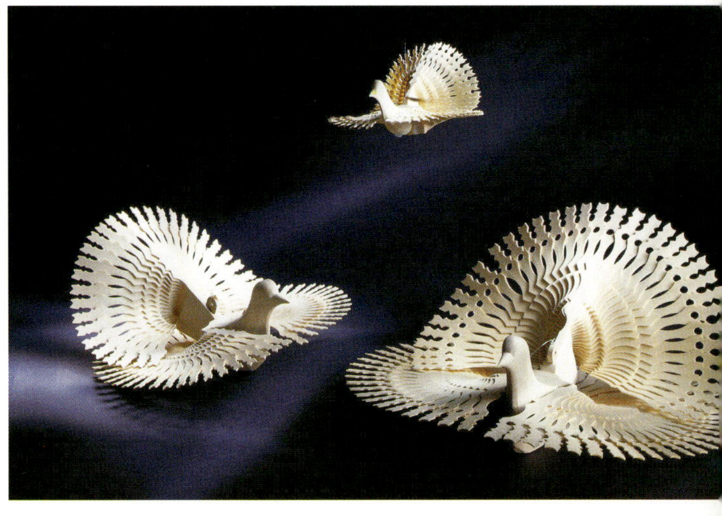

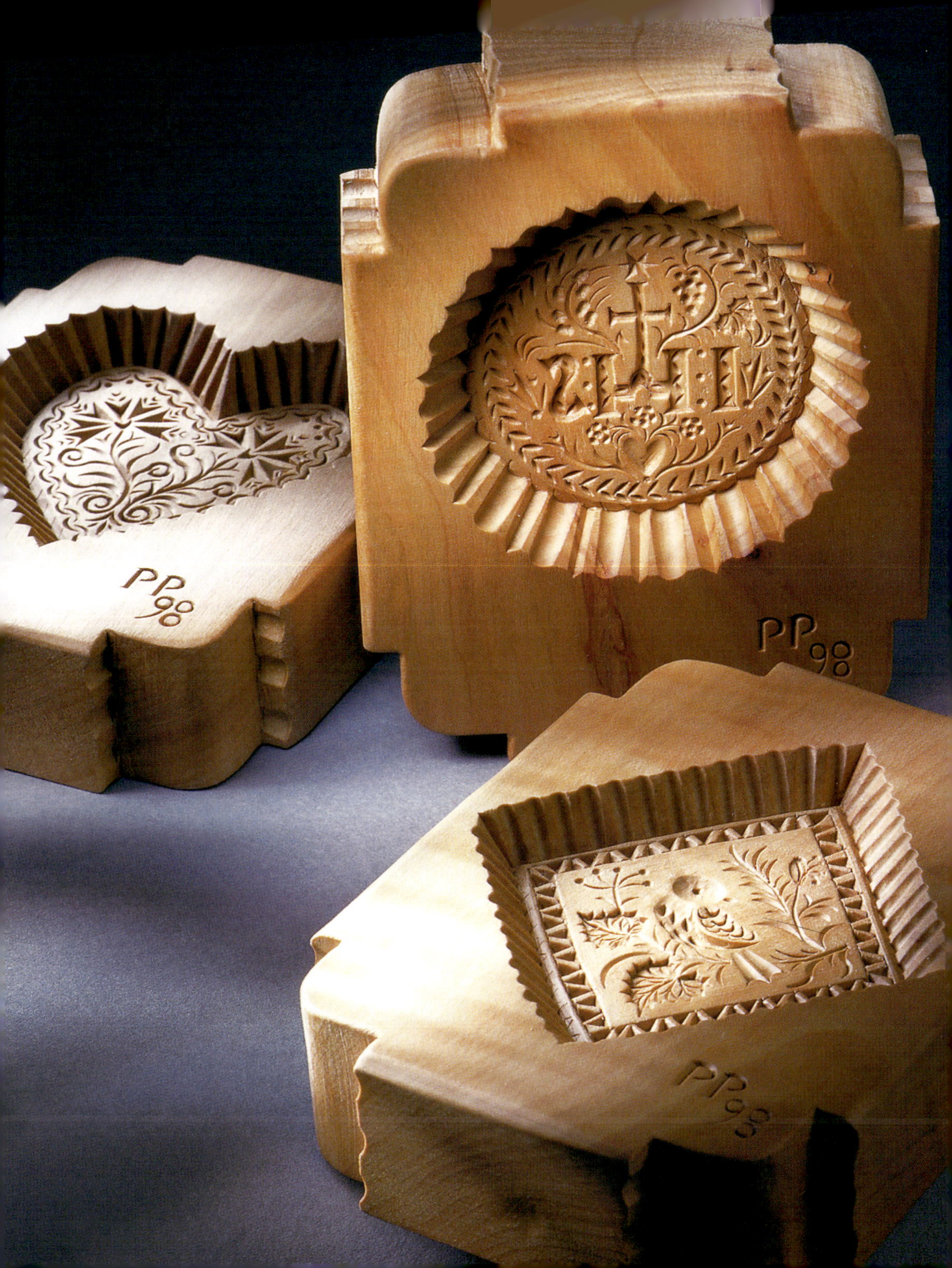
PP98
PP98
PP98

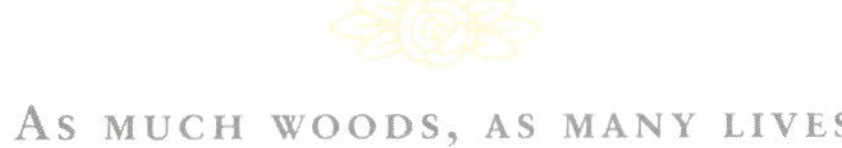

So many woods, so many colours ►

Stanislav Šalamon from Maribor is Slovenia's foremost intarsia artist and continues the rich tradition of this handicraft with great artistic expression. A distinguishing feature of his work is its orientation, since his motifs are drawn from the wealth of Slovene ornamentation characterizing various periods of history and the traditional patterns found on embroidery, lace, etc. A carefully thought out methodological model allows him to choose which ornamentation he can use for new compositions in the technique of wood intarsia. He exclusively employs natural veneers from the many types of wood that grow in Slovenia. Thus he has created an exceptional palette of colour, including shades of colour whose genuinely natural source can only be confirmed by detailed inspection.

The Crèche Figures of Franjo Srnel ▼

Setting up a Christmas crèche became a mass phenomenon only in the early 19th century when many gifted individuals and handicraft workshops undertook the carving of wooden Nativity figurines. Although paper, clay, plaster, and plastic figurines later appeared on the market, the carving of wooden figurines has survived to the present. There are relatively few masters in this field, but their carvings retain all the technological characteristics of genuine handwork with the knife and chisel.

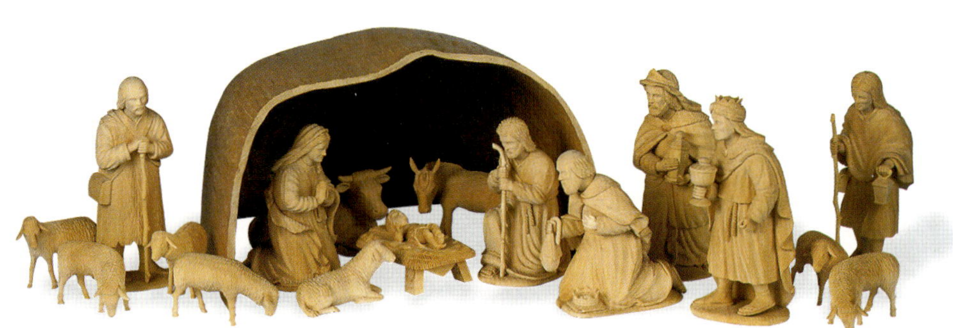

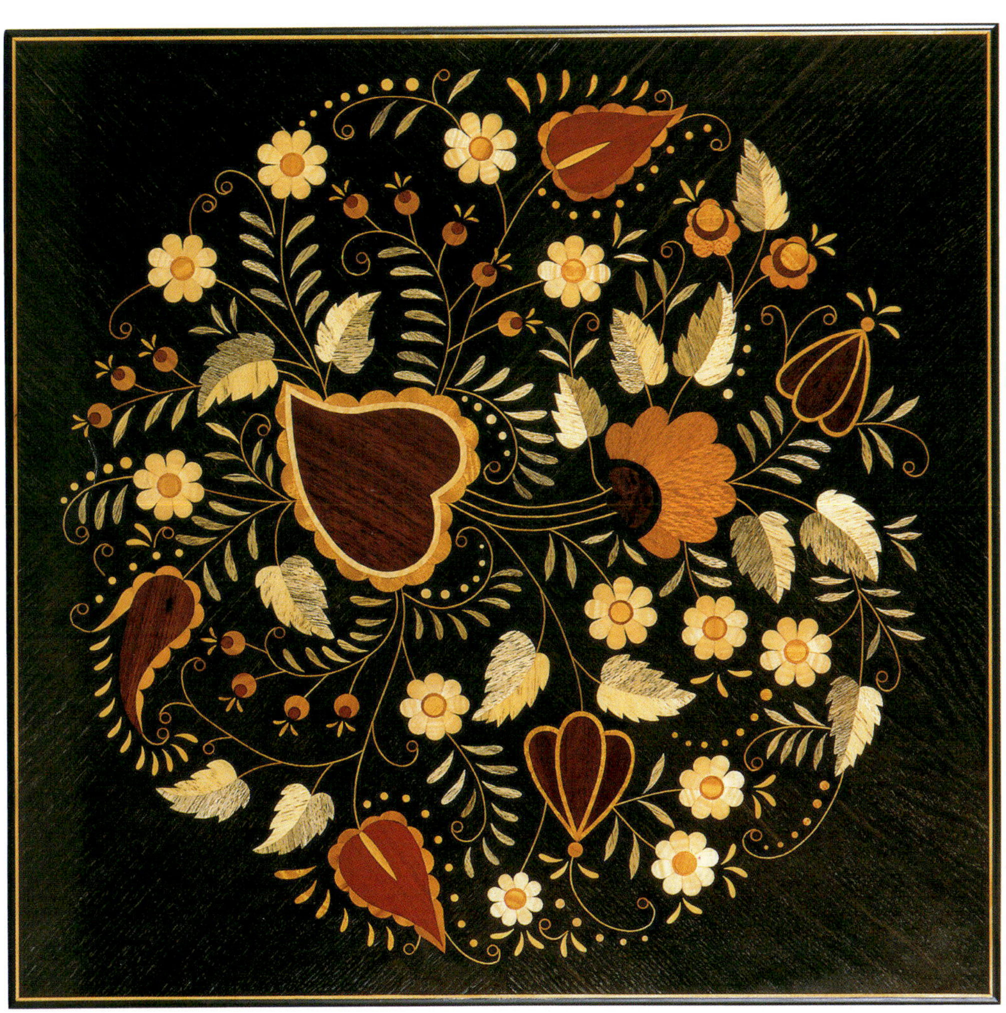

Wood and magical violin sounds ►

Manufacturing violins and other stringed instruments is a family tradition in the Demšar family, who lived in the ancient barrelmaking and woodworking environment of the Selška dolina valley in Gorenjska. **Vilim Demšar** today continues this rich family tradition in his eminent workshop in the heart of Old Ljubljana. A musician himself, the master early realized that the rich family experience must be augmented by greater knowledge of sonority and resonance based on new empirical studies carried out with modern research tools. Thus Demšar's workshop produces outstanding instruments such as the tonally improved *Tartini* violin created in cooperation with designer **Oskar Kogoj** for the 300th anniversary of the birth of the great violinist and composer Guiseppe Tartini (1692-1770) from Piran.

The bow as a synthesis of technological knowledge and design ▼

Every type of wood has its specific properties, and only an extraordinary knowledge of the characteristics of wood and a mastery of techniques could lead to the outstanding handicraft activity developed by **Franc Oblak** from Radovljica in Gorenjska. From his workshop come the highest quality competition and sport bows, individually tested by Oblak who is an archer himself. Among many types of bows from his workshop is the bow made in collaboration with the internationally recognized Slovene designer **Oskar Kogoj** that is one of the items in Kogoj's *Nature Design* collection.

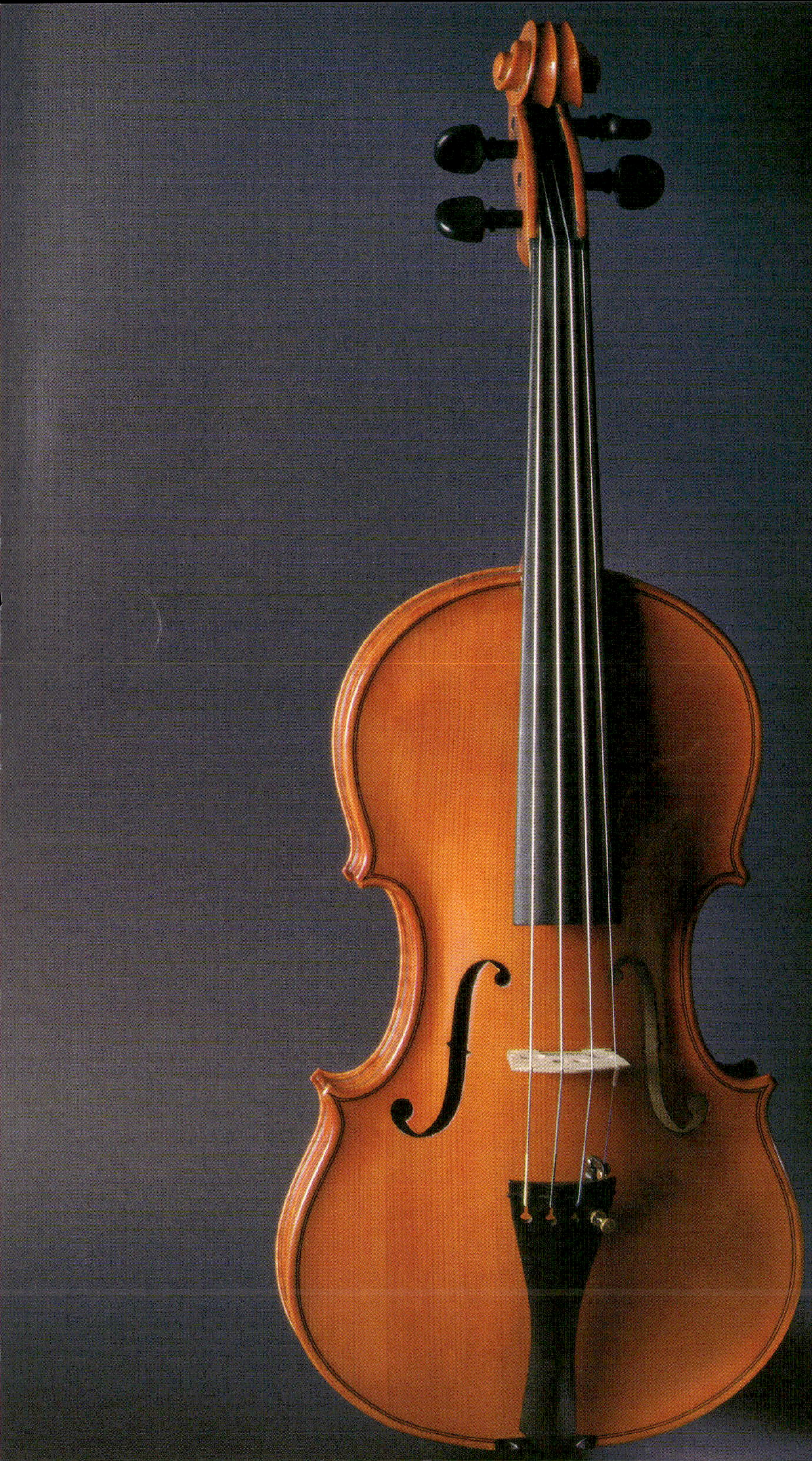

Janez Golob, top woodturner

Woodturning is a branch of *suha roba*. It offers a unique design and creative challenge that combines the highest knowledge of wood and its properties and potential and the discovery of new shapes. Architect Janez Golob turns bowls from various kinds of wood native to Slovenia (oak, maple, elm, pear, acacia, beech, etc). His products belong in the framework of unique personal design where the designer himself directly shapes an individual item and is not merely the designer of a shape made by a journeyman woodturner.

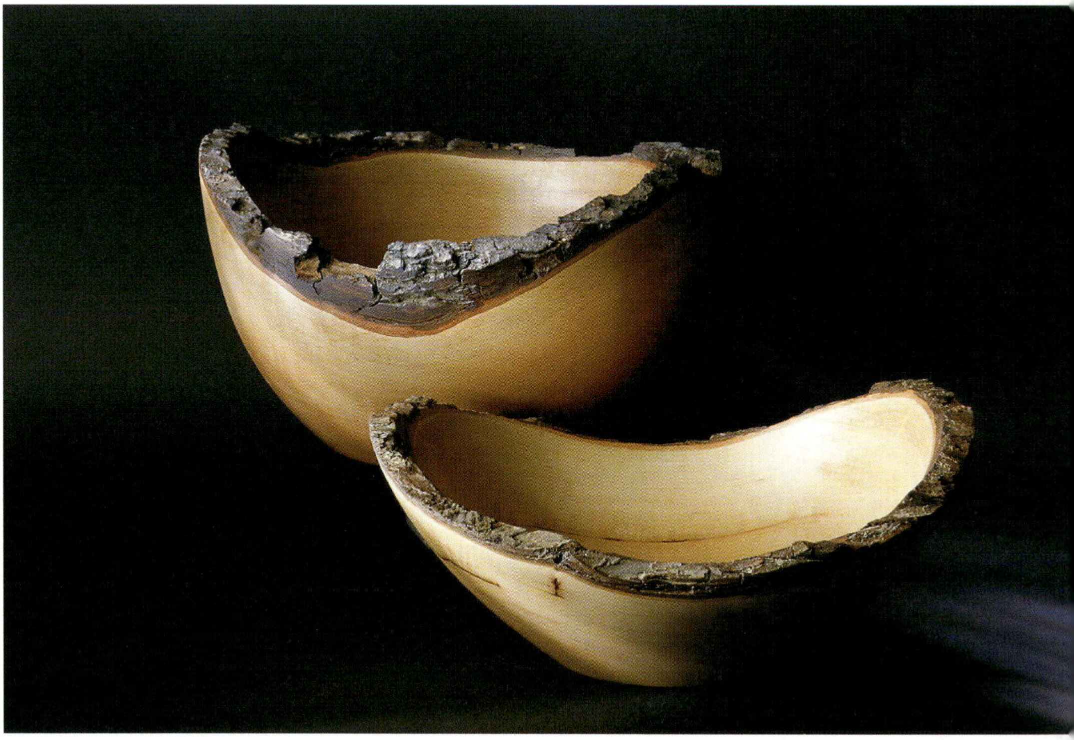

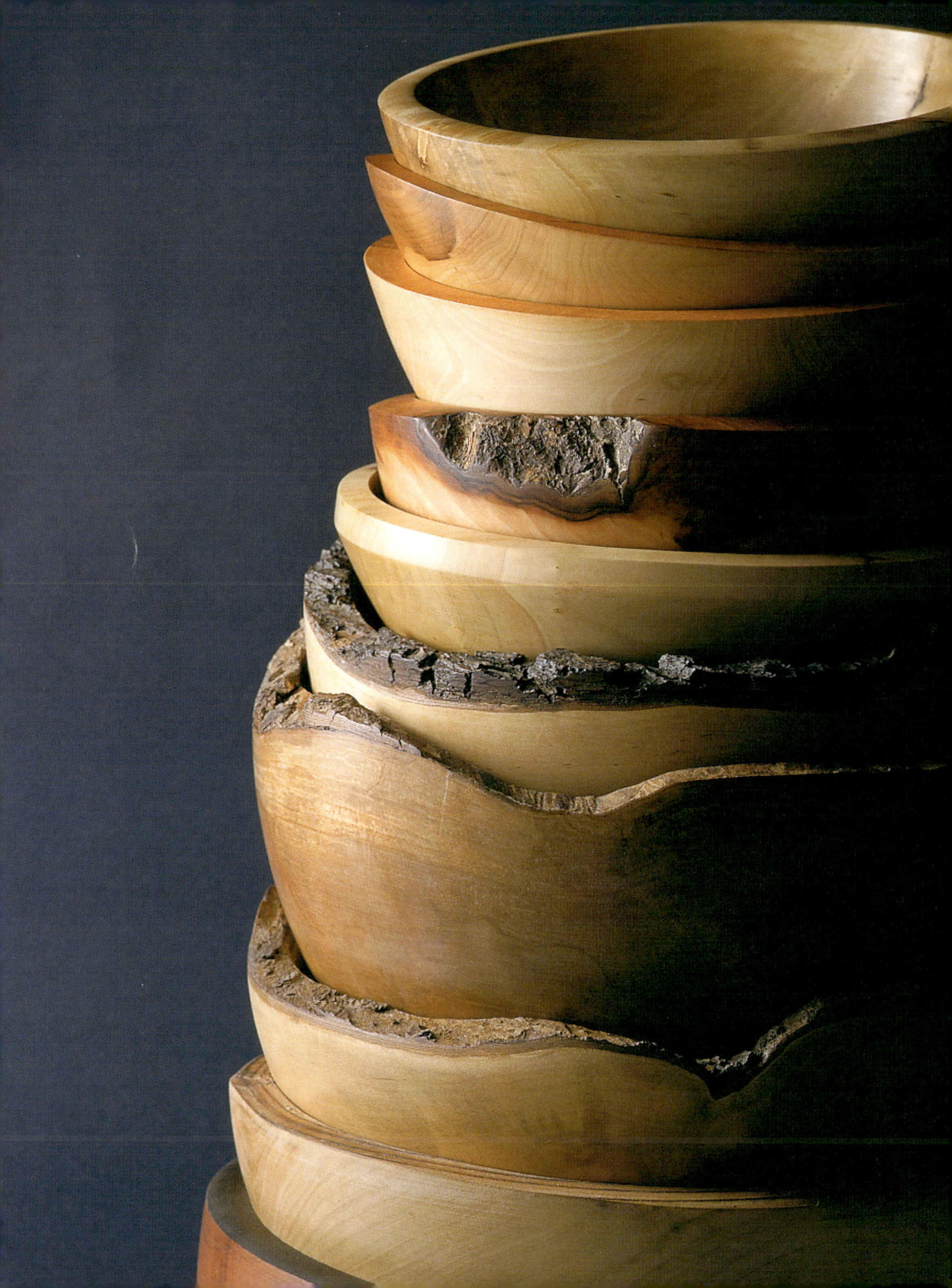

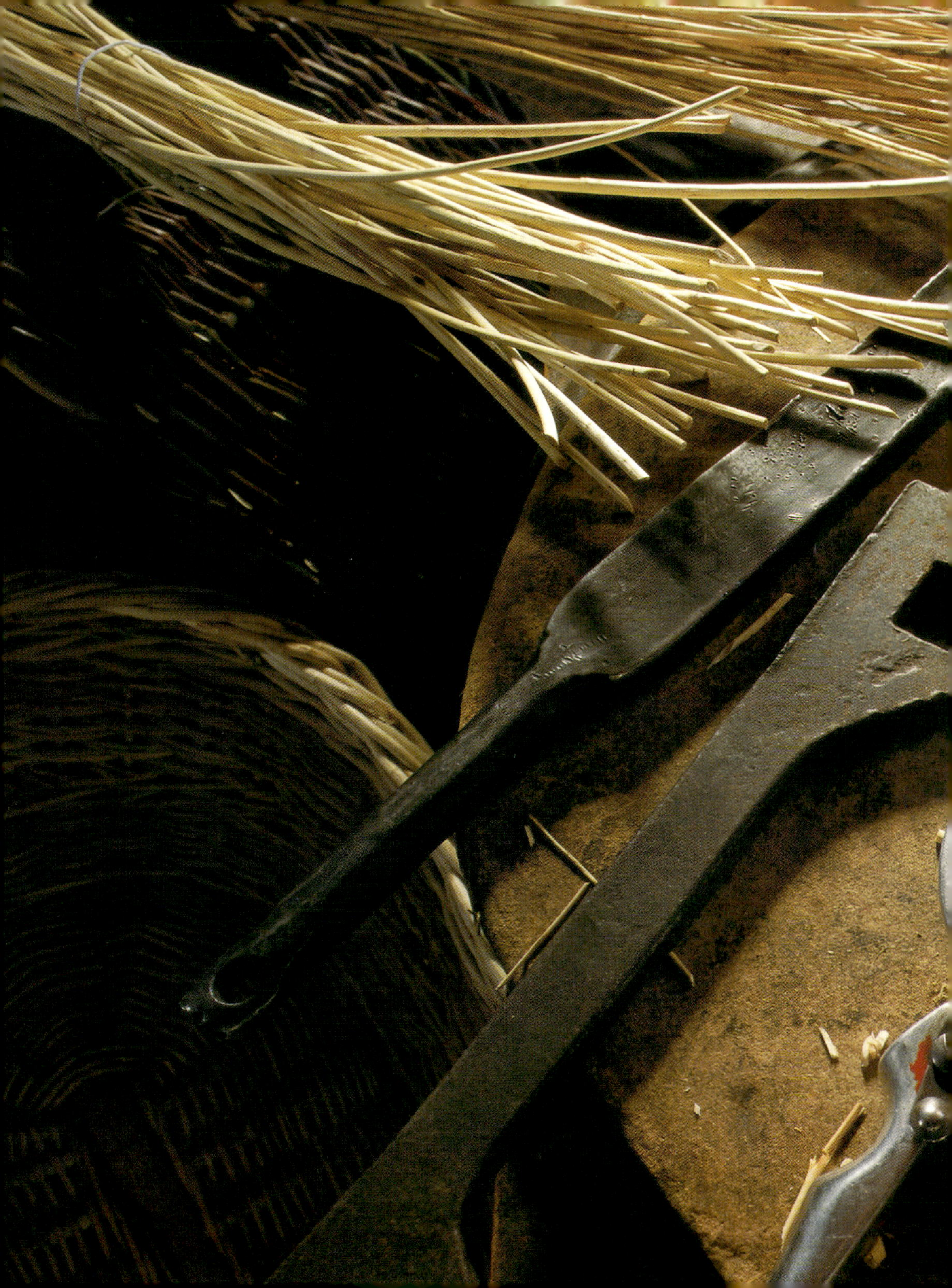

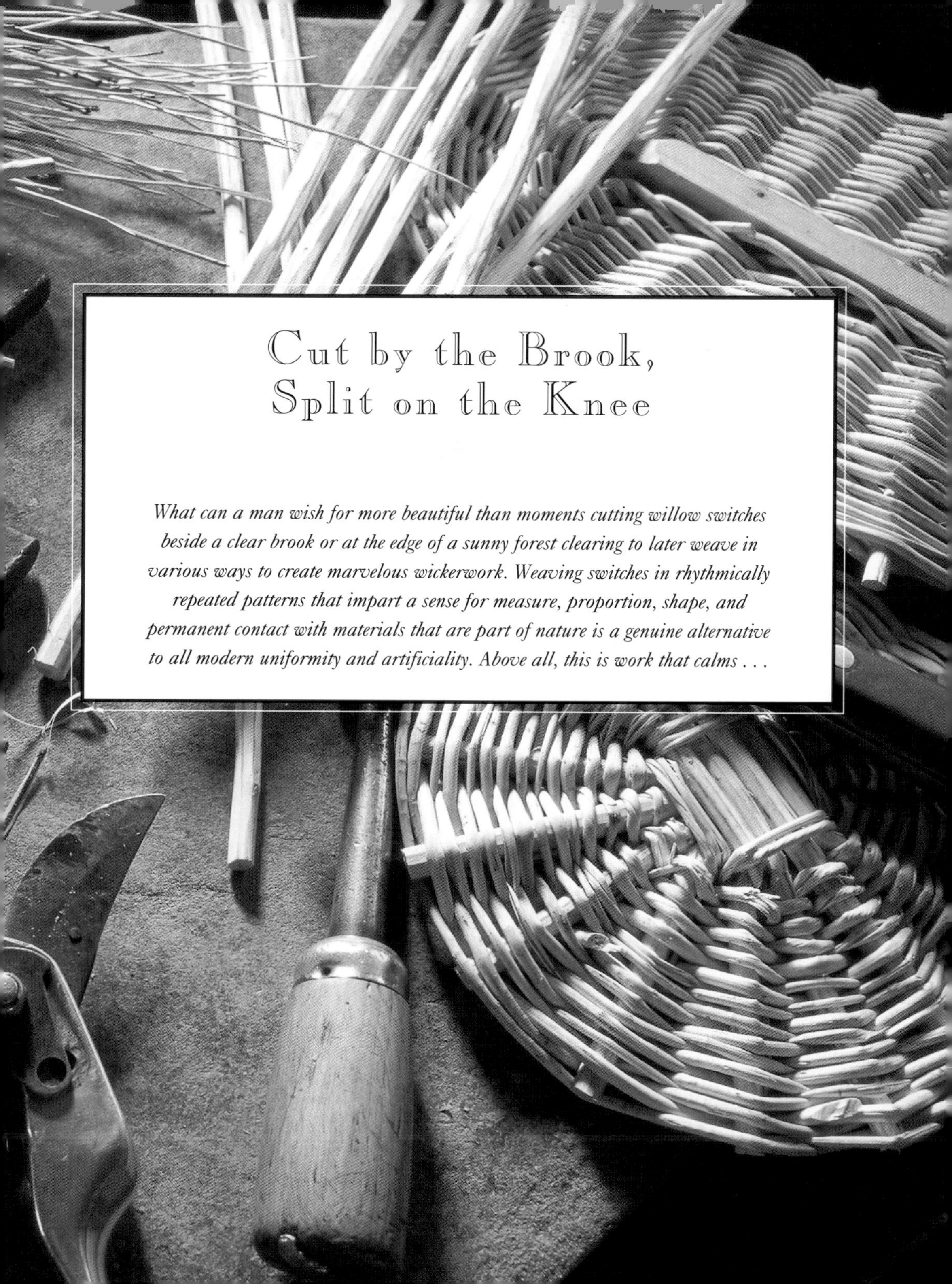

Cut by the Brook, Split on the Knee

What can a man wish for more beautiful than moments cutting willow switches beside a clear brook or at the edge of a sunny forest clearing to later weave in various ways to create marvelous wickerwork. Weaving switches in rhythmically repeated patterns that impart a sense for measure, proportion, shape, and permanent contact with materials that are part of nature is a genuine alternative to all modern uniformity and artificiality. Above all, this is work that calms . . .

Various types of osiers, reeds, and wood shavings are the basic materials for wickerwork. Items made from straw and corn husks will be presented in a separate chapter, even though they form part of traditional and modern wickerwork in Slovenia.

Wickerwork is among the oldest handicraft activities that people undertook originally to satisfy their own needs, and wickerwork items served the widest variety of purposes in everyday household use. Great attention was subsequently devoted to wickerwork, particularly in the period of Austro-Hungarian mercantilism and physiocracy. The authorities strove to improve wickerwork skills with new knowledge and instituted appropriate training courses and wickerwork schools. The fruits of this work are still being harvested today, even though little attention or concern is given nowadays to training in this branch of handicrafts. In spite of this, there are wickerwork craftsmen virtually everywhere in Slovenia today. Wickerwork is not limited to rural areas, and even modern urban areas boast individuals skilled in wickerwork knowledge and creativity. Of great concern is the fact that wickerwork skills are too little employed as one of the possible forms of rehabilitation or work for the mentally or physically handicapped, in school programs, etc. Nevertheless, despite this criticism, which applies not only to Slovenia but abroad as well, I believe that our wickerworkers create a truly varied range of products relative to form, technological realization, and function. The cultural heterogeneousness of Slovenia is also reflected in the diversity of wickerwork products. Repetitions of historical memory are naturally in the foreground, bearing in mind that traditional items have today acquired completely new uses and are no longer found only in specific geographical areas. Thus, many items that only a few decades ago still had various specific uses in rural households have today acquired new functions in modern urban environments. Among all handicraft activities, wickerwork is most largely based on traditional models and least influenced by various modern design modifications. Although the wickerwork craft boasts the greatest number of craftsmen and the greatest variety of products, completely modern approaches to wickerwork have been mastered by only a handful of individuals, and we have not even one creative wickerwork workshop, let alone any wickerwork training centers. However, from this point of view, history is our teacher and offers excellent instruction through suitable manuals and professional literature on wickerwork. Along with itinerant wickerwork courses organized by the Austro-Hungarian monarchy, excellently organized wickerwork lessons began in the Wickerwork Department of the School for Wood Industry and Crafts (*Šola za lesno industrijo in obrt*) in Ljubljana during the 1894–1995 school year. The State Wickerwork School operated from 1908 to 1935 in Radovljica and from 1928 to 1939 in Ptuj. These are only a few basic details from the rich past and above all experience that is reflected in our efforts today. Parallel with wickerwork education, there was development in the areas of technology and raw materials. Thus, for example, great attention was paid to growing willow, a field essential for guaranteeing suitable quality wickerwork material. In addition to the exploitation of the immediate natural environment (willow growing beside streams and rivers and other bushes and trees providing suitable wickerwork materials), properly maintained willow plantations were an excellent source of raw material. It is therefore not surprising that these professional efforts bore their first fruit as early as 1935 when Slovene willow growers were awarded a gold medal in Solun in Greece for the highest quality cultivated willow in Europe. Undoubtedly, this fact belongs to the history of international recognition of Slovene trademarks.

The basic wickerwork material in Slovenia is still switches from bushes and trees and the wicker made from them. Among wickerwork materials, the most frequently used include hazel, willow, chestnut, pine, beech, and hornbeam, other plants such as briar, reeds, clematis, and various types of strong grasses. The rich wickerwork knowledge of some individuals is slowly making its way back into school programs, and some schools are trying to acquaint the young with the basic techniques of weaving wicker as a most original and most basic way of encouraging a sense for esthetics, patience, and a systematic approach to work.

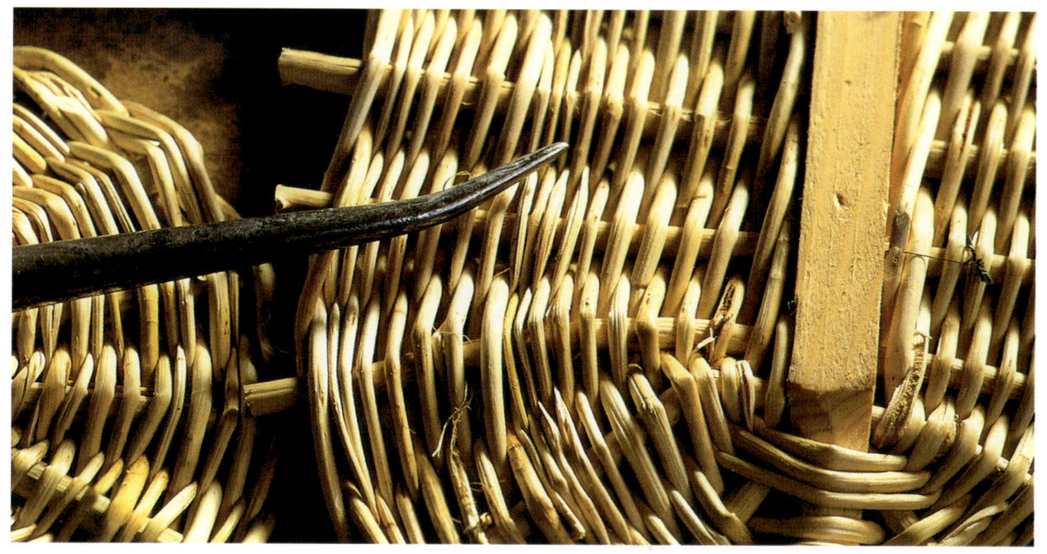

MARJAN GOLMAJER – WICKER IN THE RIGHT HANDS ►

Distinctive shapes and the interweaving of different coloured switches are the special features of Marjan Golmajer's wickerwork. From his workshop in the old Gorenjska town of Radovljica come single-handled and double-handled wicker baskets of many sizes, umbrella stands, clothesbaskets, and round straw breadbaskets. All are the work of an outstanding master with a great sense of design and symmetrical rhythm of weaving. His great wickerwork skill is undoubtedly the consequence or, to put it more accurately, a surviving echo of the former famous wickerwork school in Radovljica.

TRADITIONAL FORMS AND QUALITY FOR MODERN LIFE ▼

There are many active wickerworkers in the wider Ljubljana area. One is **ALOJZ ZAVIRŠEK** from Šmarje-Sap near Grosuplje. The range of his products includes typical single-handed and double-handed baskets of various shapes and sizes. We can consider them local types more or less distinct from those of other Slovene regions. It is interesting that the richness of Slovene wickerwork is also reflected in terminology. For any one type of basket, for example, there are many different local names, a unique illustration of Slovenia's diverse cultural mosaic, its heritage, and its modern times. As his basic wickerwork materials, Zaviršek employs blanched hazel wicker and clematis switches, making his work particularly recognizable.

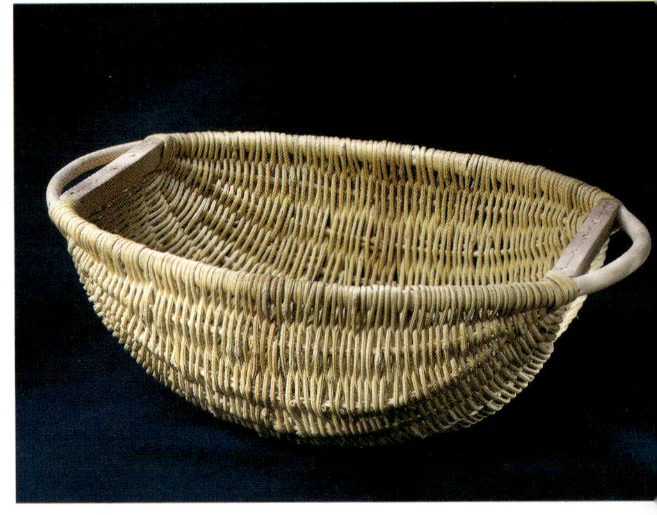

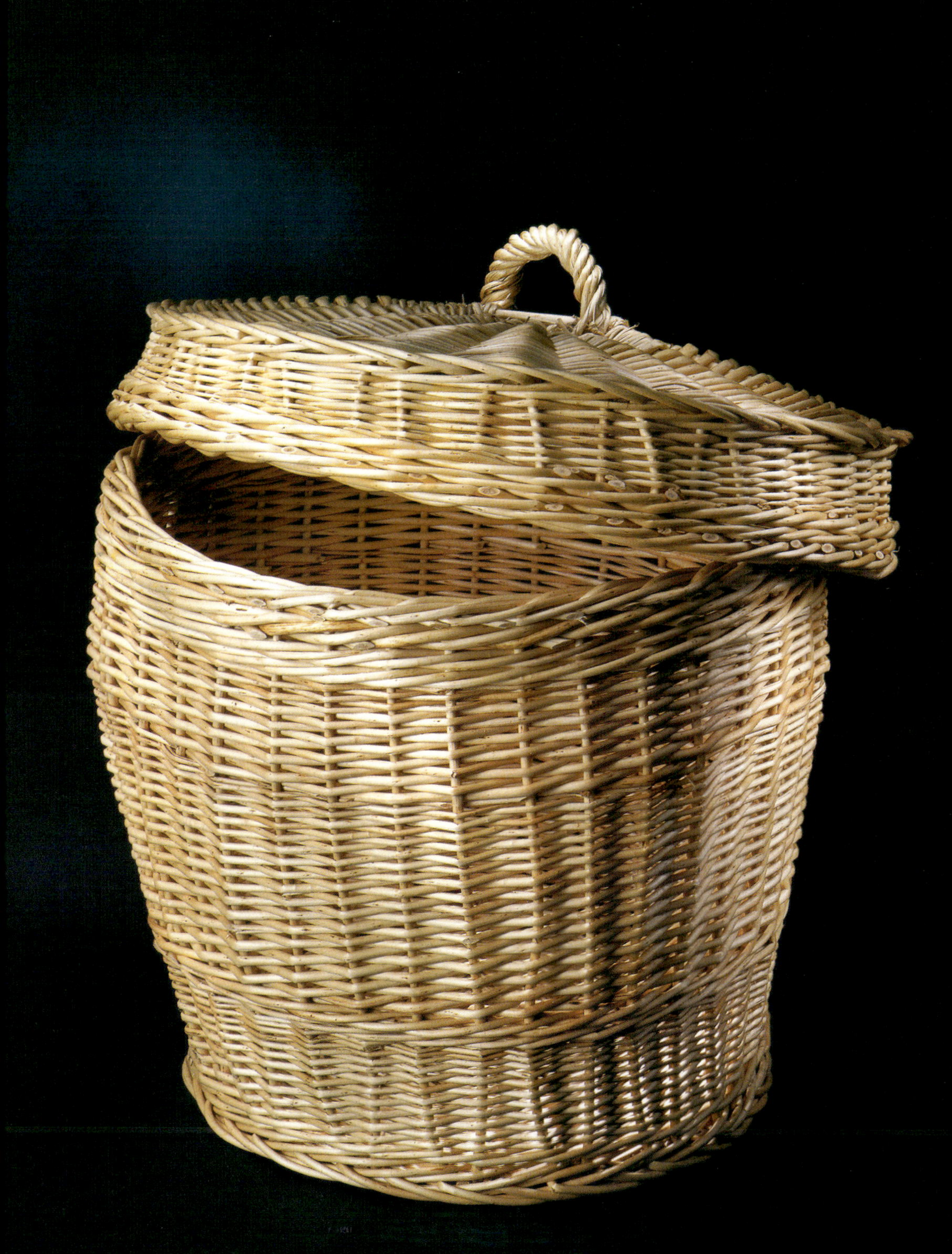

Master Matija Zupan teaches the young ►

Relatively few wickerworkers in Slovenia pass their rich knowledge and experience on to the young. The reasons for this are various. Apart from purely personal reasons is the fact that we have few organized forms of training for wickerwork artisans. One of the exceptions is Matija Zupan who teaches a wickerwork course as an extracurricular activity at the primary school in Preddvor near Kranj. He acquaints his students with typical local wickerwork items that are recognizable examples of Slovene wickerwork, including double-handled and single-handled baskets and shoulder baskets. The latter were a typical implement for transporting things, especially in the alpine world where they were used in everyday work and the care of the cattle (transporting fodder) as well as for carrying various burdens for longer distances.

Good bottles for good wine ▼

In the village of Sabonje near Ilirska Bistrica, **Alojz Možina** specializes in covering bottles with blanched willow wicker. Covering bottles in wicker is still quite a widespread activity in Slovenia. This is not really surprising, since Slovenia is a country of top quality wines and excellent winegrowing regions. The patient, painstaking, and universally high quality covering of bottles is therefore a unique expression of the regard Slovenes have for their wines. Along with wine, other beverages are also stored, transported, and offered in these protected and attractively decorated bottles.

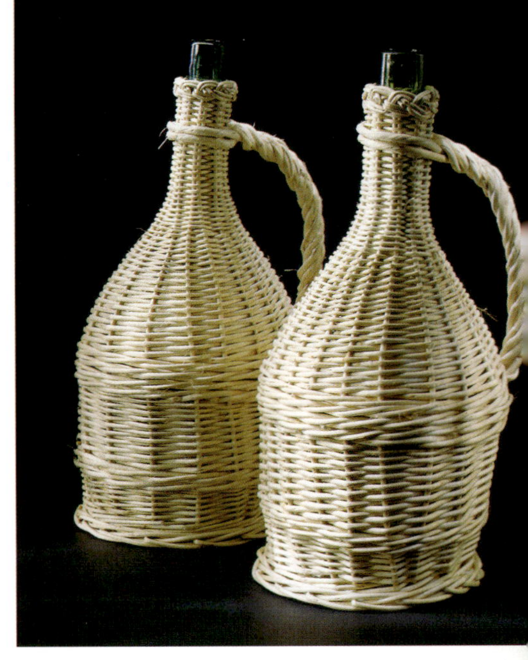

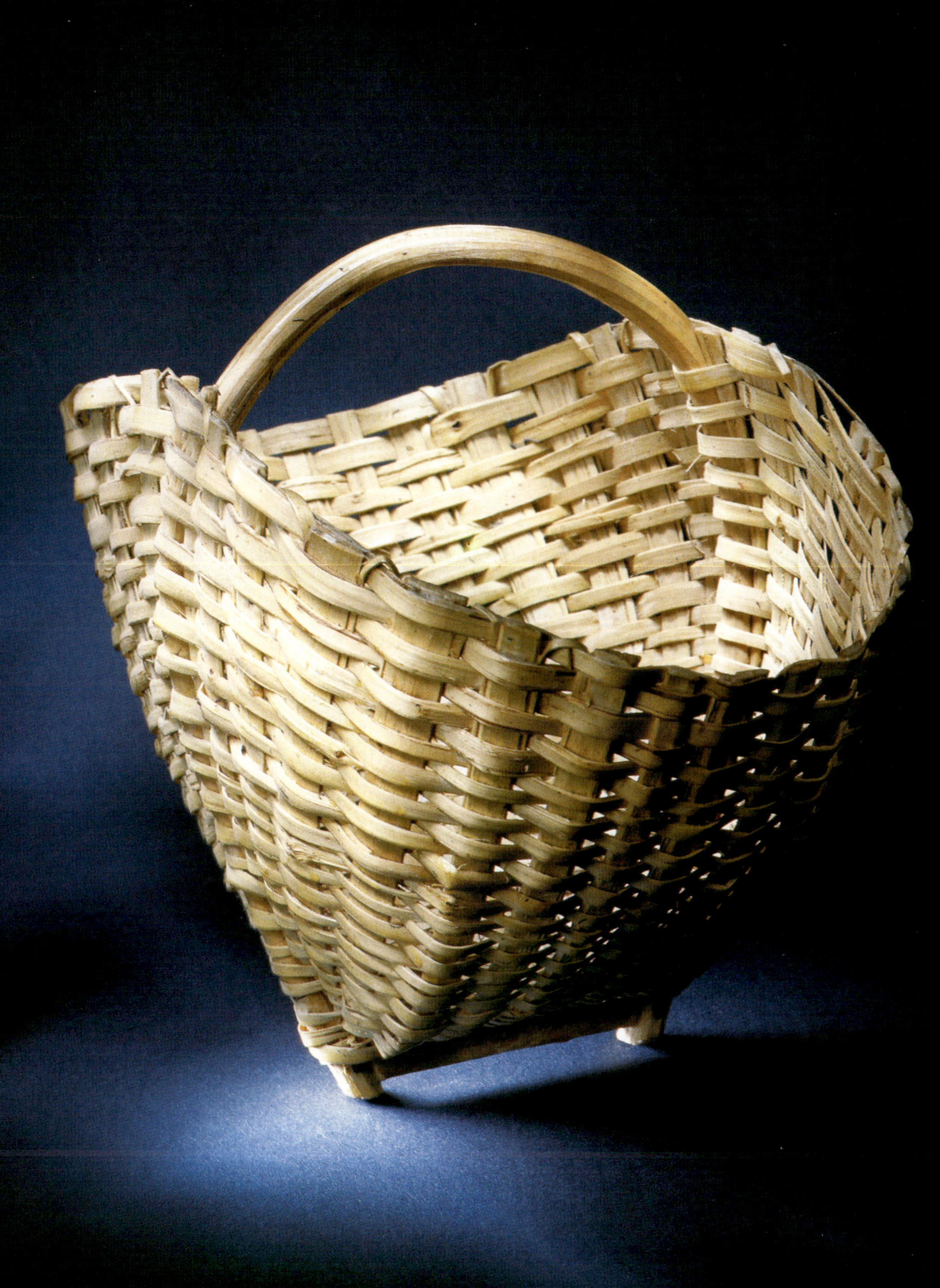

Tightly covered bottles ►

Covering bottles with wicker has both practical and decorative significance. This branch of wickerwork developed particularly in the winegrowing regions of Slovenia. The quality of the wickerwork is judged primarily by the strength of the wicker covering that provides the bottle with necessary protection against bumps and jarring and also by the esthetic appearance created by the rhythmic weave of the wicker itself. Some wickerworkers arrange a small gap just below the neck of the bottle by skipping several lines of wicker, and through this window we can see when the wine reaches the neck as it is poured. Among the outstanding creators of wicker-covered bottles is **Štefan Kalšek** from Žiče in Štajerska, the site of a Carthusian monastery known throughout Europe in the Middle Ages.

From teaching the young to a gift for the Pope ▼

Tončka Jemec is also passing her rich and excellent wickerwork skills on to the young, and naturally she makes outstanding wickerwork herself. Her somewhat modified range of products is a consequence of the proximity of Ljubljana and is largely oriented toward usefulness and adapted to the urban lifestyle. A special feature of her wickerwork activity lies in the special pleasure of discovering and seeking various new products and techniques. She strives to achieve completely unique solutions with her wickerwork technique and thus demonstrate the creative possibilities of woven wicker. She made one such item in 1996 when she created an enlarged rosary in wickerwork as a gift from Slovene pilgrims to the Pope in the Vatican.

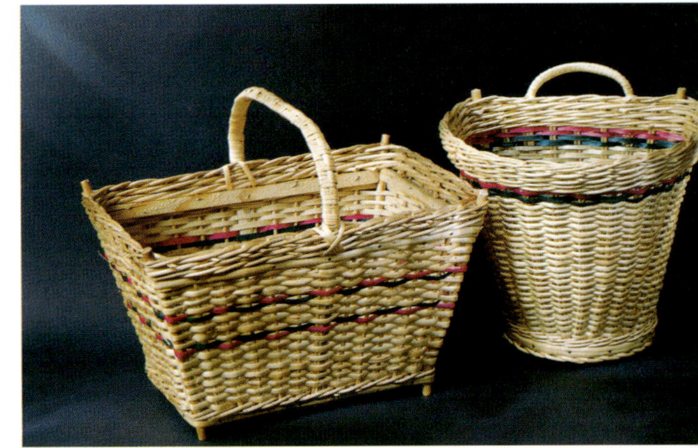

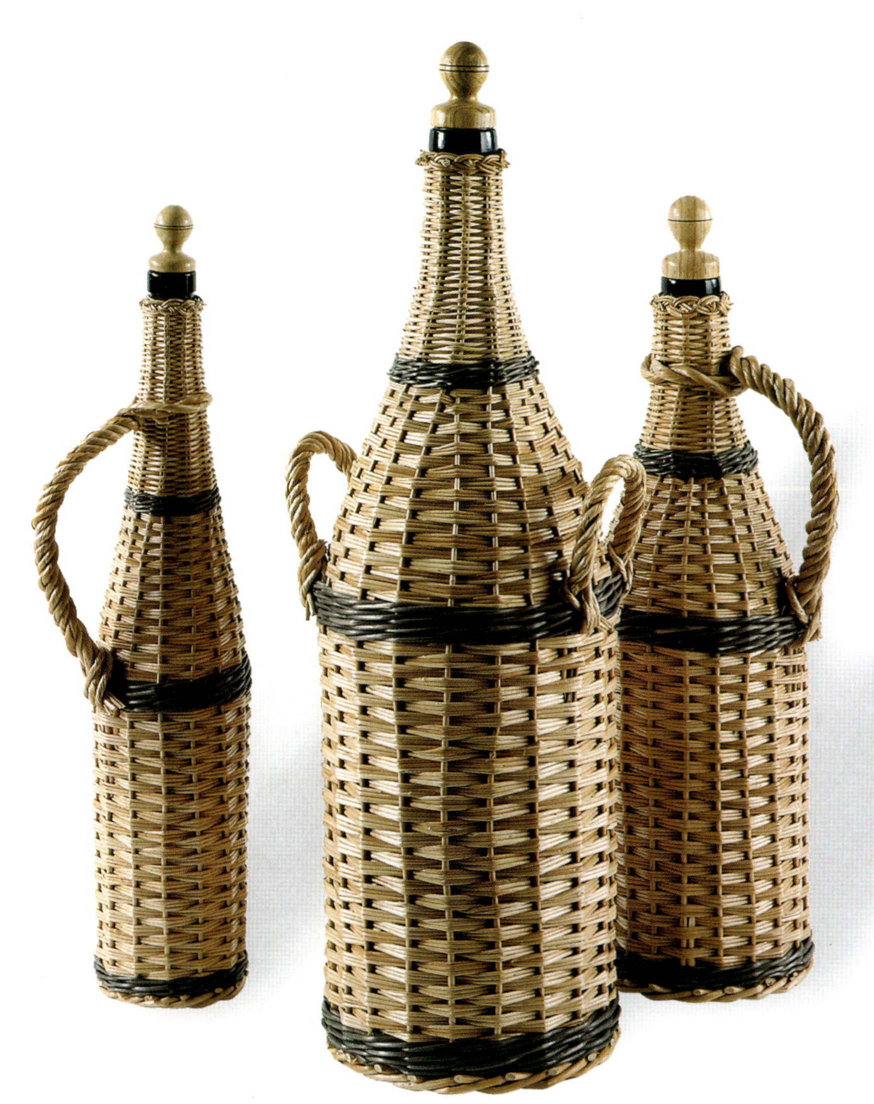

Ana Marija Klančičar from Dolenjske Toplice ►

Various types of willow and hazel wicker comprise the basic raw material for wickerwork in Slovenia. The use of this material reflects a unique form of symbiosis between man and his natural environment in the past when wickerwork handicraft activities were much more widespread than they are today. Cultivated willow plantations and areas along brooks and rivers where willow trees grew offered fresh shoots and one- and two-year-old osiers every year. Year after year, nature thus provided material wickerworkers later used to make their products. By annually cutting willows and other waterside bushes and trees, they cleared the riverbanks, which today are frequently too overgrown since this handicraft activity is waning. The balance between man and nature is therefore damaged as this and other handicraft fields die out.

Wickerwork and rituals ▼

There are many excellent wickerworkers active in southeastern Slovenia. One is **Janez Hočevar** from Škocjan, who weaves single- and double-handled baskets of various types. Due to the quality of their carefully selected materials and the richness of their final production and decoration, Hočevar's baskets could be ranked among the special wickerwork used for holidays and special occasions, for example, at Easter when Easter dishes are carried in them to church for blessing. Apart from their traditional uses, these and similar wickerwork items nowadays also serve as high quality and original packaging for various business and protocol gifts.

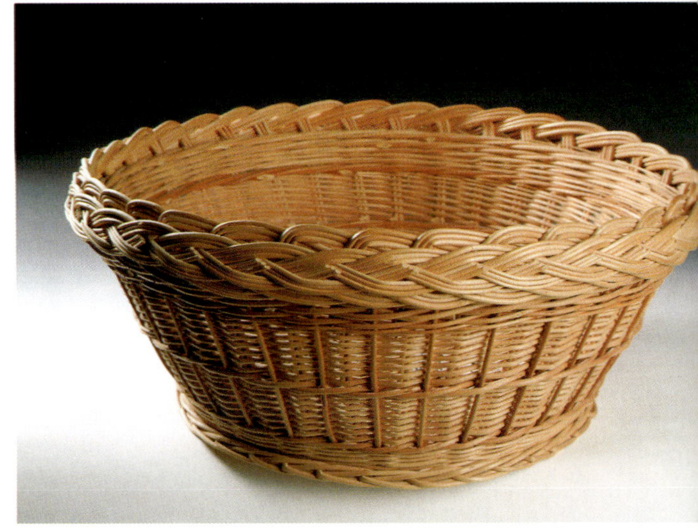

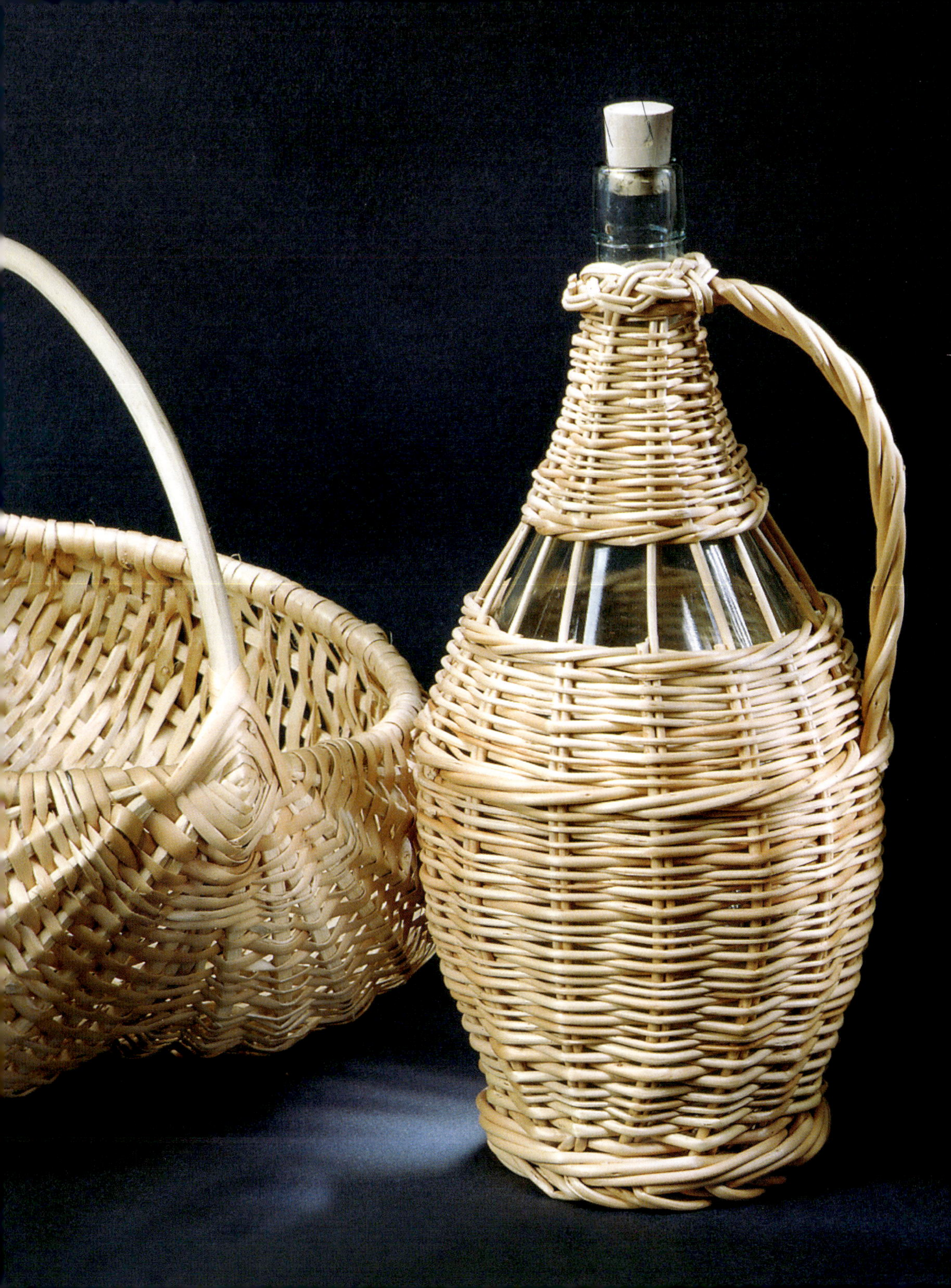

Switches and wood shavings woven into the Palm Sunday *butarica*

One of Christian holidays of the Easter period is Palm Sunday. Naturally, the roots of this holiday reach back much farther into pagan times when ancient peoples believed in fertility gods and offered them gifts every year in the spring. The Slovene *butarica* or bundle of switches and wood shavings naturally has an additional iconography, reminding us of Christ's arrival in Jerusalem where the people joyously awaited him with palm fronds. In Slovenia, the weaving of bunches of spring flowers and shoots into *butarice* takes innumerable forms and shapes. The youngest of these forms developed after World War I in the Ljubljana area, and they are still made on farms in the vicinity of the city. The greatest mastery has been achieved by the **Mrvar** family, who use the original techniques of arranging wood shavings to create new designs.

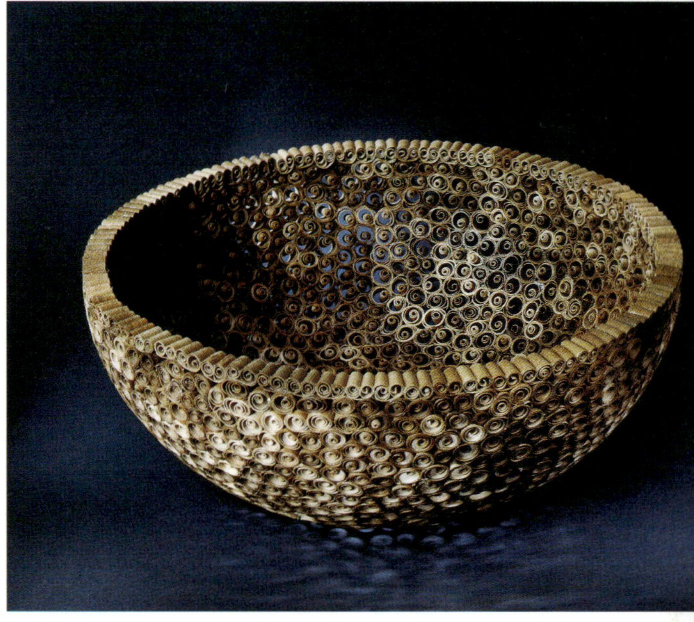

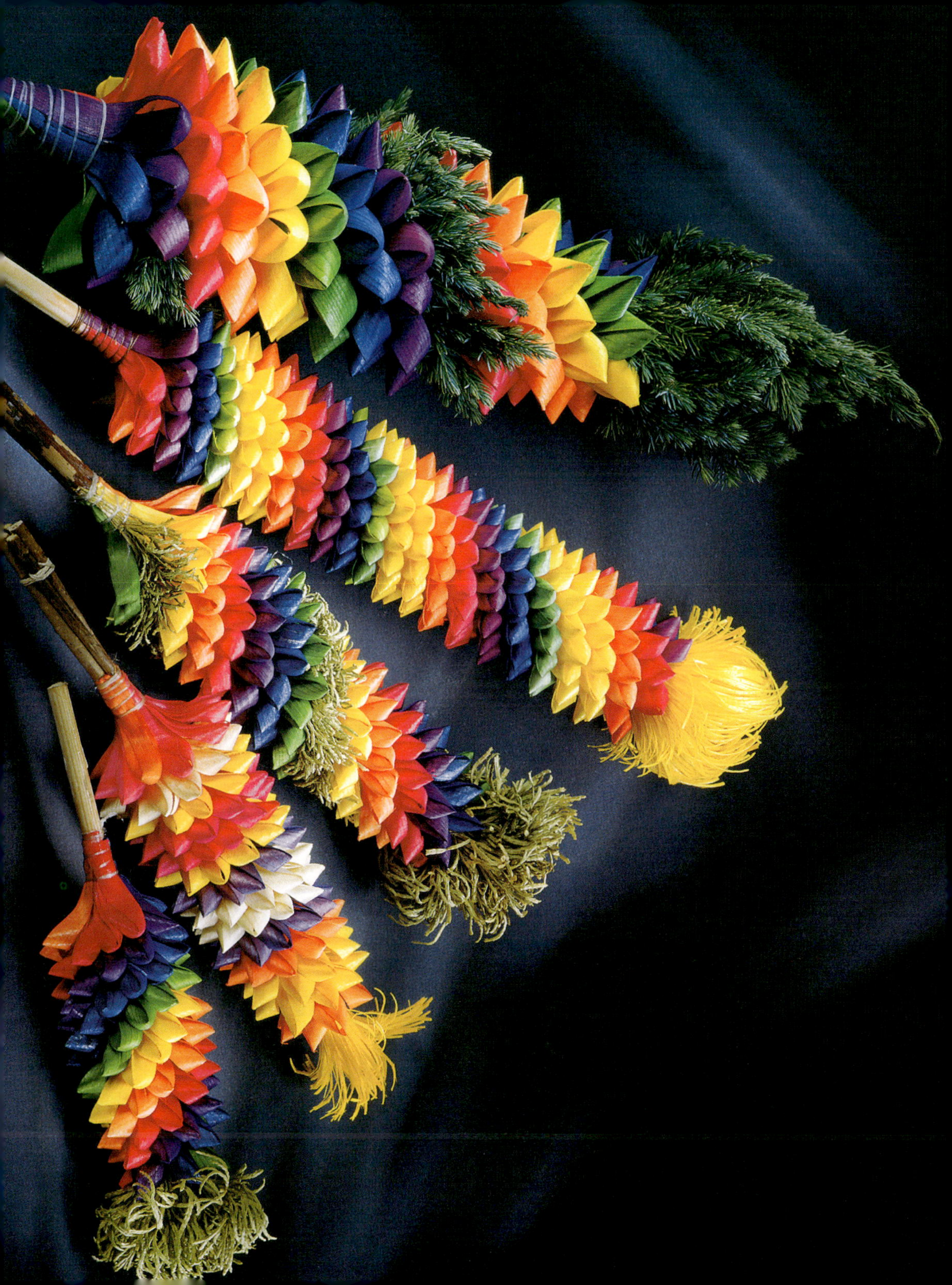

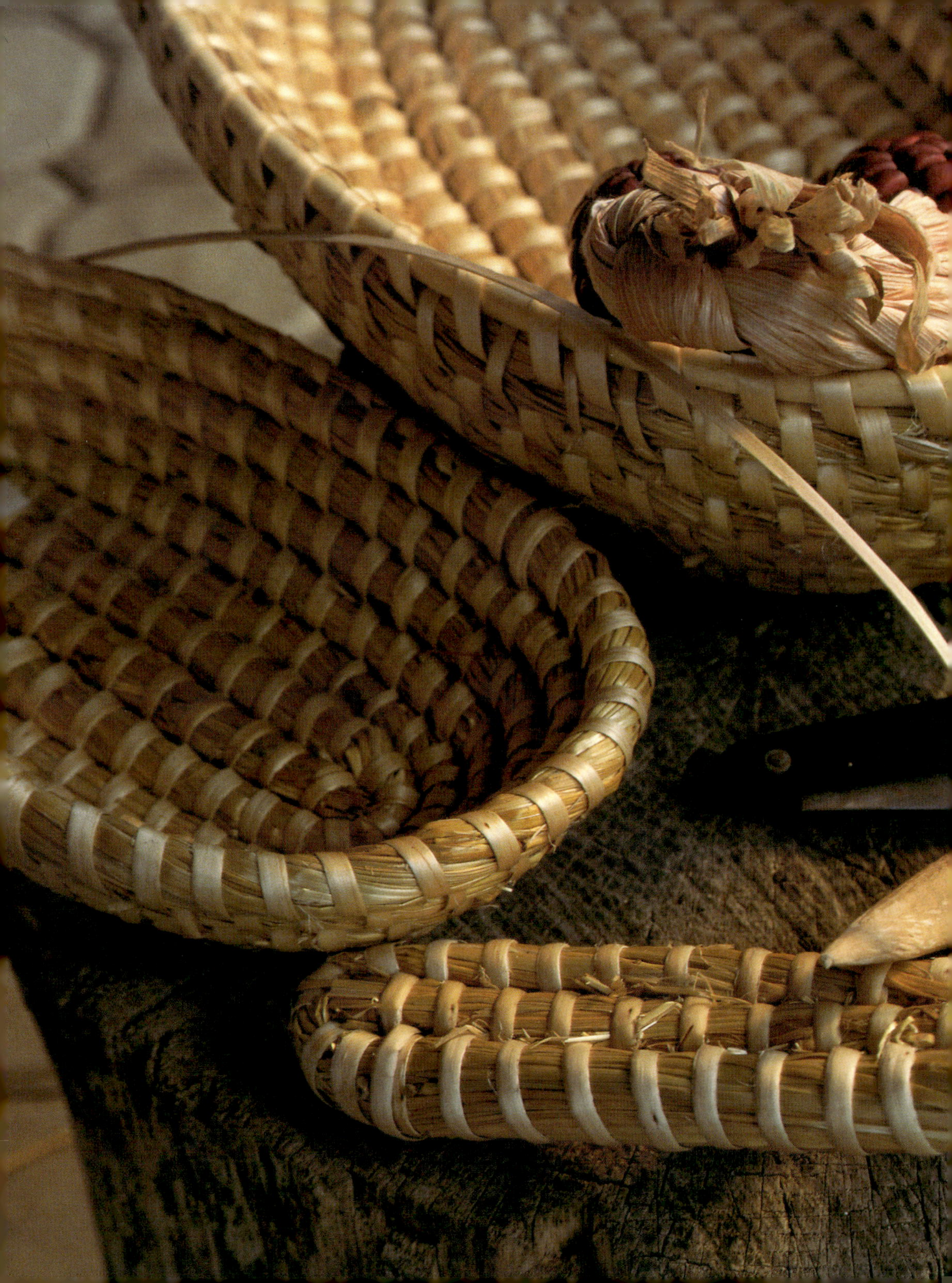

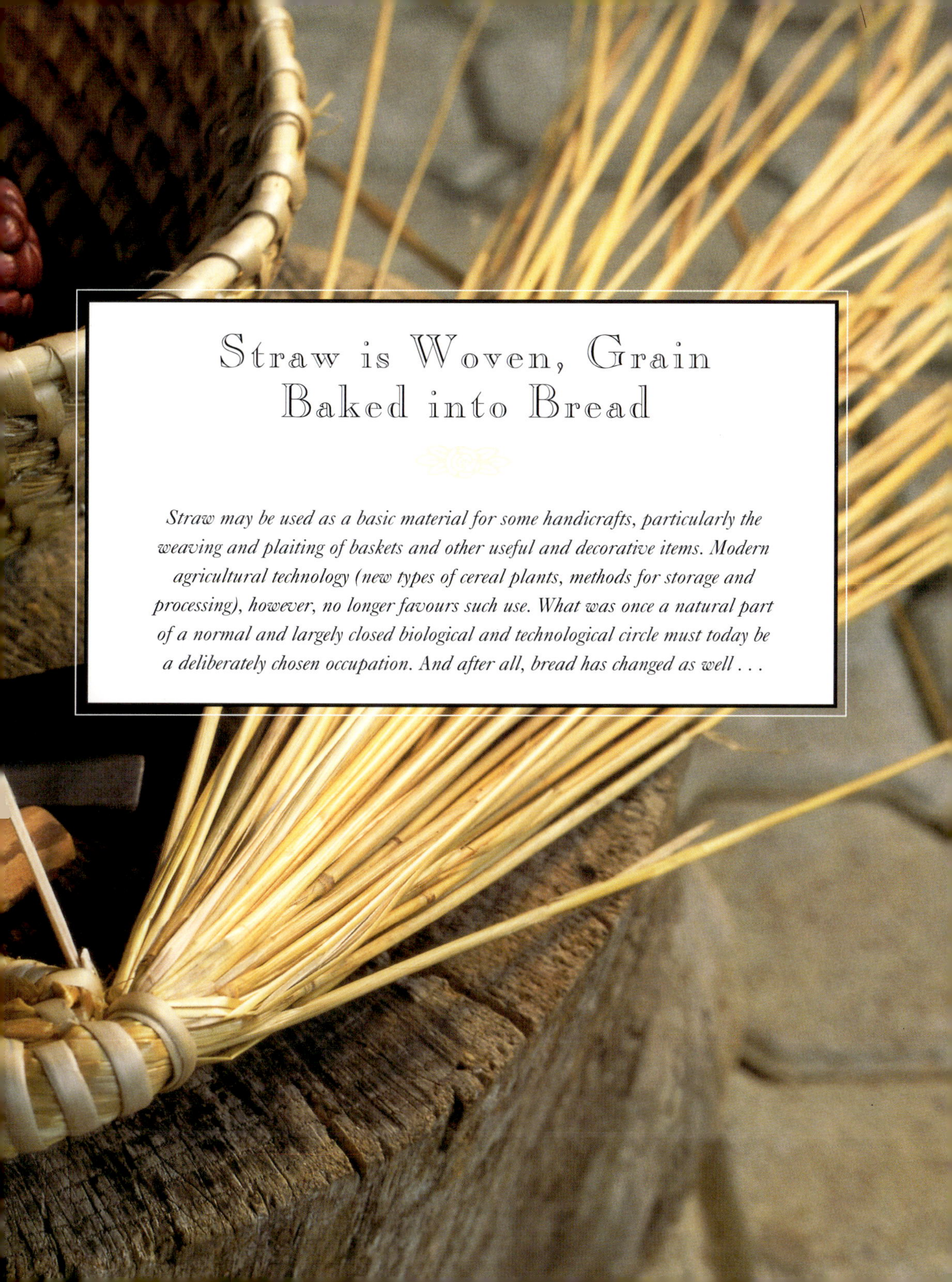

Straw is Woven, Grain Baked into Bread

Straw may be used as a basic material for some handicrafts, particularly the weaving and plaiting of baskets and other useful and decorative items. Modern agricultural technology (new types of cereal plants, methods for storage and processing), however, no longer favours such use. What was once a natural part of a normal and largely closed biological and technological circle must today be a deliberately chosen occupation. And after all, bread has changed as well . . .

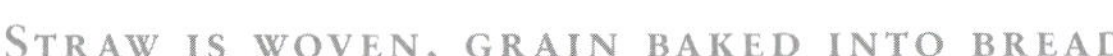

A founder of the Basketweavers Association ►

Anton Zakrajšek is one of our younger wickerworkers and is one who deserves much credit for the renewed flowering of wickerwork in southeastern Slovenia (Mirna, Trebnje). Some years ago he was one of the founders of the local Basketweavers Association, the only association of its kind in Slovenia. This master makes cables of straw wrapped with thin wicker and binds them to create excellent wicker baskets of a type that were indispensable in past centuries for storing grain, various garden produce, and dried fruit. Some were also used as beehives.

From cereals for cereals ▼

Franc Jeriha from Prežganje near Ljubljana is an excellent basketweaver who makes shallow straw breadbaskets called *peharji* and the specially-shaped one-handled baskets once used for sowing wheat in the fields. Their asymmetrical shape, which resembles an oversized bean, is explicitly adapted to the human body and the arm motion used to broadcast seeds. Today, the uses for such baskets have gone beyond their original purpose, and they have become unique handicraft masterpieces that add both function and beauty to our daily lives.

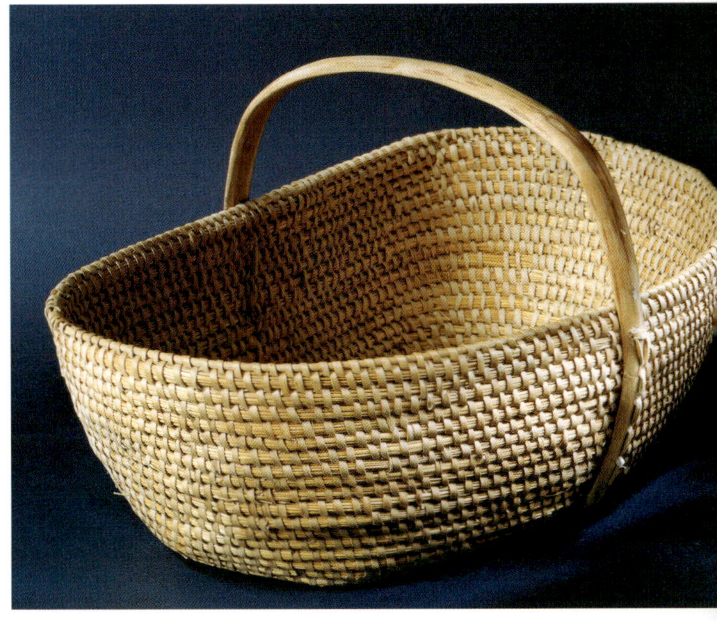

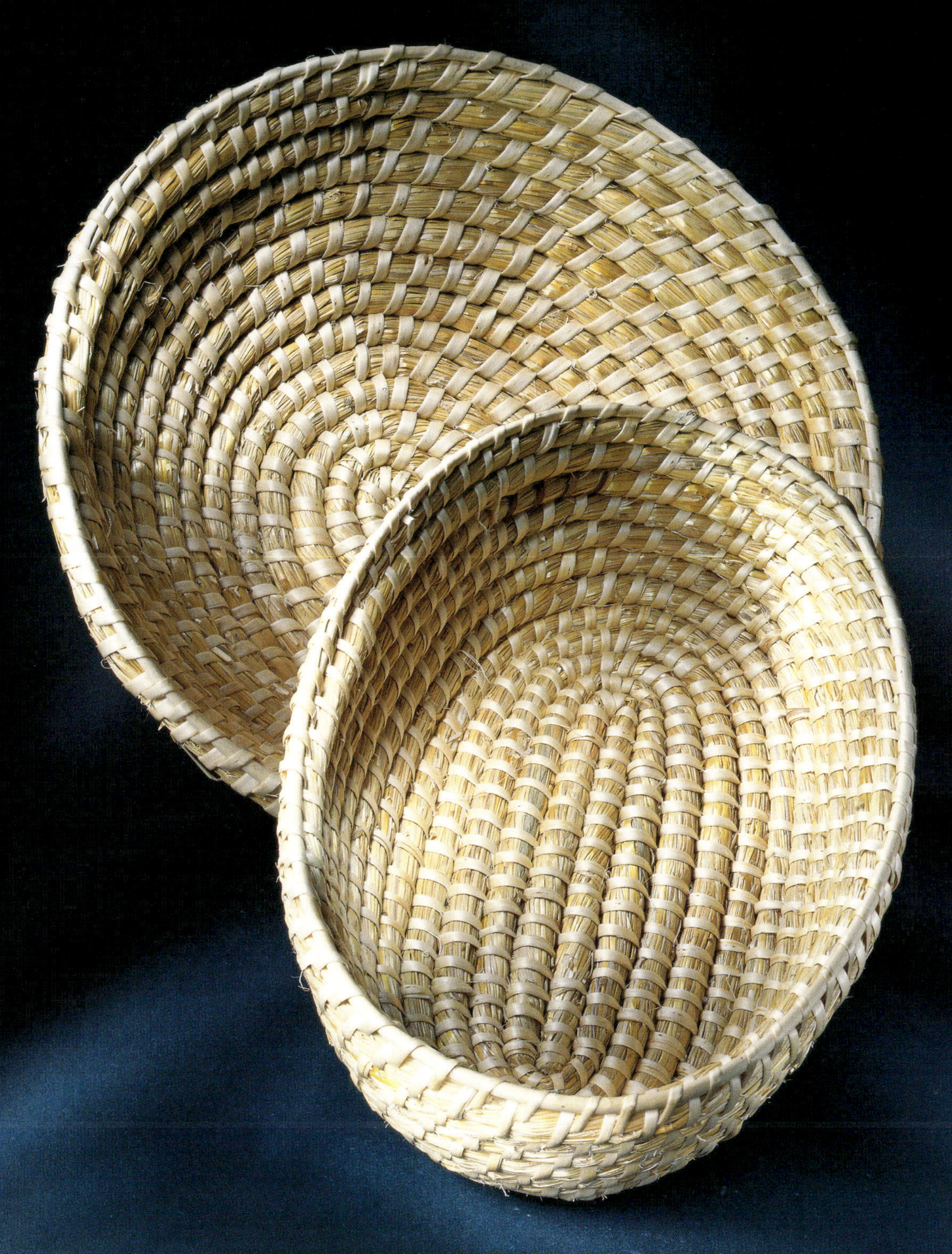

STRAW CHANDELIERS – A MEMORY OF ANCIENT HARVEST RITUALS ►

In Prekmurje, the northeasternmost part of Slovenia and the heart of its Pannonian region, the custom of making of decorative chandeliers and other hanging ornaments from straw has survived. The origin of this type of ornament so characteristic of Prekmurje farm households is somewhat obscure, and there are only hypothetical links to the other cereal growing regions of Europe's Pannonian world. These chandeliers are most often associated with the decoration that enhanced the festive holiday atmosphere on farms at the end of the harvest. There are very few craftsmen still making these handicrafts today, among them **IVAN** and **BERNARDA ŽIŽEK** from Lipovci.

THE STRAW BAGS OF MATILDA PROSENC ▼

In the 18th century, the authorities began to encourage a special cottage industry based on straw in Domžale, Mengeš, Kamnik, and nearby villages. Whole families braided straw plaits that were then used to make various items such as straw bags, straw hats, slippers, small boxes and bowls, wainscoting, etc. In time, factories were built to produce straw hats, but the raw materials, straw plaits, were still woven in homes and cooperative relationships were formed with companies. After World War II, however, this industry disappeared completely and the skill of braiding plaits along with it. Today, straw plaits are imported from distant countries such as China. Among the obstacles to the further development of straw bag making is the dependence on traditional models and patterns and the lack of modern design approaches.

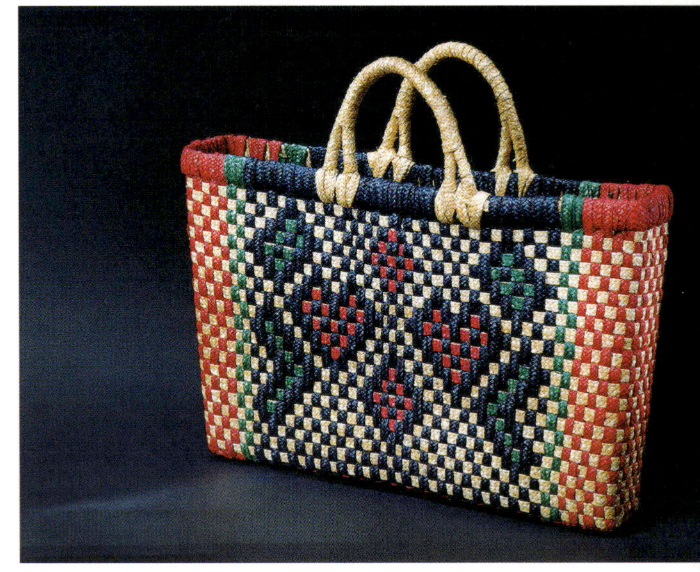

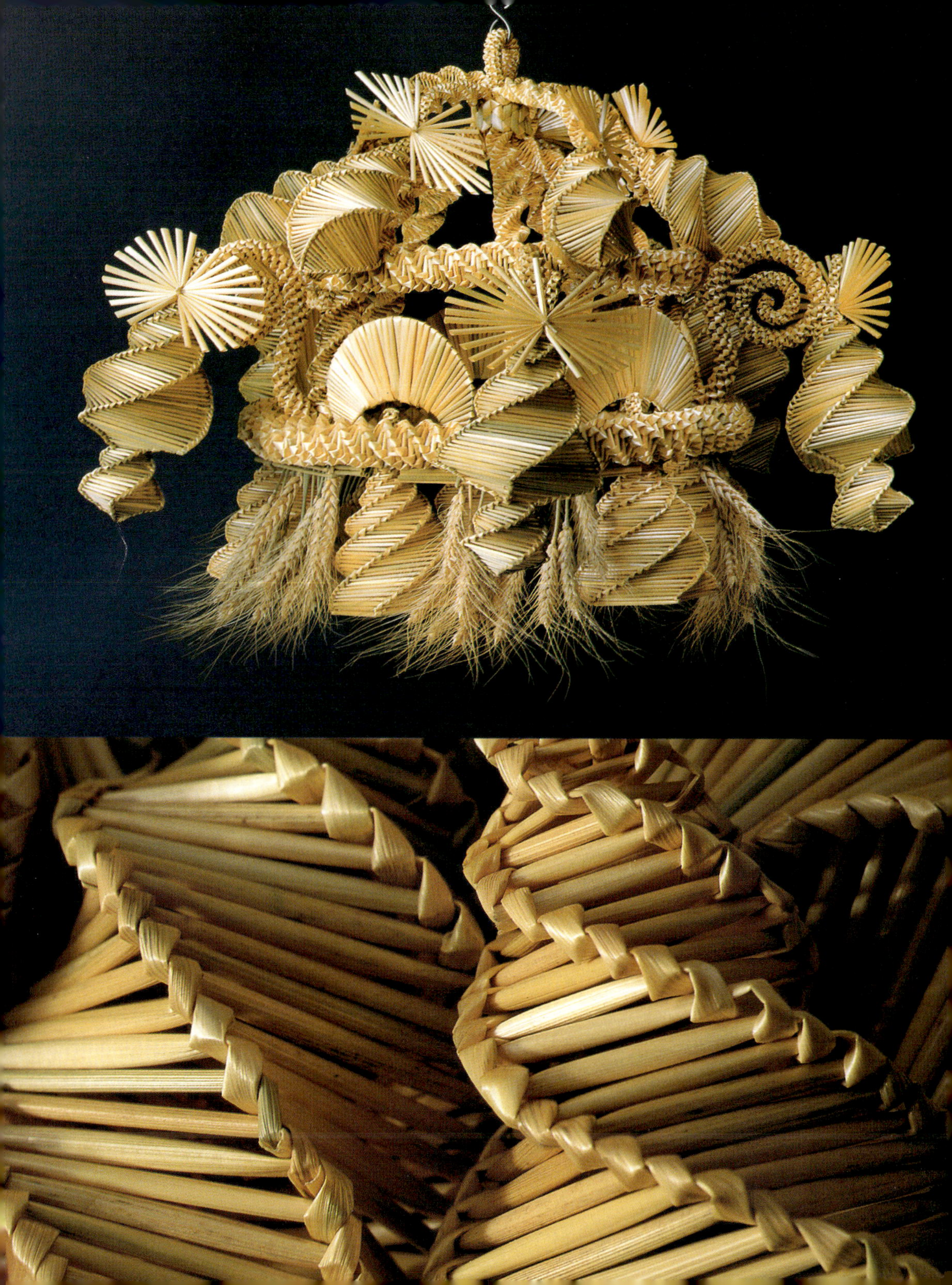

Veronika Starin's straw bags

These tall and narrow straw bags made from natural and coloured plaits of wheat straw are known as "*kranjski cekar*" after the Province of Kranj (Carniola, Krain), which from 15th century onwards was the central province of Slovene ethnic territory. In the past, the term "*Kranjec*" was synonymous with "Slovene." The production of these bags was linked to the extensive cottage industry of making straw hats that began developing in 18th century. Today, only a modest historical memory remains of this once widespread occupation.

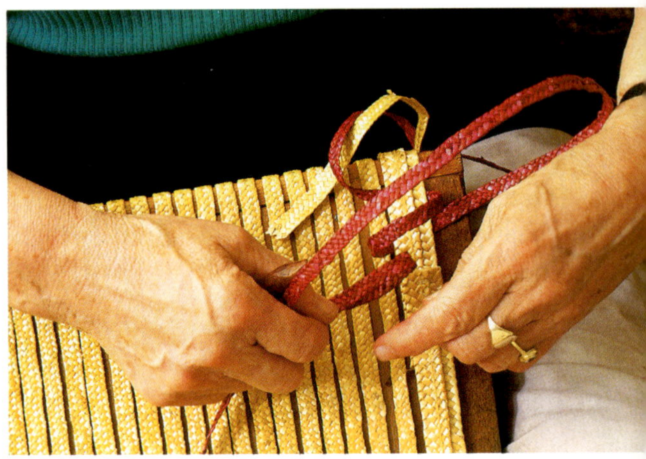

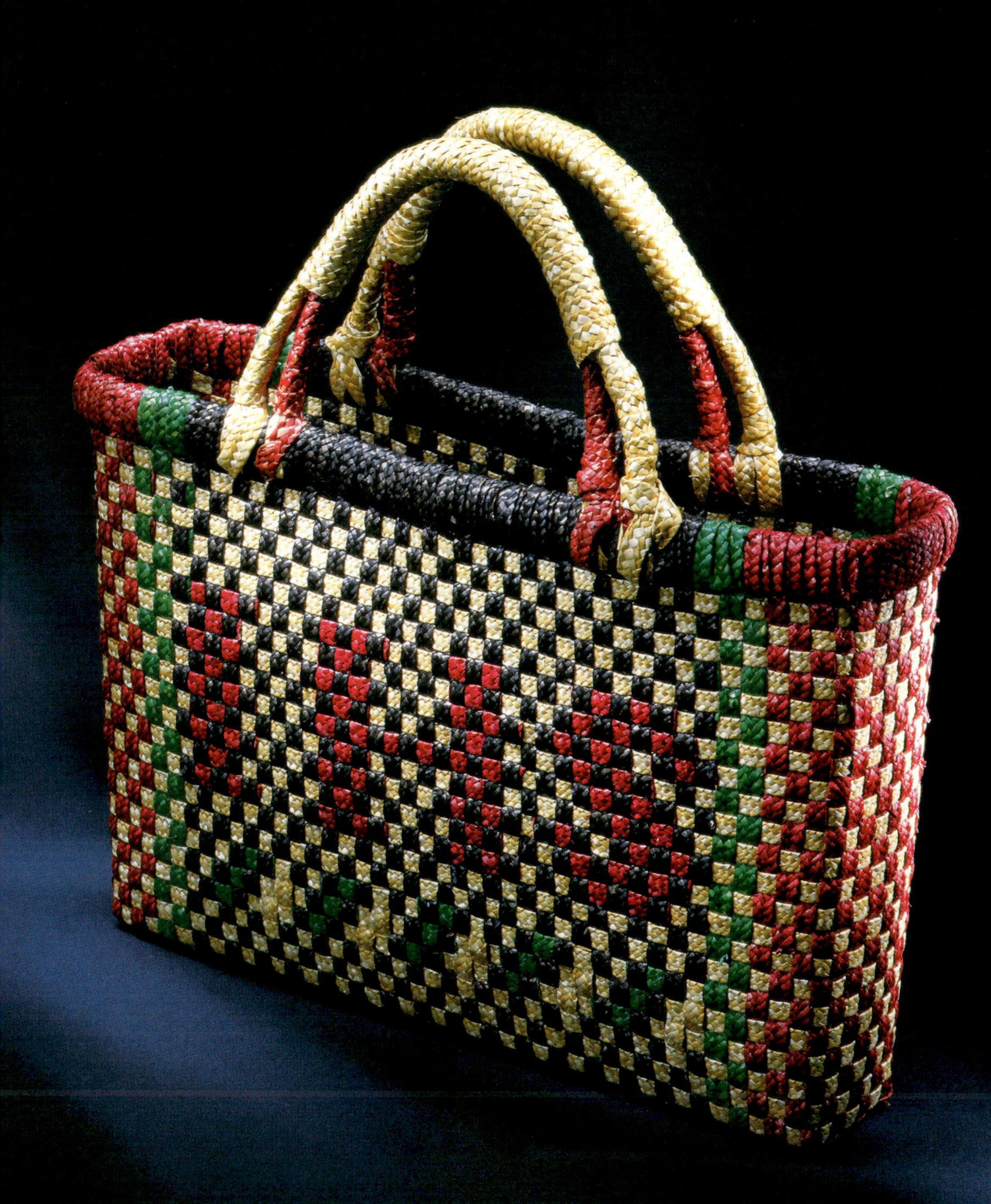

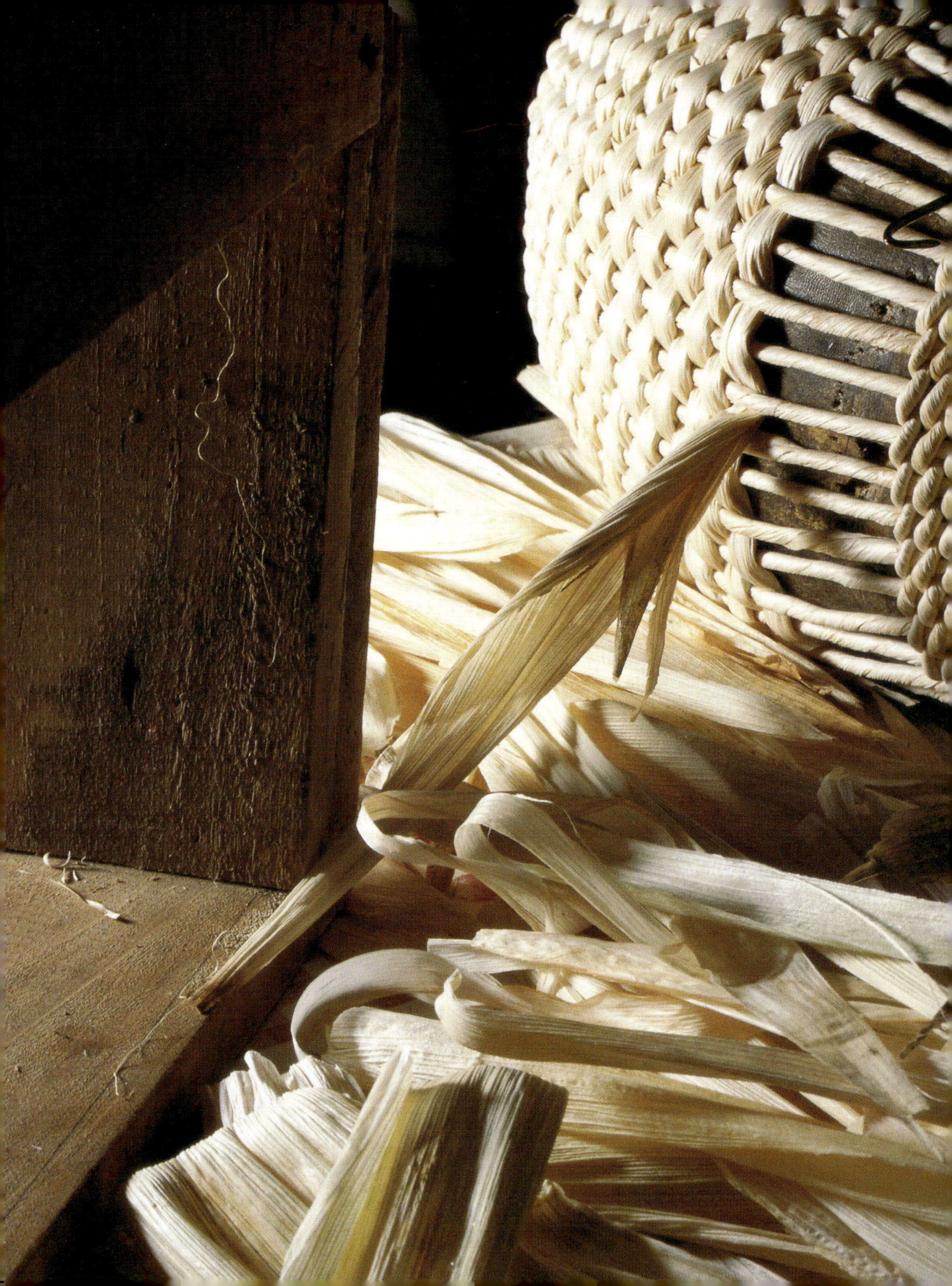

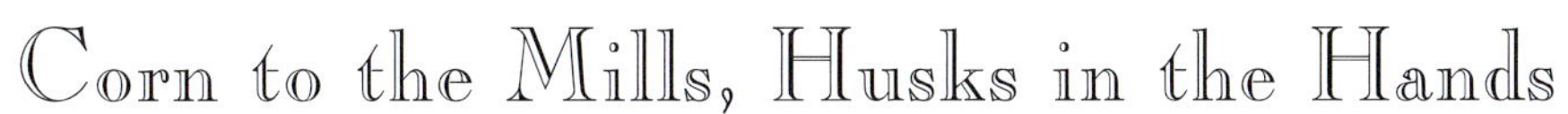

Corn to the Mills, Husks in the Hands

Like other countries, Slovenia acquired many new things in the course of history. Among the farm crops introduced was corn, which spread like many other cultural elements into Slovene territory from the west and east. Slovenes always knew how to adapt every newly-acquired innovation to their needs and way of life, and corn was no exception. Thus, all parts of the corn plant became useful, from the kernels to the husks, from which superb items are still produced with deft fingers.

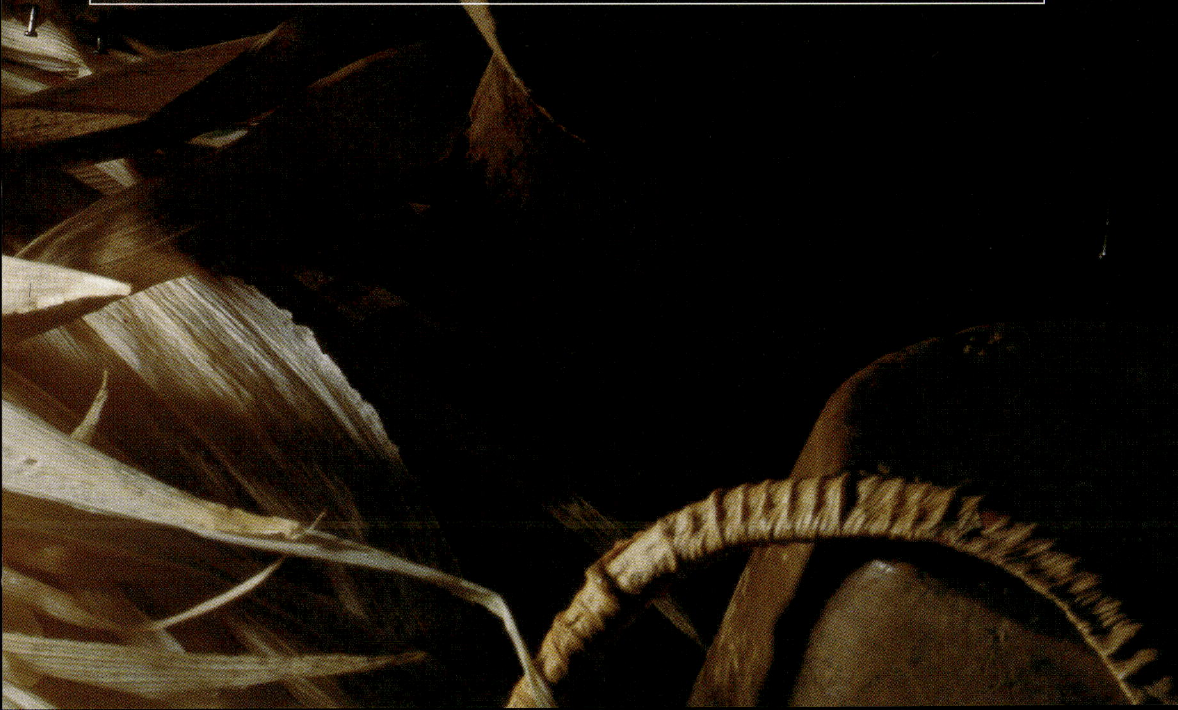

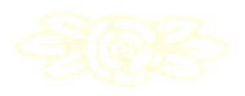

Corn husks and the fashion creations of Stanislava Vauda ►

The creations of Stanislava Vauda, a young fashion designer from Ptuj, are an excellent example of building on our heritage through modern design. For her, corn husks have become a basic material in the design of clothing. This innovative technological and design approach to corn husks should not be considered merely an alternative application or even provocation to bring new materials into design. Undoubtedly, new alternatives exists, but Vauda's work represents a challenging encounter between the body and the masterpieces of nature, returning to the oldest messages of human history when plant leaves or animal skins protected and at the same time marked and differentiated human communities in a special way.

Creative as well as sociable ▼

In Prekmurje, the weaving of items from dried and suitably prepared corn husks by farm wives and girls began to flourish after World War II as a source of additional household income. However, this craft has declined greatly in recent years. Changes in the technology of corn production have played their part as well. **Marija Rajtar** is one of the last excellent corn husk weavers. Working at home, she whiles away the time in the pleasant company of other village women who help her making straw bags, handbags, slippers, doormats, breadbaskets, decorative flowerpots, and stands for wine bottles and spices.

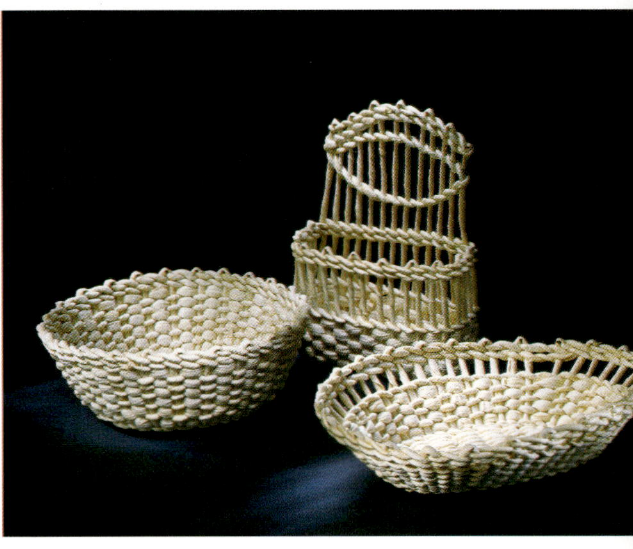

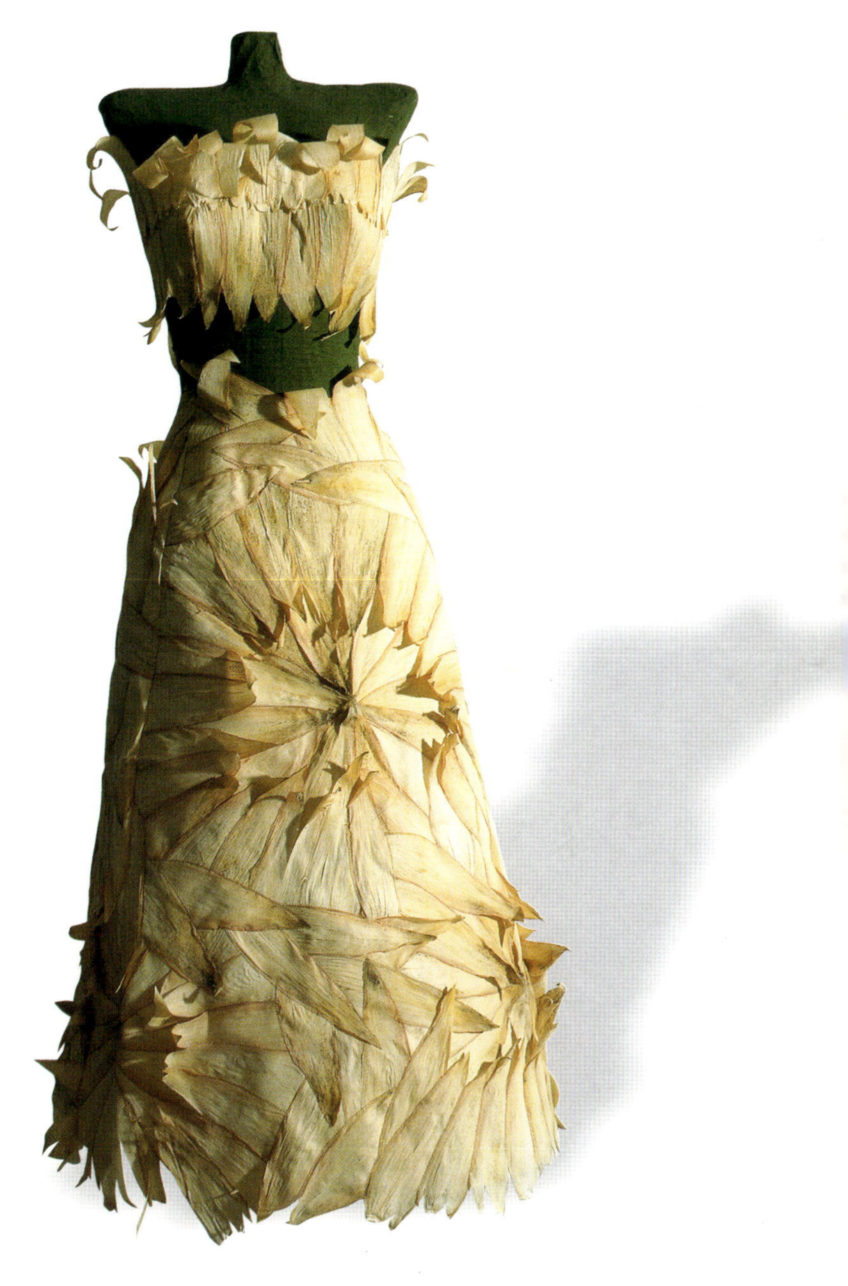

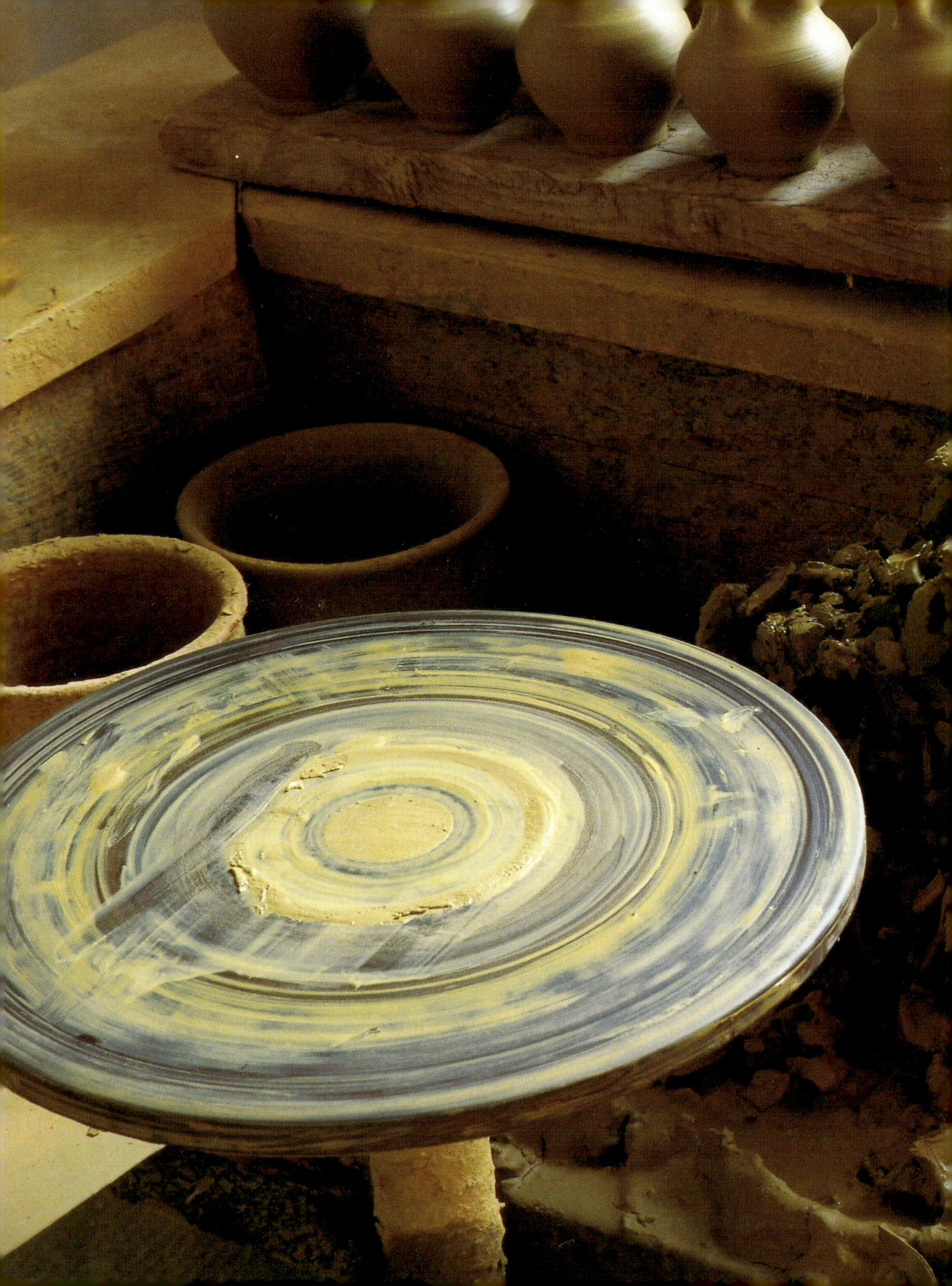

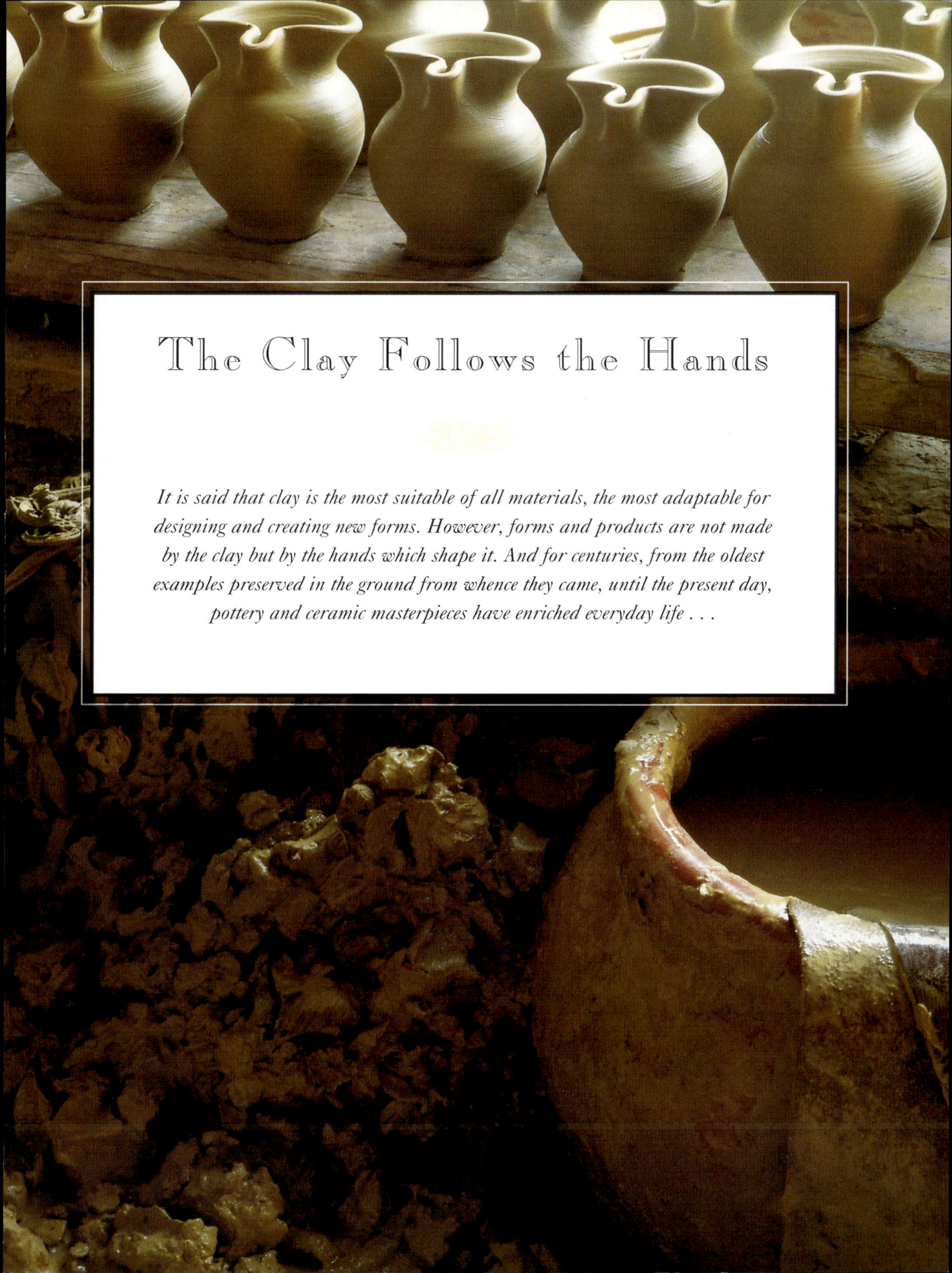

The Clay Follows the Hands

It is said that clay is the most suitable of all materials, the most adaptable for designing and creating new forms. However, forms and products are not made by the clay but by the hands which shape it. And for centuries, from the oldest examples preserved in the ground from whence they came, until the present day, pottery and ceramic masterpieces have enriched everyday life . . .

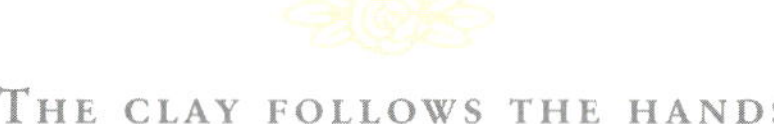

Three generations of potters in the Nosan family ►

Typical of the pottery produced by the Nosan family (grandfather **Jakob**, son **Jakob**, grandson **Aleš**, and son-in-law **Adi Sinanovič**) in Prigorica are figurines that often contain a whistle. With these figurines, the family carries on one of the most recognizable pottery traditions in the Ribnica Valley. They also use traditional methods for glazing and firing their products, achieving the most varied visual effects using different kinds and colours of clay. Along with the most diverse farm and wild animals, they produce a whole range of completely modern motifs with depictions of various human figures, occupations, and activities. They also make purely functional pottery such as bowls, pots, drinking cups, and flower vases.

A little horse that "whistles in the ass" ▼

In addition to the Nosan family in Prigorica, the Ribnica Valley boasts the **Bojc** family of potters, who work in nearby Dolenja vas. Among their most familiar products are little horses with whistles in their tails that are jokingly said to "*piskajo v riti*" or "whistle in the ass." They also make clay figures of St. George on his horse, a woman with her hands raised in prayer or supplication, and various whistles and "warbling" figurines. Water is poured into the latter so that warbling is heard when they are blown through. Of all potters from pottery centers in Slovenia, the potters of the Ribnica Valley produce the most figural pottery, including toys for children, whistles, and even Nativity figures for the traditional crèches arranged in homes at Christmas.

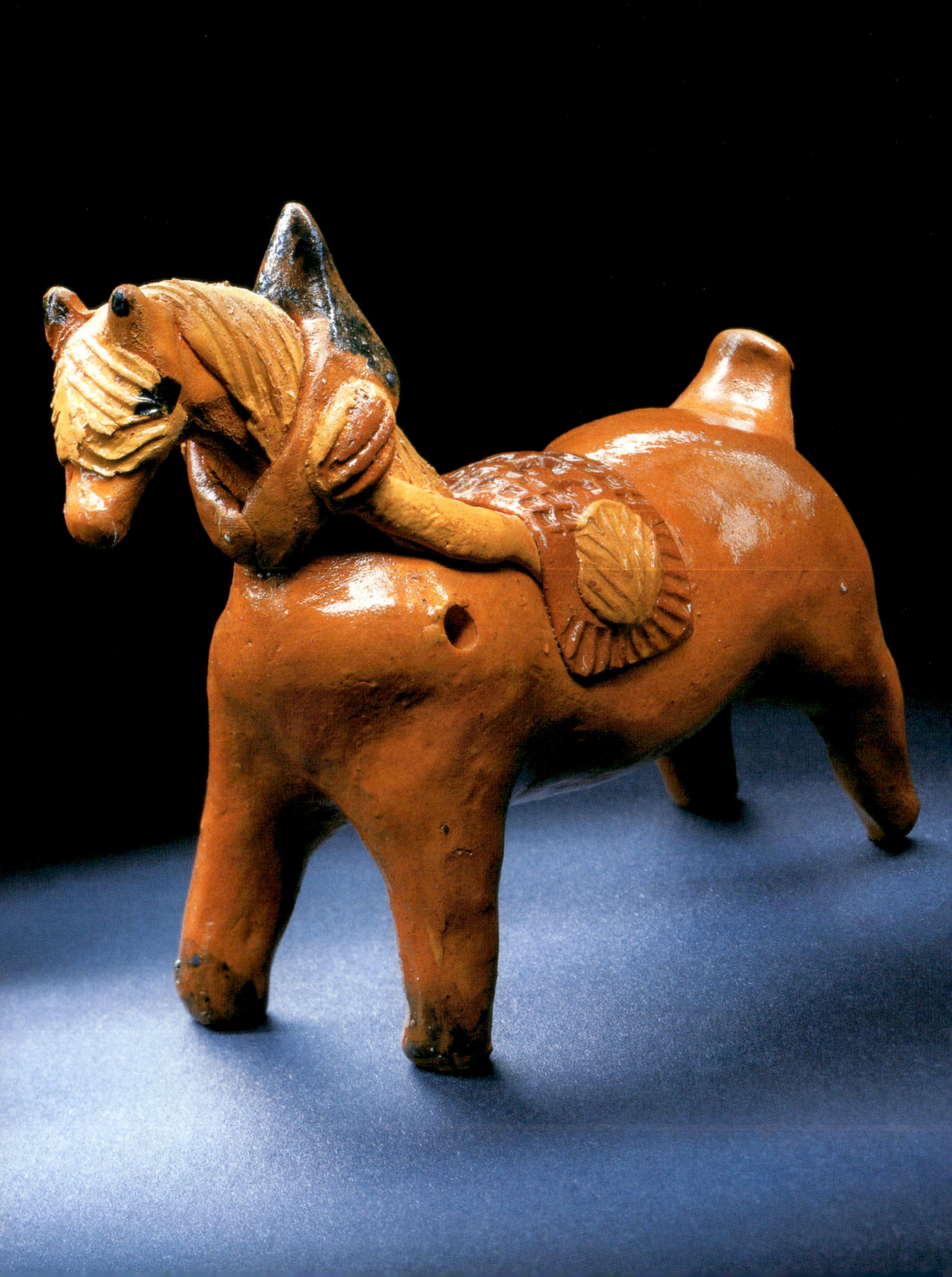

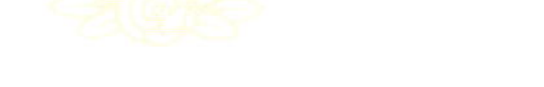

THE MOST BEAUTIFUL BIRD AND TRADITIONAL BOWLS ►

The traditional **PUNGERČAR** pottery workshop in the village of Gruča pri Šentjerneju in south-eastern Slovenia contributes two items of recognizably characteristic Slovene pottery that continue our rich heritage. The first is a wine pitcher in the form of a rooster. The rooster, a typical holiday dish in this winegrowing region of Slovenia, also appears in a local folk song praising this "most beautiful bird." The second line of distinctive products comprises remarkable bowls decorated with white lines and stylized patterns. These patterns are a continuation of traditional motifs and their derivations, and in their simplicity and artistic purity these bowls are examples of top quality craftsmanship.

POTTER FRANC BUSER AND HIS TRADITIONAL SHAPES ▼

Franc Buser is the only traditional potter left in the wider Celje area. His products preserve all the features long typical of pottery in this part of Slovenia, including shape, colour, and the uses of individual items. However, many traditional uses have today given way to completely new purposes. Function is superseded by decorative purposes or new uses have been found. Thus, a masterfully crafted pitcher formerly used primarily for storing homemade apple vinegar or carrying water is today used as a wine pitcher on special occasions or even a business gift.

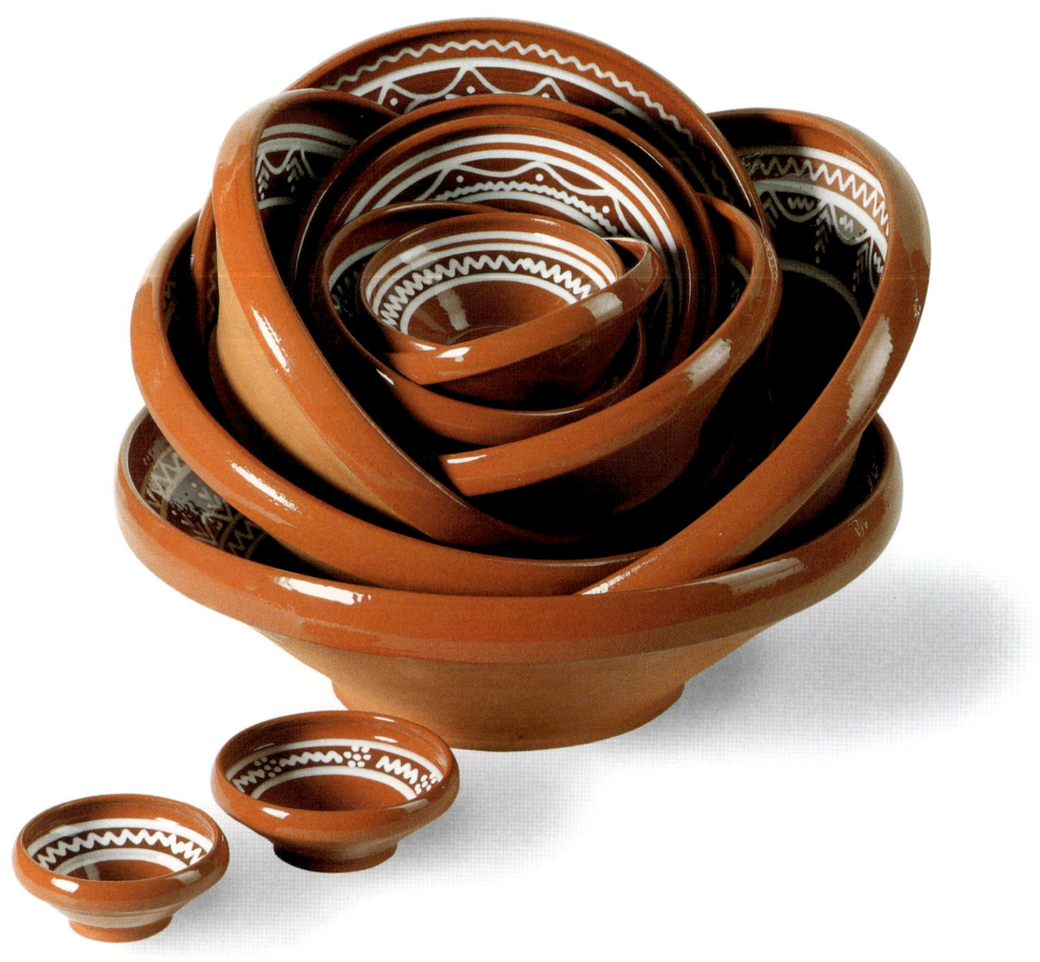

NEW PATHS THAT RESPECT THE HERITAGE ►

In Komenda near Kamnik, the former estate of the Maltese Knights Hospitallers and the home of the great European apiculture expert, priest, and patron of the arts Peter Pavel Glavar (1721-1784), **FRANC KREMŽAR** continues the rich tradition of this once important pottery center. The highest levels of skill and technique rank him among Slovenia's leading potters. He has developed a whole series of useful and decorative products and has exhibited at numerous exhibitions at home and abroad. His outstanding products include molds for baking potica, a traditional Slovene cake, various baking dishes, bowls, roasting pans, pitchers, earthenware vessels for wine and brandy, glasses, etc. He even makes sacral vessels from fired clay, an original gift for newly-ordained priests and other clergy. He works with numerous well-known designers to realize their ideas for furnishing rooms with fired clay objects.

GOLDEN WINE IN BLACK "*PÜTRE*" ▼

Potter **ŠTEFAN GOMBOC** from Tešanovci in Prekmurje makes one of the specialties of the pottery heritage of this part of Slovenia, bellied jugs of smoked or black clay used for carrying and drinking water and wine. The throat of these jugs is narrow, and the handle is hollow and has a small hole in its upper part. Liquids remained cold for a longer time in such jugs and were only drunk through the hole in the handle while the mouth of the jug stayed corked. With their pure form, these Prekmurje jugs or "*pütre*" are primarily decorative items today.

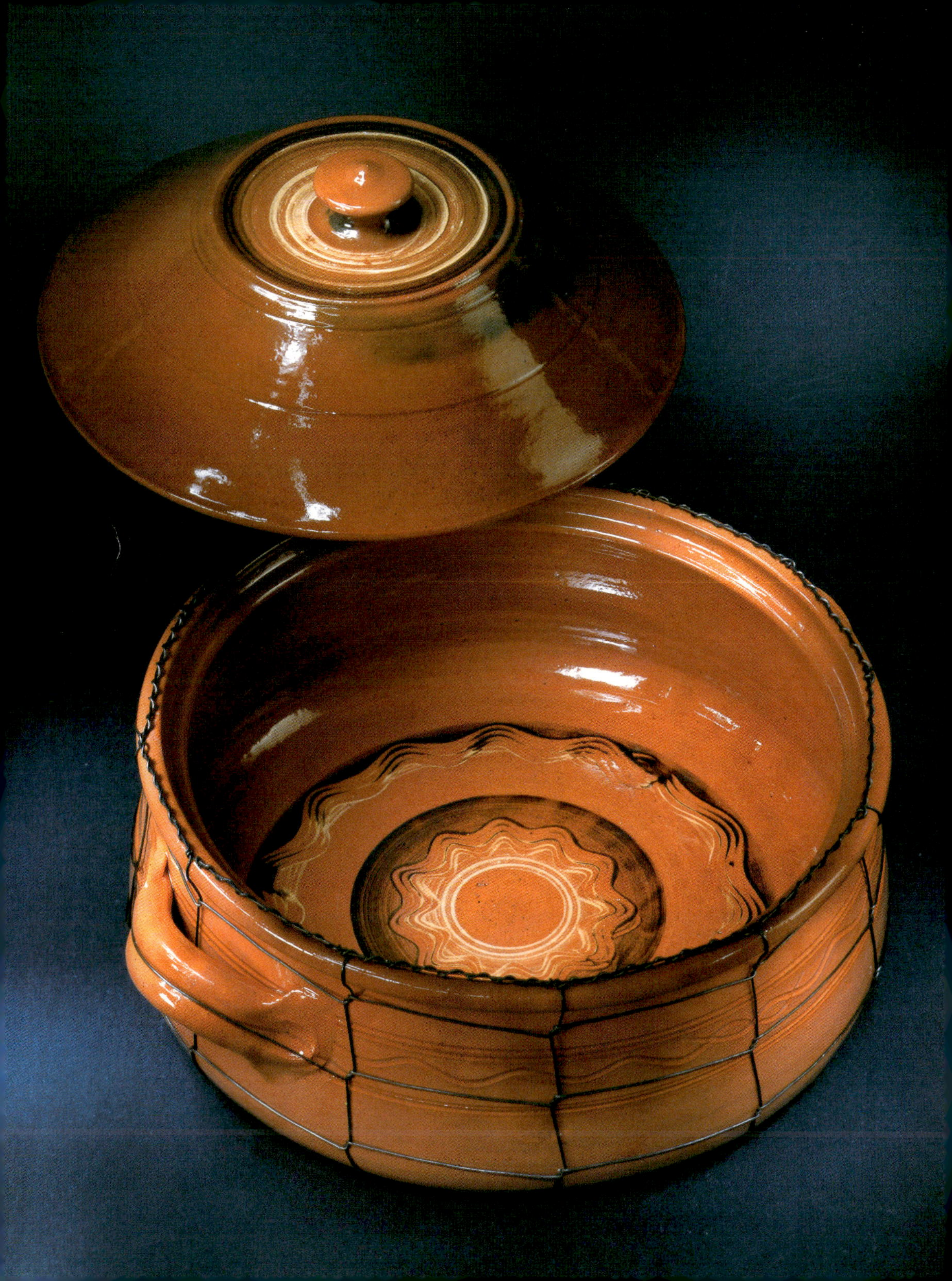

Modern design and traditional pottery ►

Slovenia's pottery heritage offers numerous possibilities and challenges for modern design. Pottery masters, who often acquired their basic skills in the family environment, naturally cannot be expected to create top quality modern designs at the same time. The repetition of traditional shapes and products is one thing, but creating new ones is something completely different. For the latter, skill and special talents must be combined. Through the collaboration of architect and designer **Matjaž Deu** and potter **Franc Kremžar**, a typical Slovene wine pitcher, the *majolika* or *ročka*, was given a new appearance while retaining all its "traditional" recognizable and functional properties, from ease of pouring and keeping beverages cool to enriching the celebratory mood around the table . . .

With smoke to black earthenware ▼

The potters of Prekmurje, the northeasternmost part of Slovenia, have preserved the traditional local characteristics of their products through a technology that also makes them unique. Their *kopaste* or tall oval kilns have seven or eight vents at the top for releasing smoke. During the firing, the kilns are loaded with heavily resinous (e.g., pine) logs that produce a thick smoke while burning. The potters then block all the vents so the smoke remains in the kiln and "walks" over the vessels baking inside. The vessels and other products thus acquire a typical black colour in place of other commonly used glazes. This traditional method of firing is used by **Alojz Bojnec** and his grandson **Tomaž** in Bogojina, a village that also prides itself on a remarkable church designed by the eminent Slovene architect Jože Plečnik (1872-1957), who incorporated works by local potters in the furnishings of the interior.

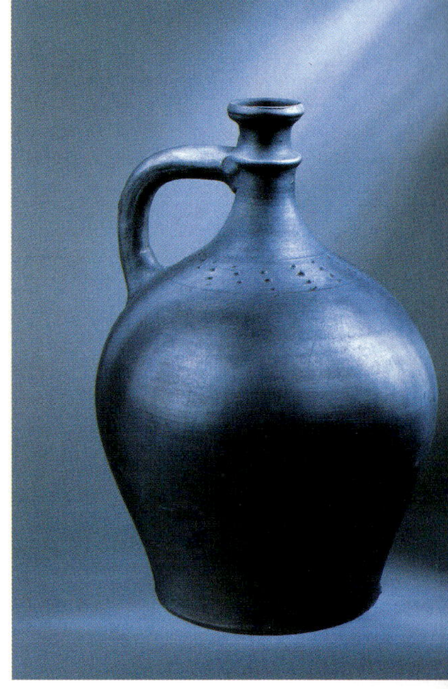

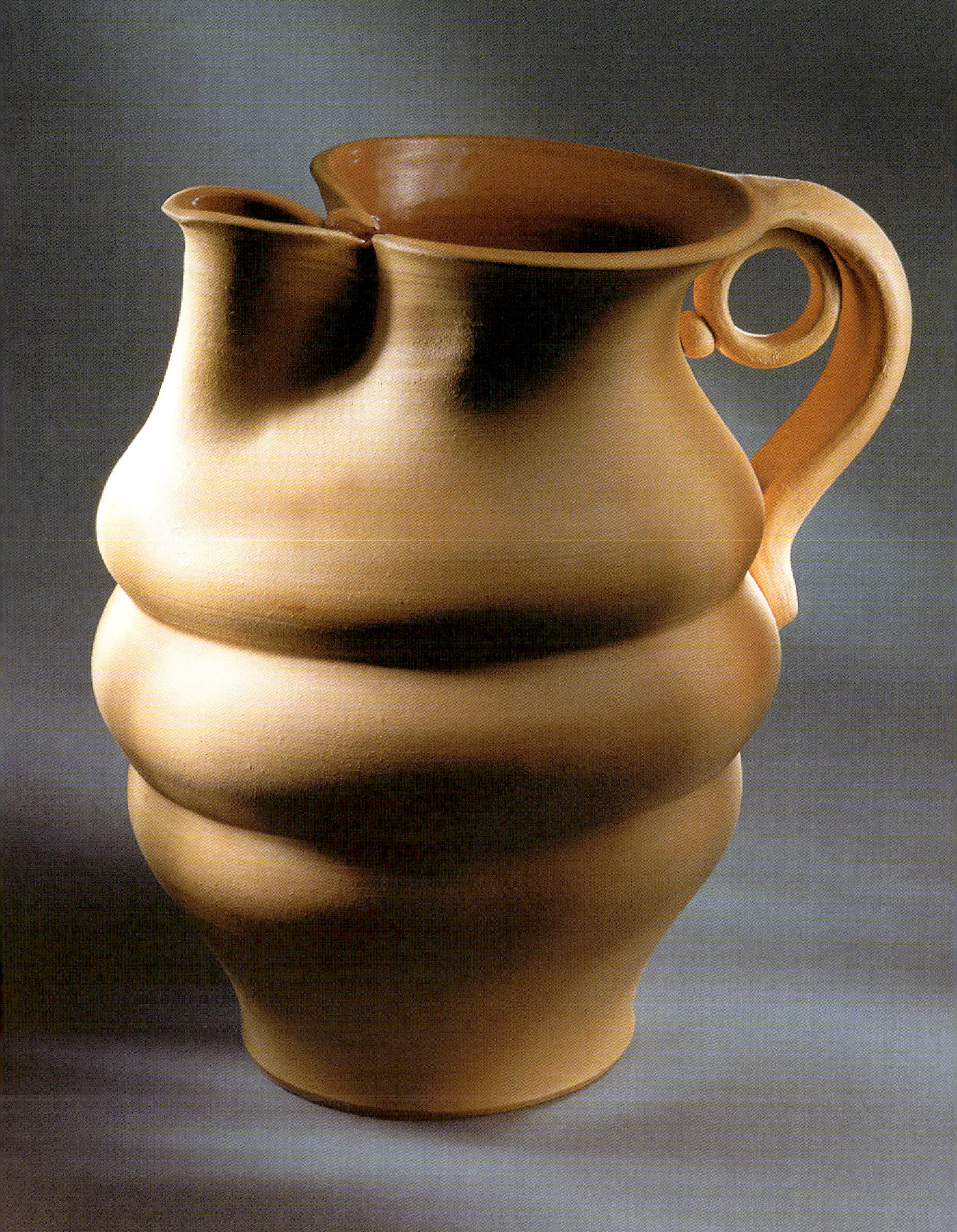

A breath of archeology ►

After several decades of stagnation (with rare exceptions), in recent years modern ceramic creativity has again begun to develop in Slovenia. While a number of courses and schools are now in operation, this is certainly not enough for truly quality progress in this creative activity and Slovene potters and ceramists have also established the Association of Ceramists and Potters, which helps significantly. There are also some exceptionally talented individuals striving to establish their own recognizable creative styles that are not merely interpretations of examples from (foreign) ceramics and pottery literature. The creative explorations of **Danica Žbontar** place her among them.

When photographs become ceramic figures ▼

At her studio in Laze on Planinsko polje, ceramist and potter **Nataša Prestor** primarily produces unique figural ceramics, particularly witty caricatures, in thematic sets, the majority based on the Slovene heritage presented in various ways and in various realizations. Foremost is the world of myth, which through her interpretations acquires an image of renewed actuality. She also brings to life subjects from old photograph albums and family photographs in three-dimensional miniature scenes. In addition, she has designed a whole series of human characters, figures from fairy tales, depictions of occupations, and finally animals through which she reminds us of the values of the natural environment that we often neglect.

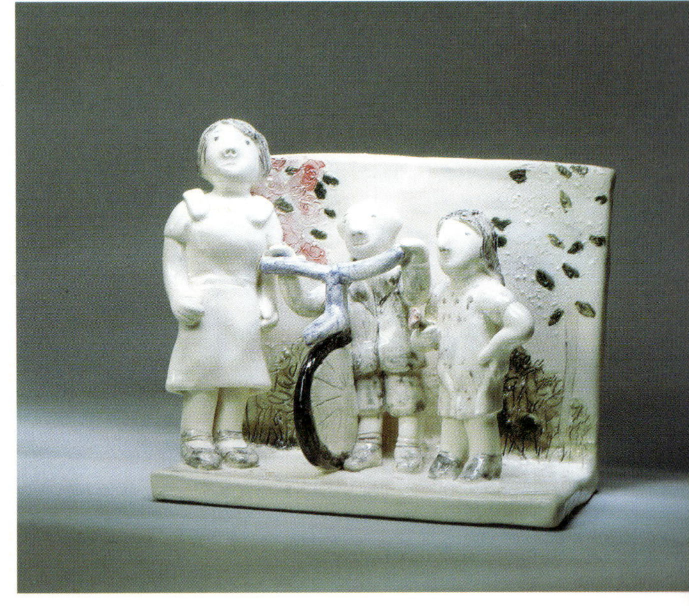

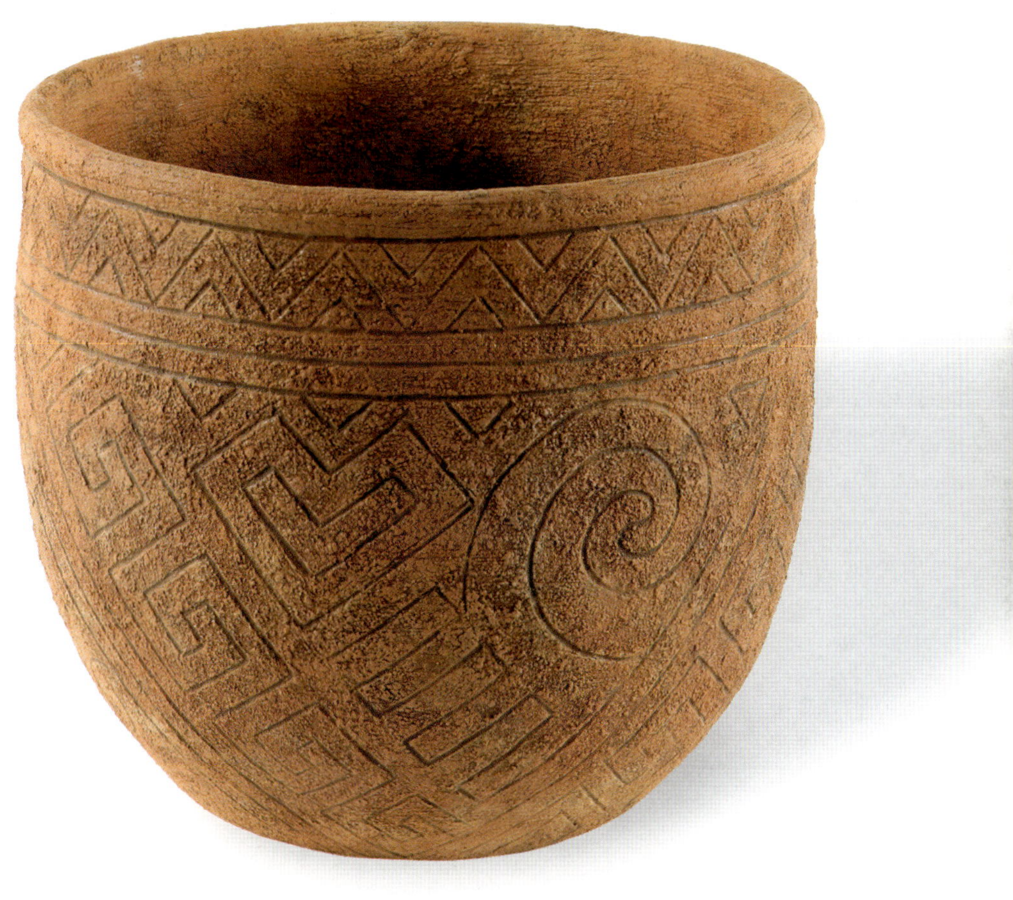

New expressive possibilities, enriched by Japanese technological skills ►
Superb ceramics technology and a deliberate philosophical model are the fundamental elements leading to the synthesis of profound introspection in the ceramics of **Majda Gregorič Trost**. Advanced training in ceramics in Japan has complemented her exceptional personal talent, and we can say that the artist has united the experience of both worlds.

Unique ceramic explorations ▼
The useful and decorative pieces by **Tanja Smole – Cvelbar** rank at the very top of unique pottery and ceramic design in Slovenia. Her works are immediately recognizable for their unique and deliberate artistic language and the synthesis of form and colourful glazes. Thus, upon closer inspection, her useful items enter the field of noble spatial sculptures.

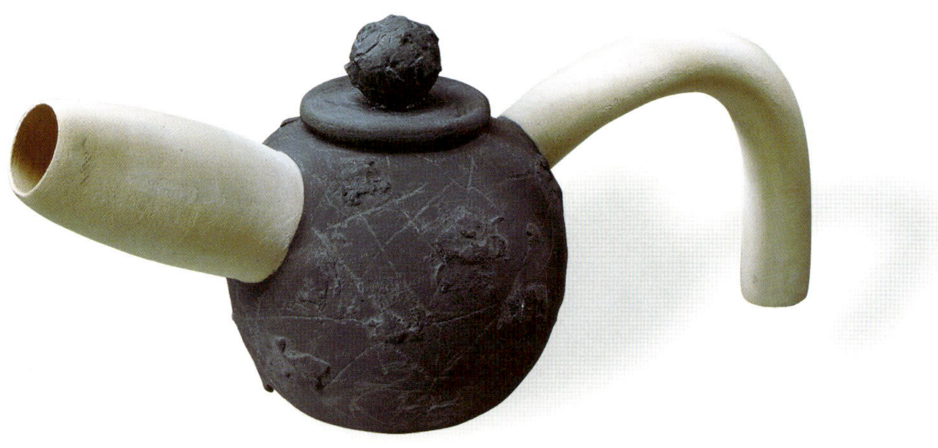

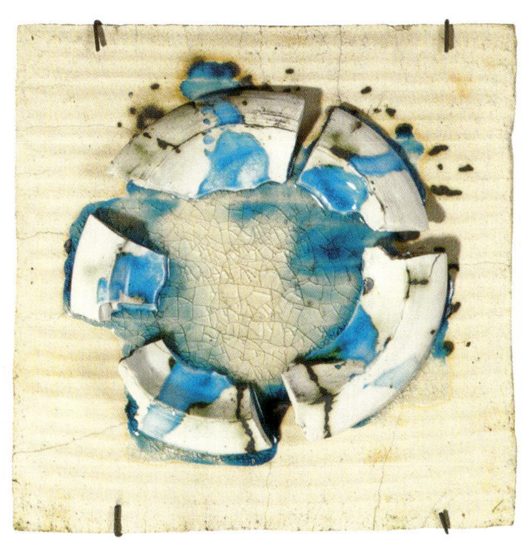
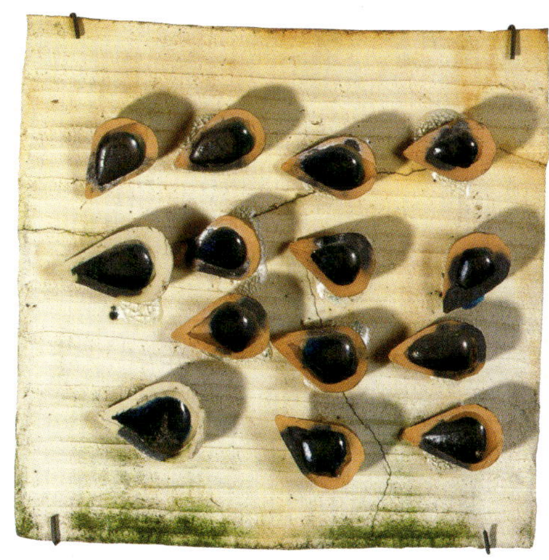
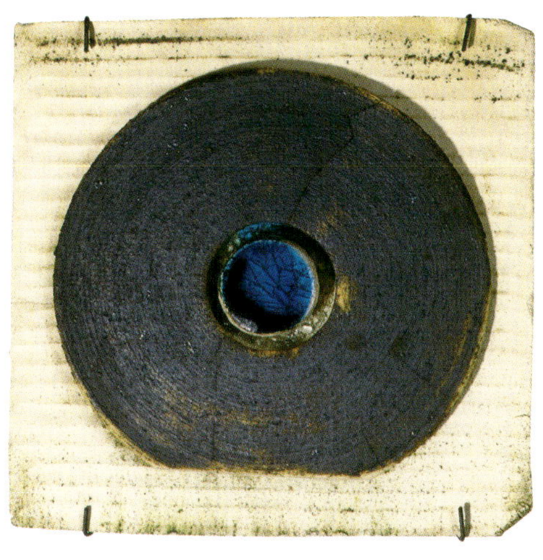
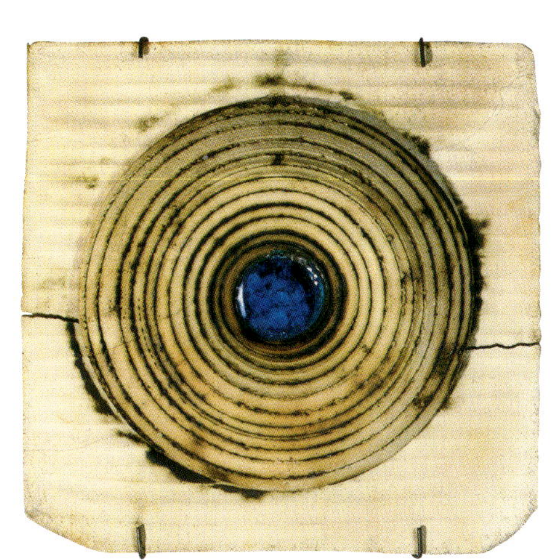
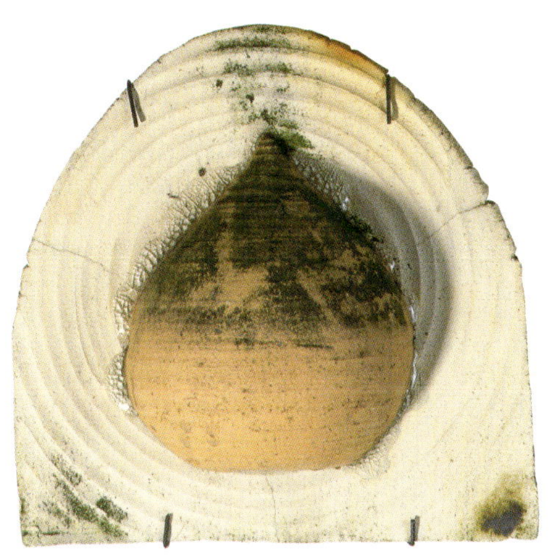
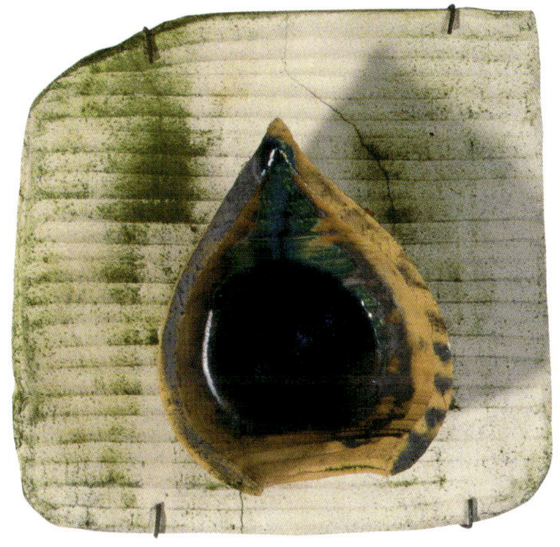

Sculpture as pottery and pottery as sculpture ►

Ljubljana sculptress **Mojca Smerdu** builds her formal "potter-sculptor's" expression on the ancient technique of shaping clay vessels by spiraling rows of rolled strips of clay. However, this is merely the means and method to achieve deeper aims and messages. Her pottery "sculptures" move us not only with their design and their superficial structure: a psychological relationship is formed that poses questions regarding our personal emptiness and the emptiness of the world in which we live. The intellectual dimensions of her creations speak primarily of their communicative role and meaning for modern man.

Ancient mysticism for new times ▼

Barbara Plevnik of Ljubljana reaches deep into the heritage in the field of ceramic creativity. Her works are not merely replicas but represent a search for creative modern solutions based on the study of the oldest testimonies of historical memory preserved by archeology. Her creations are therefore filled with the spirit of ancient cultures, but nevertheless their mysticism can be accepted in modern times, though naturally in different relationships and significance than in prehistory. The activity itself, that is, pottery and ceramics, is one of the oldest handicrafts, and the study of these oldest testimonies offers excellent creative starting points.

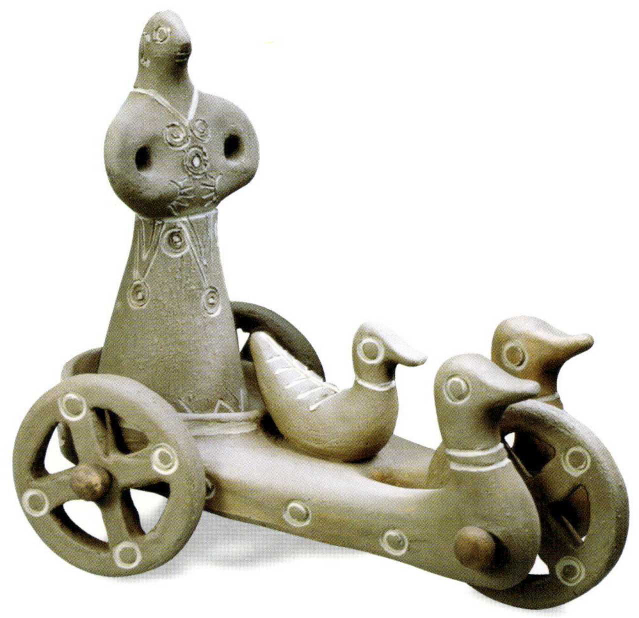

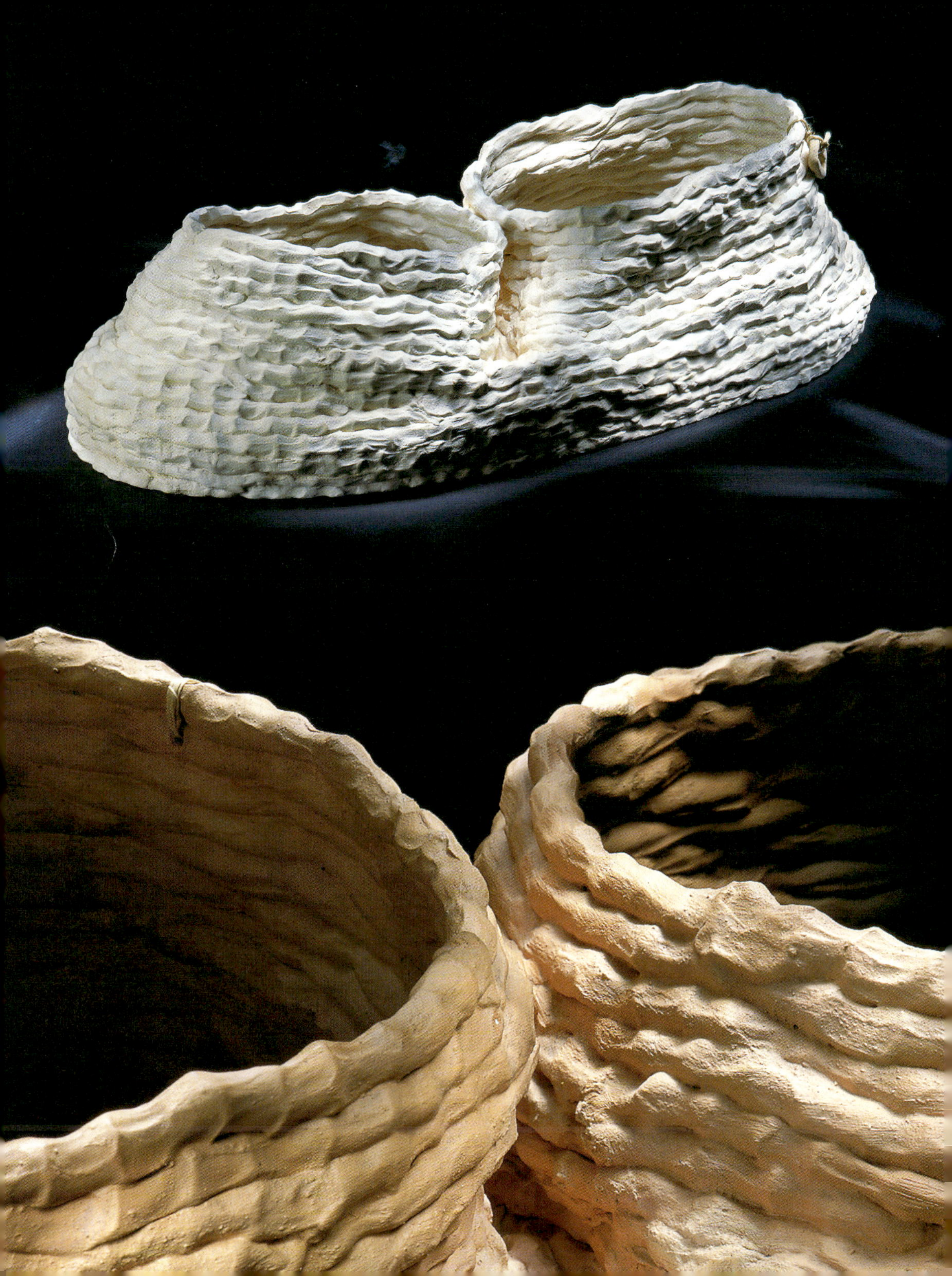

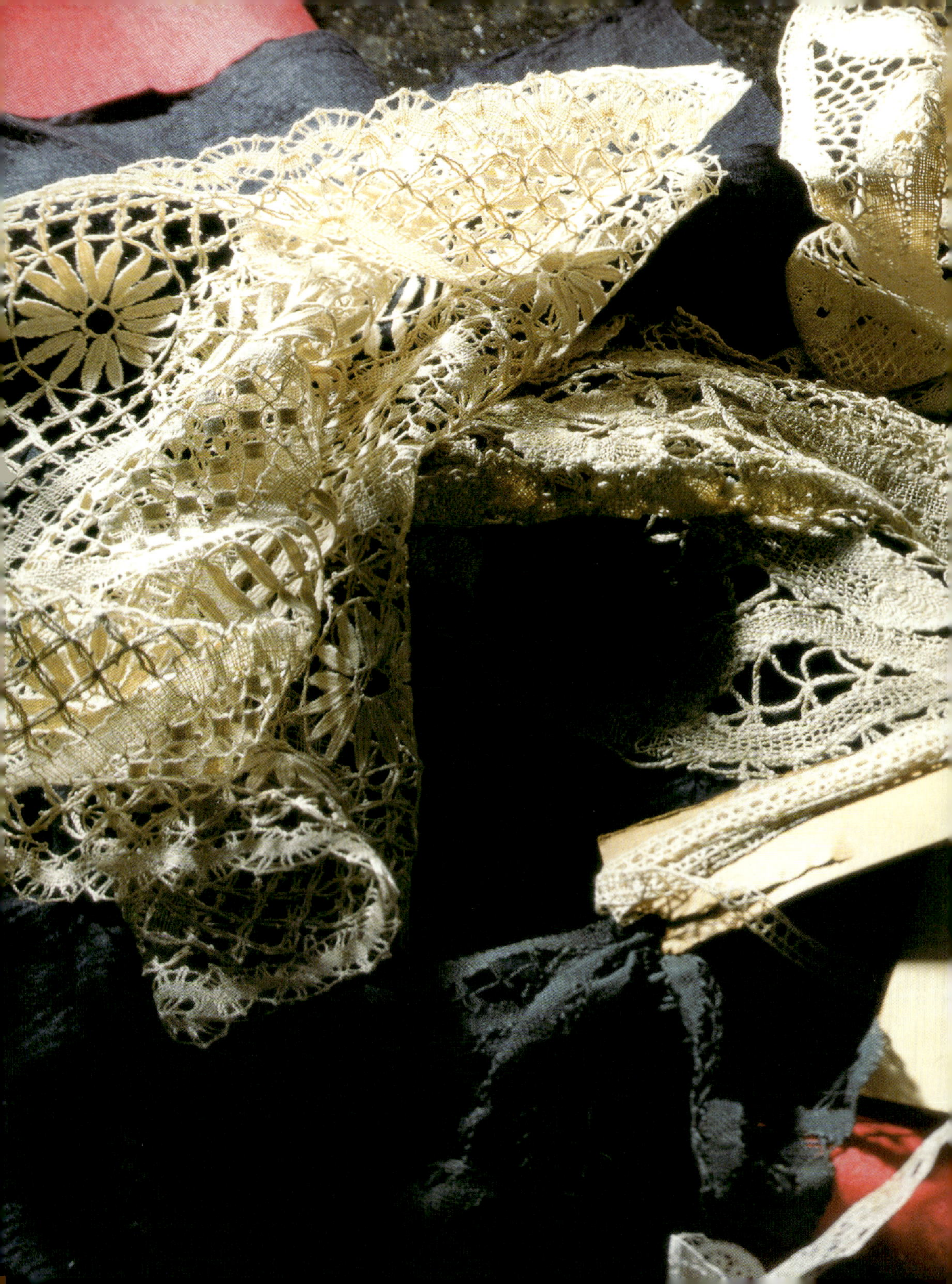

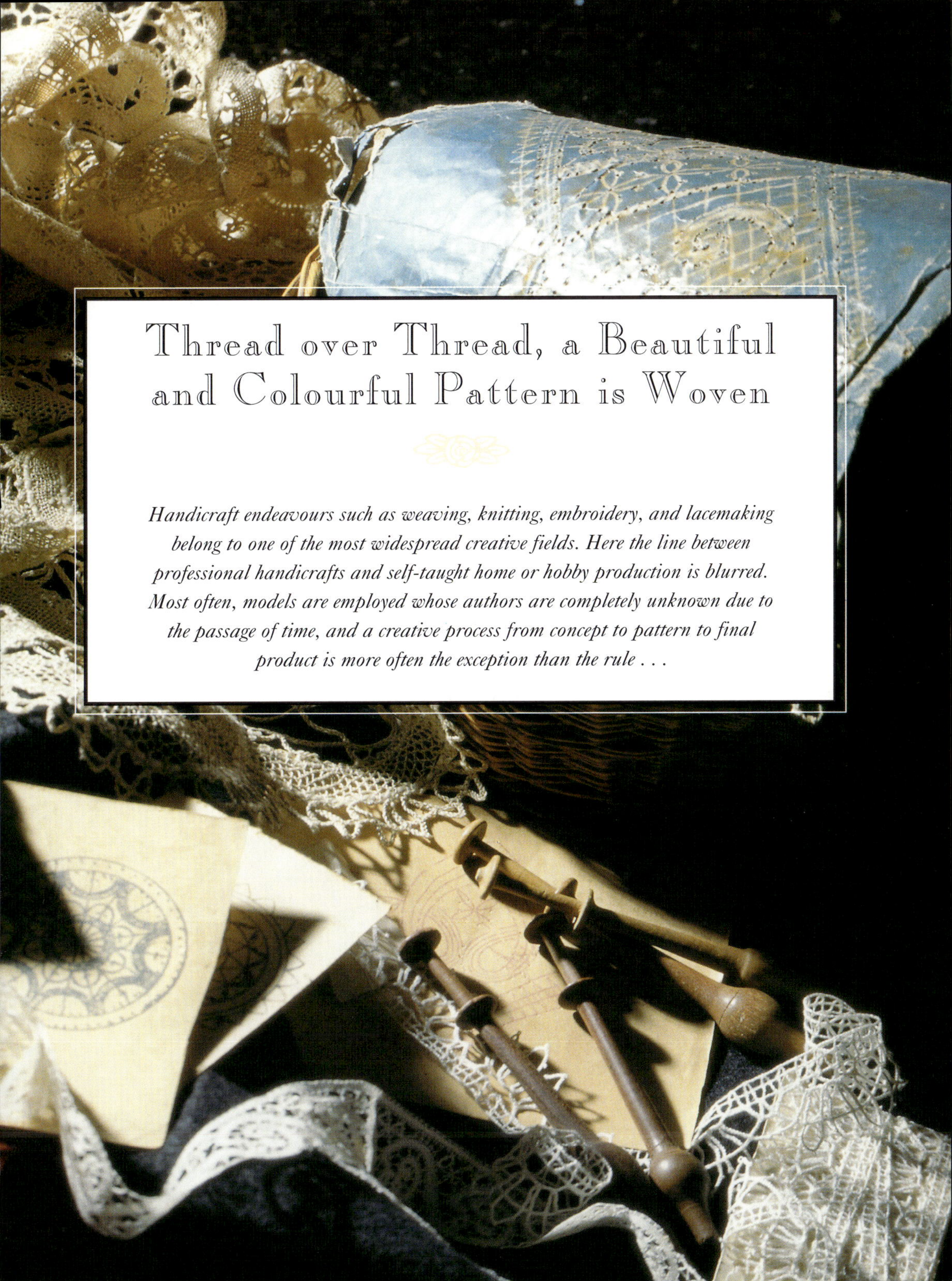

Thread over Thread, a Beautiful and Colourful Pattern is Woven

Handicraft endeavours such as weaving, knitting, embroidery, and lacemaking belong to one of the most widespread creative fields. Here the line between professional handicrafts and self-taught home or hobby production is blurred. Most often, models are employed whose authors are completely unknown due to the passage of time, and a creative process from concept to pattern to final product is more often the exception than the rule . . .

MARICA CVITKOVIČ, ONE OF THE LAST "TRADITIONAL" WEAVERS ►

Traditional linen weaving survived the longest in Bela krajina in southeastern Slovenia, even into the first years after World War II. Today, Marica Cvetkovič from Adlešiči is the last traditional weaver to sow flax every year to spin into linen thread. On her loom she weaves linen cloth from which characteristic Bela krajina linen items are then made. Some are decorated with typical red and blue ornaments embroidered using an old cross-stitch technique. Among her best-known products are the woven towels (*otirači*) of Bela krajina that supposedly first appeared in the 15th century. Today these items from our heritage have acquired new uses, usually as curtains.

EMBROIDERY, A SPARE TIME ACTIVITY FOR WOMEN AND GIRLS ▼

Embroidering with needle and thread on a background of cloth is a very widespread handicraft activity that only began to develop strongly in the 19th century but soon became the most common home handiwork for women. Today we can speak of a genuine rebirth of embroidery, especially in the Slovene countryside since this handicraft is being developed as an additional source of income on farms. The products are suitable for the interior furnishing of farm households, while on tourist farms they contribute to the souvenir offer. The products of **ANAMARIJA DIJAK** rank among the highest quality needlework.

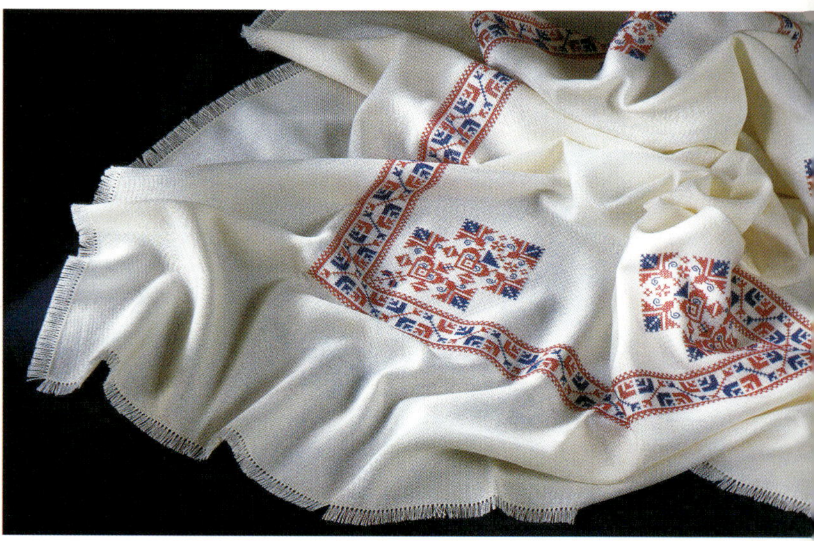

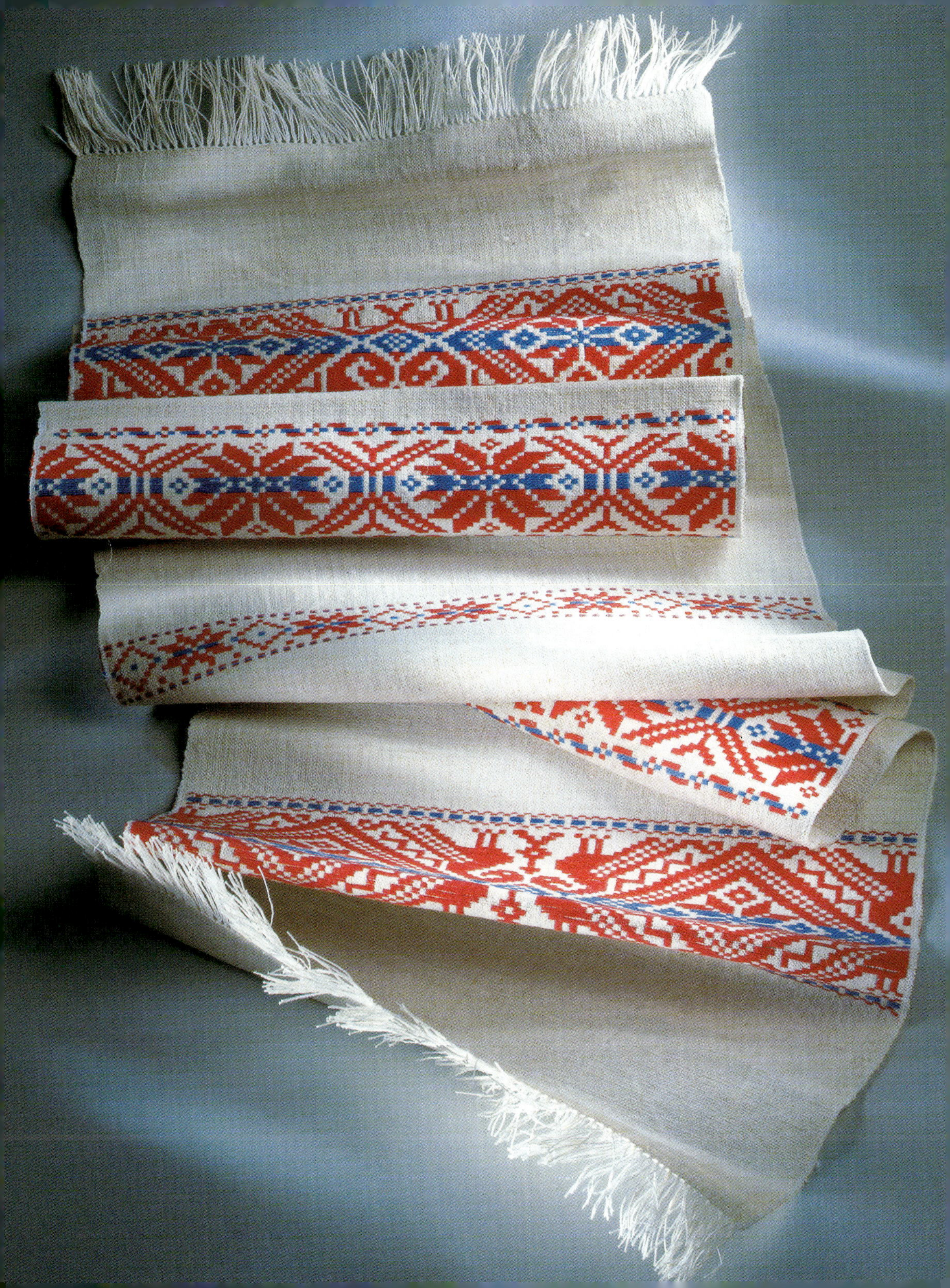

The Anton Primožič Company, established in 1888 ►

The three major lacemaking centers in Slovenia are Idrija, Železniki, and Žiri. The trademark of Žiri bobbin lace is linked to the renowned Anton Primožič Company established in 1888 that still operates today and has a sales gallery in the center of Žiri. The awareness of belonging to a family tradition is felt by its youngest member **Tadeja Primožič**, who has enhanced her basic lacemaking skills with postgraduate studies at Ljubljana University. This means an excellent foundation based on scientific research work. The latter offers completely different starting points based on a practical knowledge of handicraft skills that have been the subject of research and planning.

The embroidered flower motifs of Rozalija Strojan ▼

Flower motifs are a characteristic feature of Slovene ornamentation. This, of course, is not surprising in such a diverse natural environment as Slovenia's. Flower motifs and their combinations with geometrical and other decorative solutions appear most frequently in embroidery, and our modern embroiderers have a truly inexhaustible treasury in the rich heritage of needlework. In our admiration, however, we often forget today that embroidery and the items decorated with it were first and foremost functionally connected to the daily life and holidays of the Slovenes.

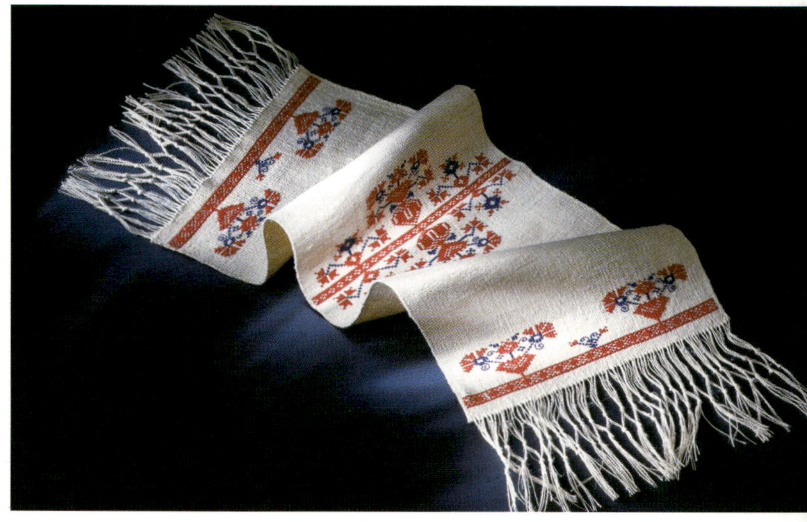

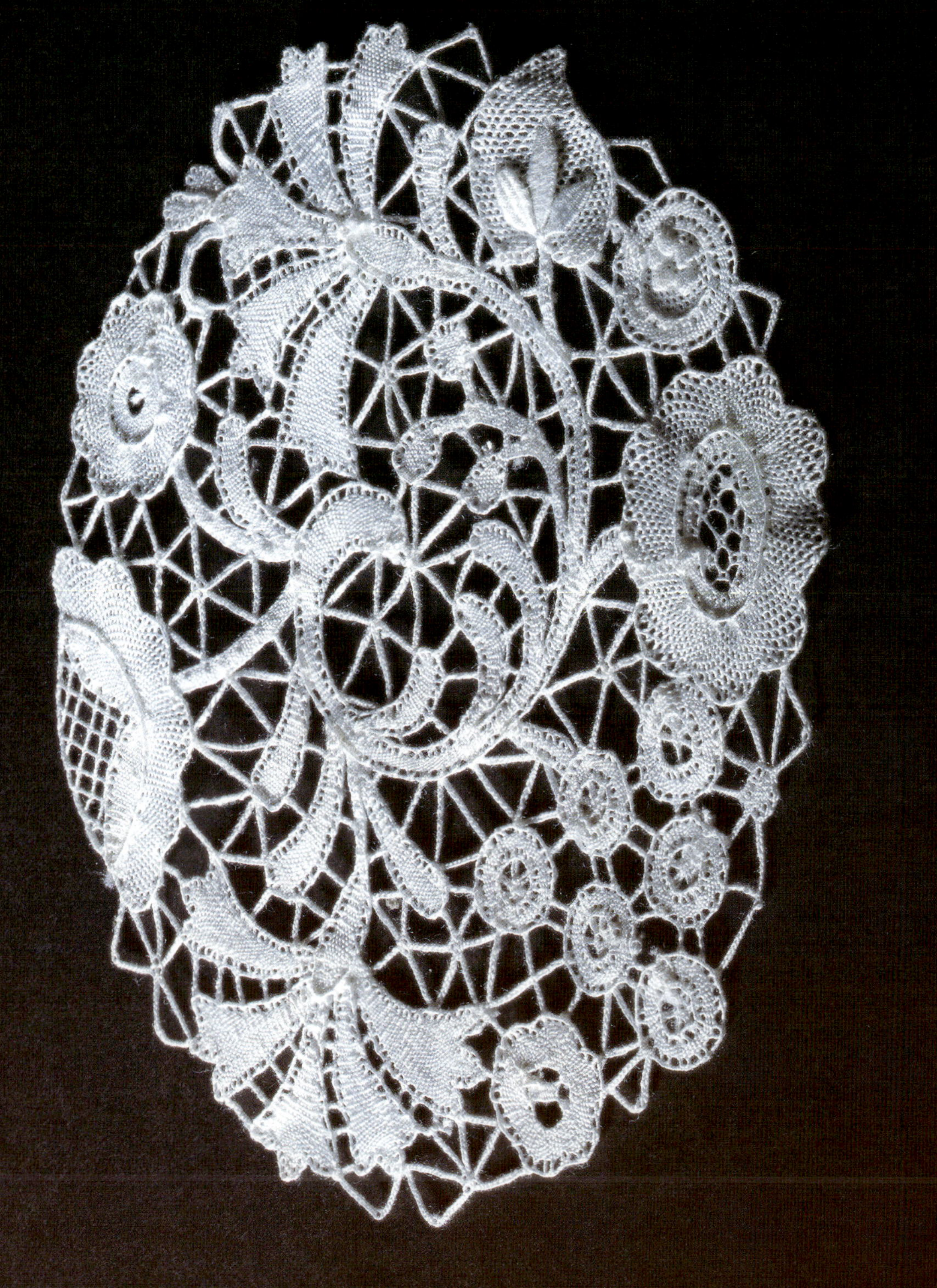

A lacemaking teacher and pattern designer ►
Teacher **Mira Kejžar** has trained several generations of lacemakers. Important are not only the excellent technical skills that she passes on to her pupils but also her personal talent expressed in numerous new designs and patterns for lace. Bobbin lace is made following a precisely-drawn pattern on paper fixed to the pillow. These patterns are mostly the work of especially talented individuals who draw patterns for lace. Individual patterns have been passed on from generation to generation, and the original designers of the oldest patterns will therefore probably never be identified.

Bobbin lace is the trademark of Idrija ▼
In 1875, **Franc Lapajne** established a company to produce and sell bobbin lace in Idrija, and a year later in 1876, our oldest school in the field of handicrafts opened here as well, the Lacemakers School (*Čipkarska šola*) that has continued its mission to the present day. It ranks among the oldest lacework schools in Europe. **Vanda Lapajne** likewise continues the work of her ancestors and the founders of the family company.

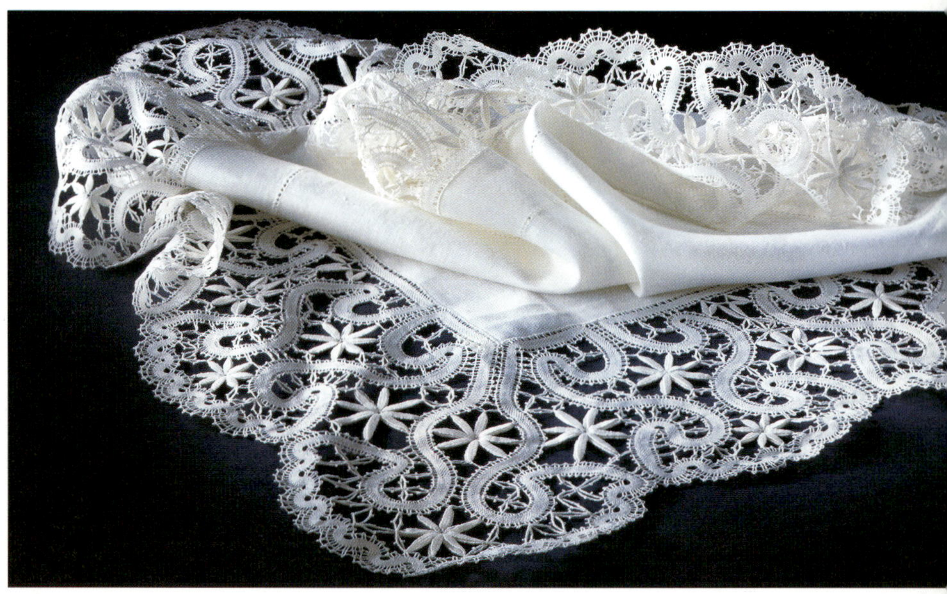

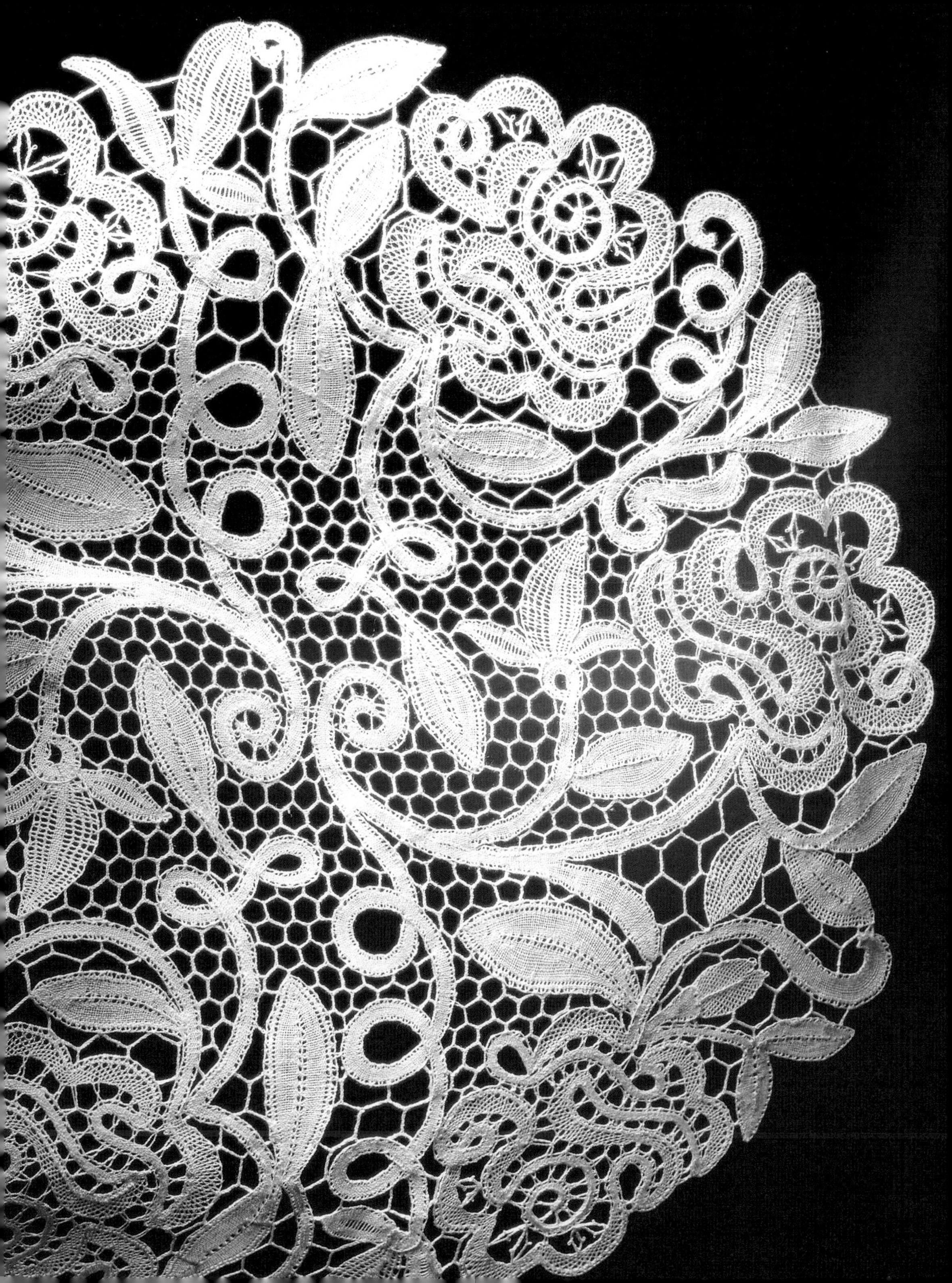

TECHNOLOGY, DESIGN, AND FUNCTION BASED ON THE HERITAGE ►

The bobbin lace works of **ANDRAŽ DEBELJAK** are an example for the future development of all handicraft branches. This young master lacemaker has not only created new patterns but has also employed new materials for his lace, replacing cotton, linen, or silk thread with thin stainless steel and gold wire. Debeljak has adapted his work methods and working tools to this new "invention." Total concentration and a mastery of bobbin work techniques are necessary to create his lacework. His wire lace products have become first class business and protocol gifts, appearing as lace pictures or incorporated in glass creations by several well-known Slovene glass designers.

FROM HERITAGE TO NUMEROUS POSSIBILITIES FOR MODERN CREATIVE EXPRESSIONS ▼

The spread of bobbin lace technology to other materials had its development. **SAŠA PUŠNAR** was among the first to make bobbin lace from wire and was also one of the first to begin creating contemporary designs in lace, in particular lace that was no longer a tablecloth, a decoration on a pillow, or a collar on a dress but rather a picture, a modern artwork. Such an orientation is essential for the future development of bobbin lacework based on the rich centuries-old heritage.

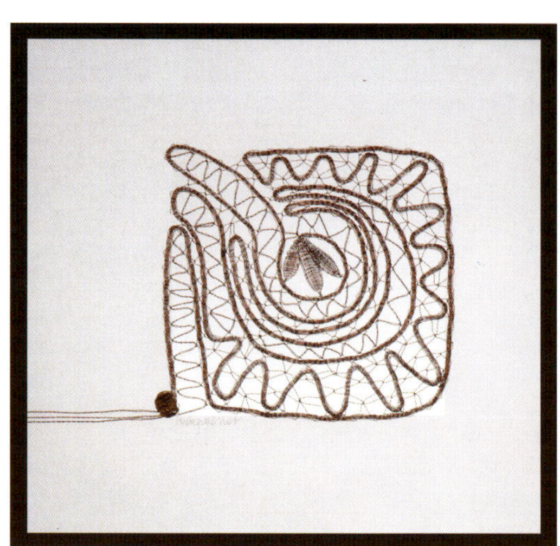

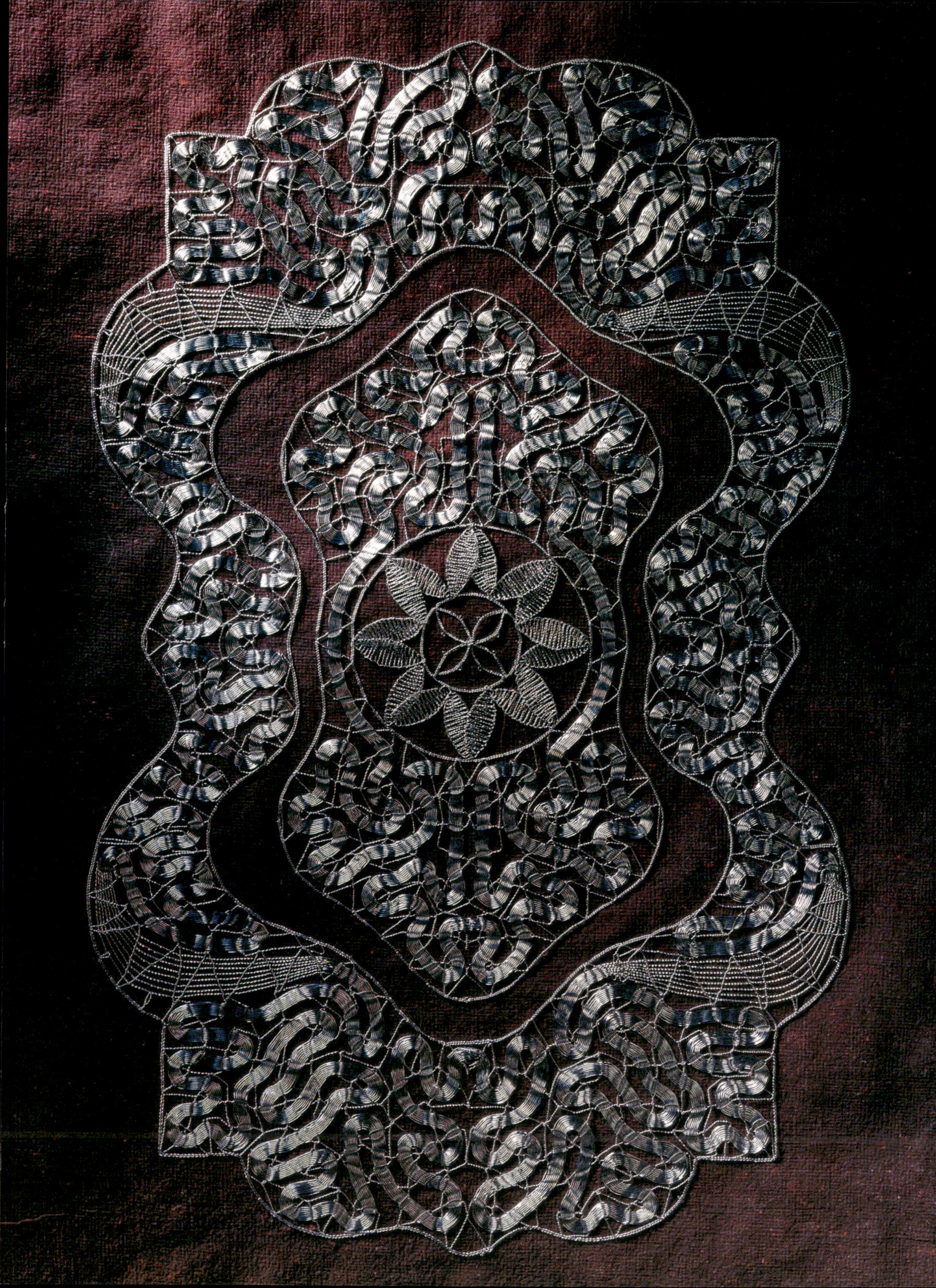

Uniquely modern specimens ►

Architect **Neda Bevk** from Ljubljana has developed completely new directions for creative unique weaving. Her fabrics, which are actually colourful woven surfaces, are made into useful and decorative products such as shawls, bedspreads, and curtains. They are distinguished by the interweaving of pure forms and the deliberate structure of the fabric. Thus she creates a palette of patterns in unison with numerous but completely harmonious colour combinations.

Handicrafts of Idrija in an intimate gallery ▼

Like all products originating in our heritage, the bobbin lace of Idrija also needs new approaches of understanding and mediation. Lace no longer comprises merely tablecloths and blouse collars but also genuine artistic masterpieces, graphics made of intertwined thread. This widens the possibilities for its application. **Studio Koder** with its sales gallery in the very center of Idrija's old town center was among the first to start breaking fresh ground for an alternative approach to designing, producing, and selling bobbin lace. A visit to this gallery is an encounter with refined products enriched with lace and its applications on the most varied personal items and products that may well enhance our home living environments.

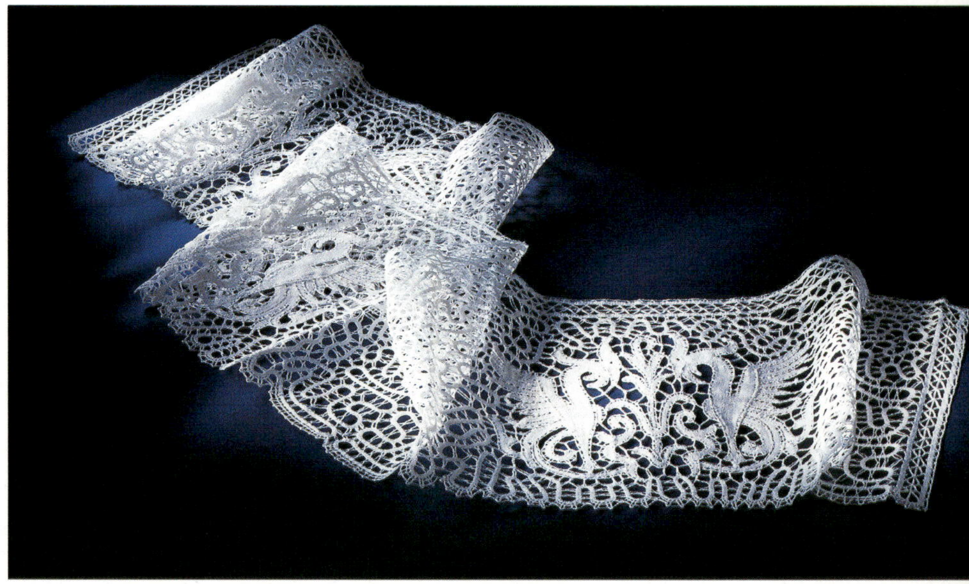

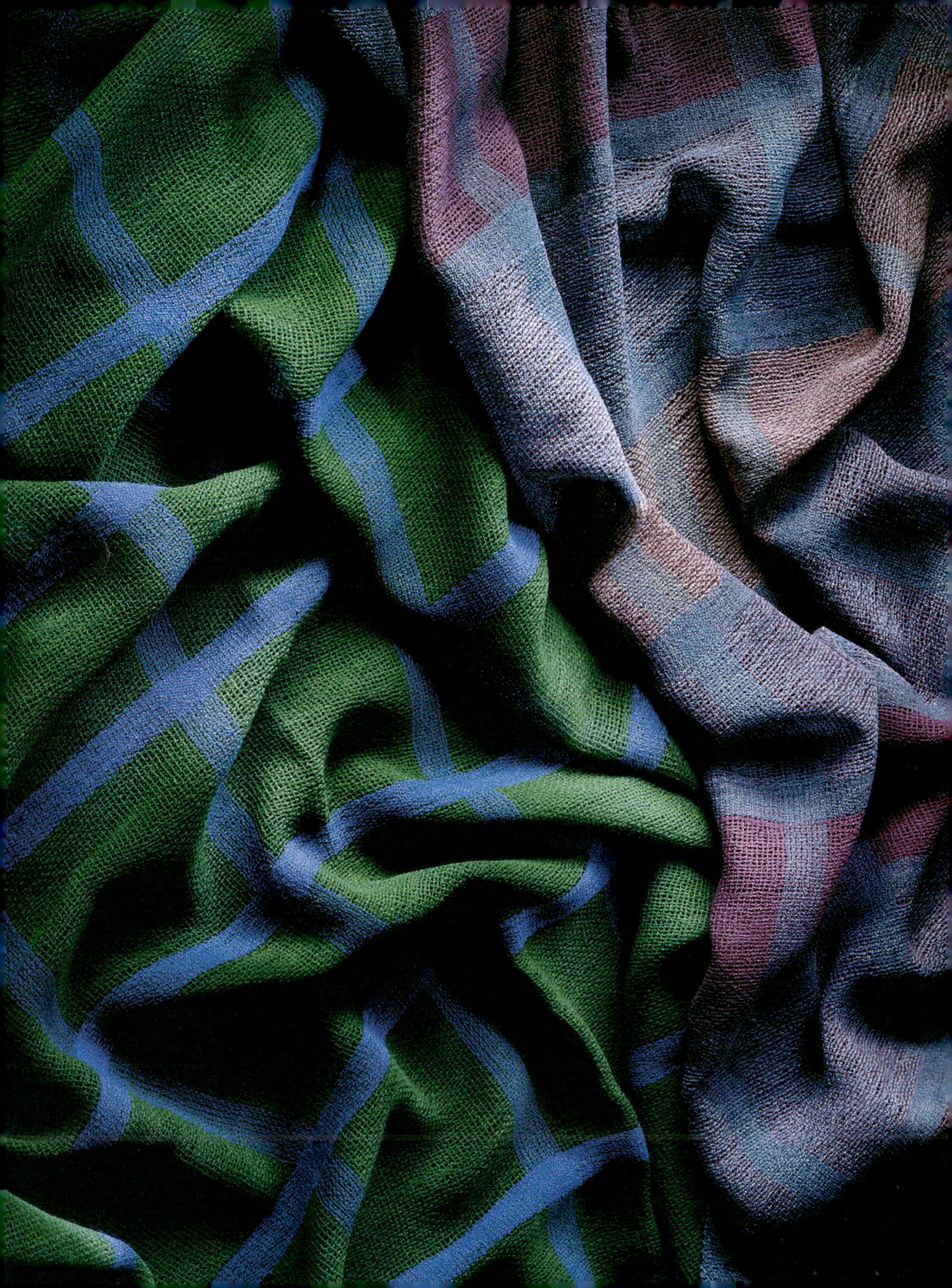

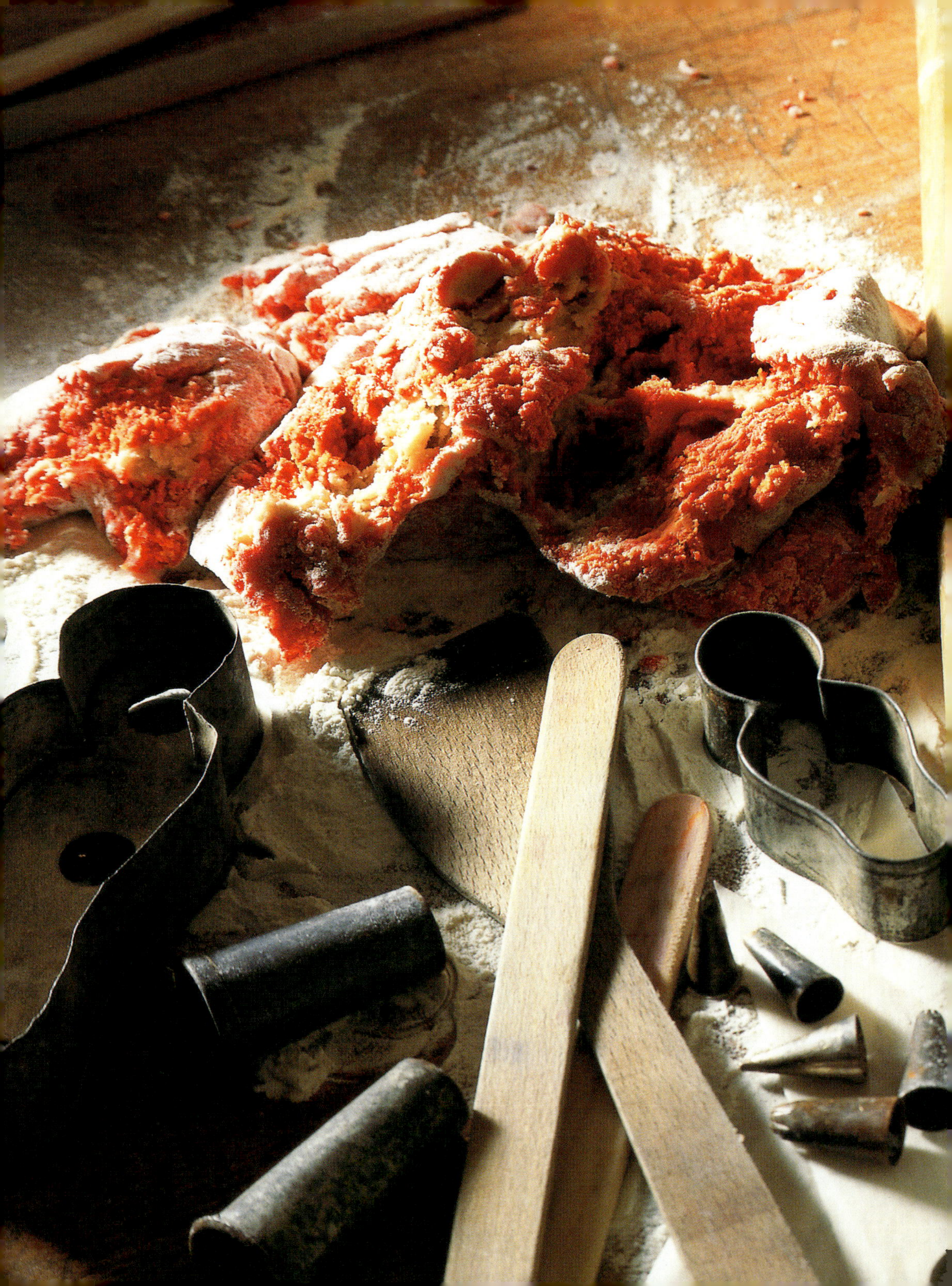

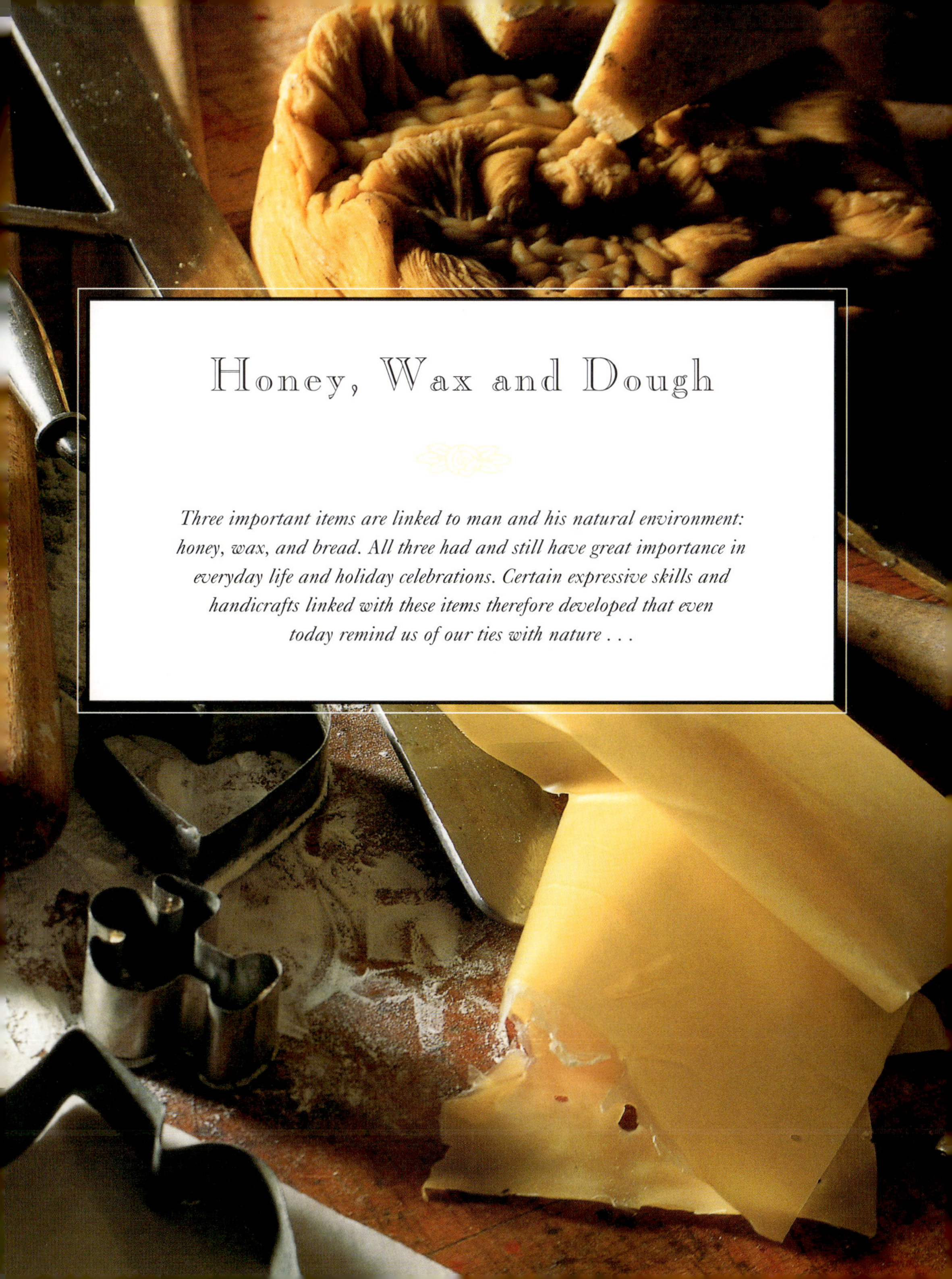

Honey, Wax and Dough

Three important items are linked to man and his natural environment: honey, wax, and bread. All three had and still have great importance in everyday life and holiday celebrations. Certain expressive skills and handicrafts linked with these items therefore developed that even today remind us of our ties with nature . . .

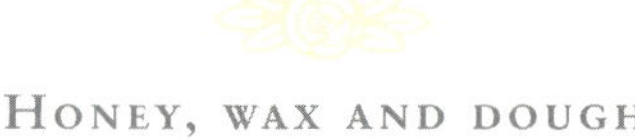

KRAJČKI ARE AMONG THE OLDEST ►
The semicircular *krajčki* ("chunks of bread") are among the oldest forms of handmade honey pastries, while heart and star shapes are also quite frequent. Such items belong with the group of various kinds of ritual breads or shaped pastries whose role was to establish bonds between the sexes and express love. They were often used as gifts in various customs and traditions. Today's products are mainly a continuation of historical memory, although some producers attempt to create new motifs as well, a reflection of creative searching and the desire for the continued development of items with a noble past. **CIRILA ŠMID** from Železniki in Gorenjska is among the best known producers of *dražgoški kruhki*.

FROM CONVENT TO FARM HOUSEHOLD ▼
Very little is known about the origins of hand-decorated gingerbread pastries made from honey dough. Some authors hypothesize that an important role was played by convents from where this handicraft skill spread to farm households and to a lesser extent to the towns. Noblewomen in castles were also said to have whiled away the time making such items. Today, the production of honey-based gingerbread pastries survives primarily in Dražgoše in Gorenjska, and they are therefore generally called *dražgoški kruhki* ("Dražgoše breads") although various individuals make decorative pastries by hand from honey dough in other places as well. One is **FRANČIŠKA ZALAZNIK** from Vrhnika near Ljubljana.

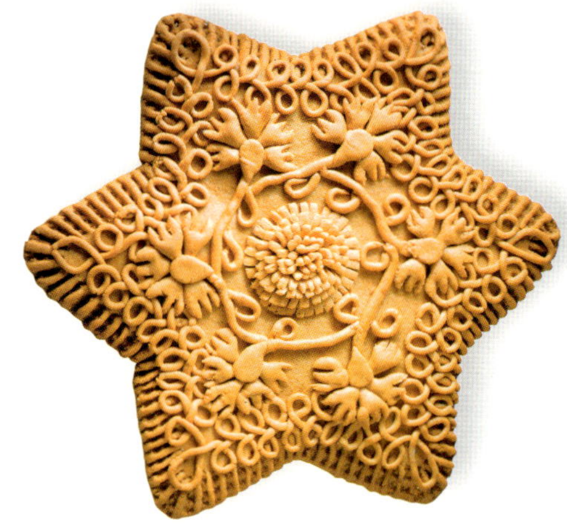

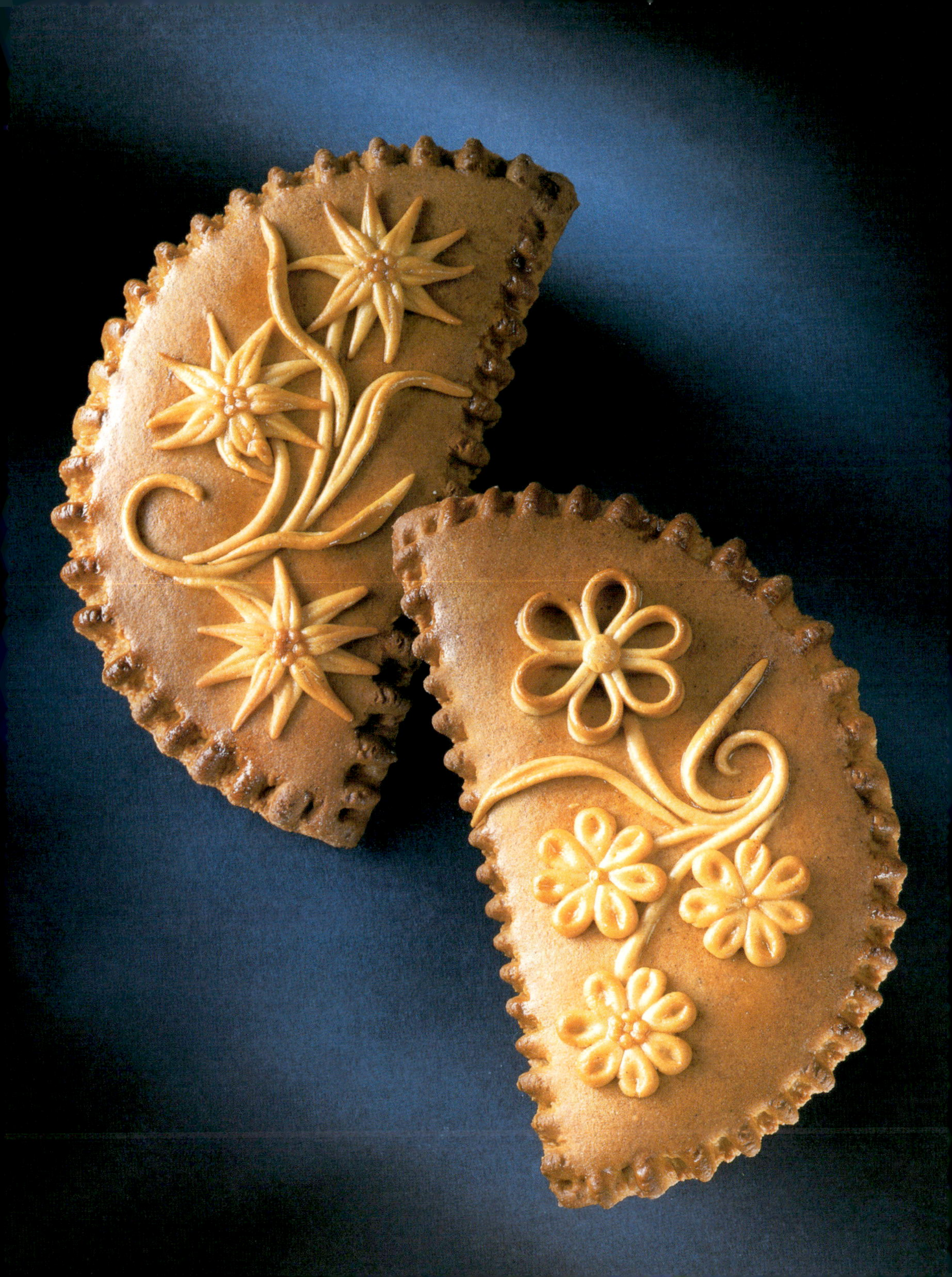

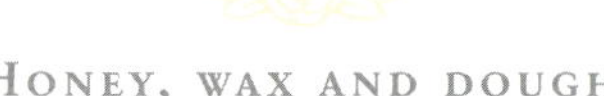

Over two hundred years of family tradition ►

Honey, wax, and dough are the basic materials of gingerbread makers and candlemakers. In the 19th century when honey, formerly the basic material, was complemented by cheaper sugar, gingerbread making developed its characteristic palette of brightly coloured and decorated products. Various gingerbread pastries are now made as presents and souvenirs using a confectioner's forcing bag and sugar icing. In first place among them are affectionate gingerbread hearts adorned with tiny mirrors and appropriate thoughts of love printed on small strips of paper. Traditional candle making is another distinctive handicraft, producing decoratively adorned candles for various ritual occasions such as christenings, confirmations, weddings, and funerals. The best known honey gingerbread and candlemaking workshop in Slovenia is in Slovenj Gradec where the master **Hrabroslav Perger** and members of his family carry on the rich tradition and develop new products as well.

Mother's best pupil ▼

Ana Selan from Ljubljana makes decorative pastries by hand from honey dough, a handicraft she learned as a girl from her mother in her native Dražgoše in Gorenjska. In past centuries–the oldest examples are from the 17th century–such pastries were made primarily for ritual purposes on major Christian holidays such as Christmas and Easter and as tokens of love. Honey pastries played their part in wedding customs as well, and in the 19th century, such pastries were often given as presents on Saint Nicholas Day. Today, these items are acquiring a distinctly decorative nature.

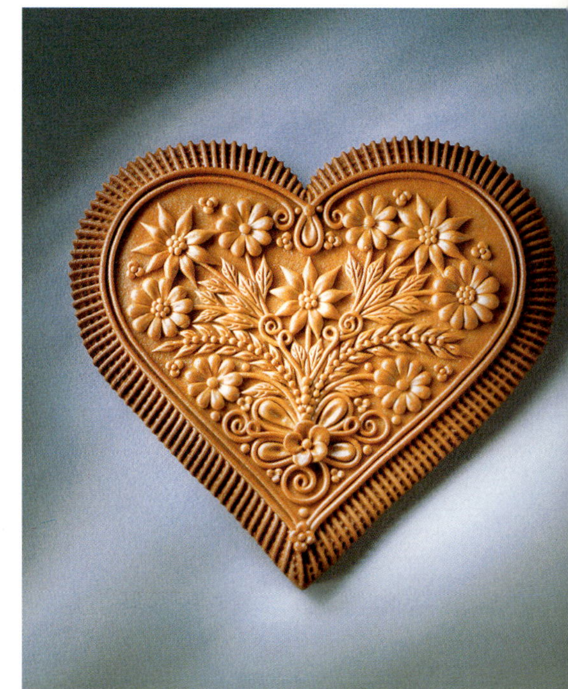

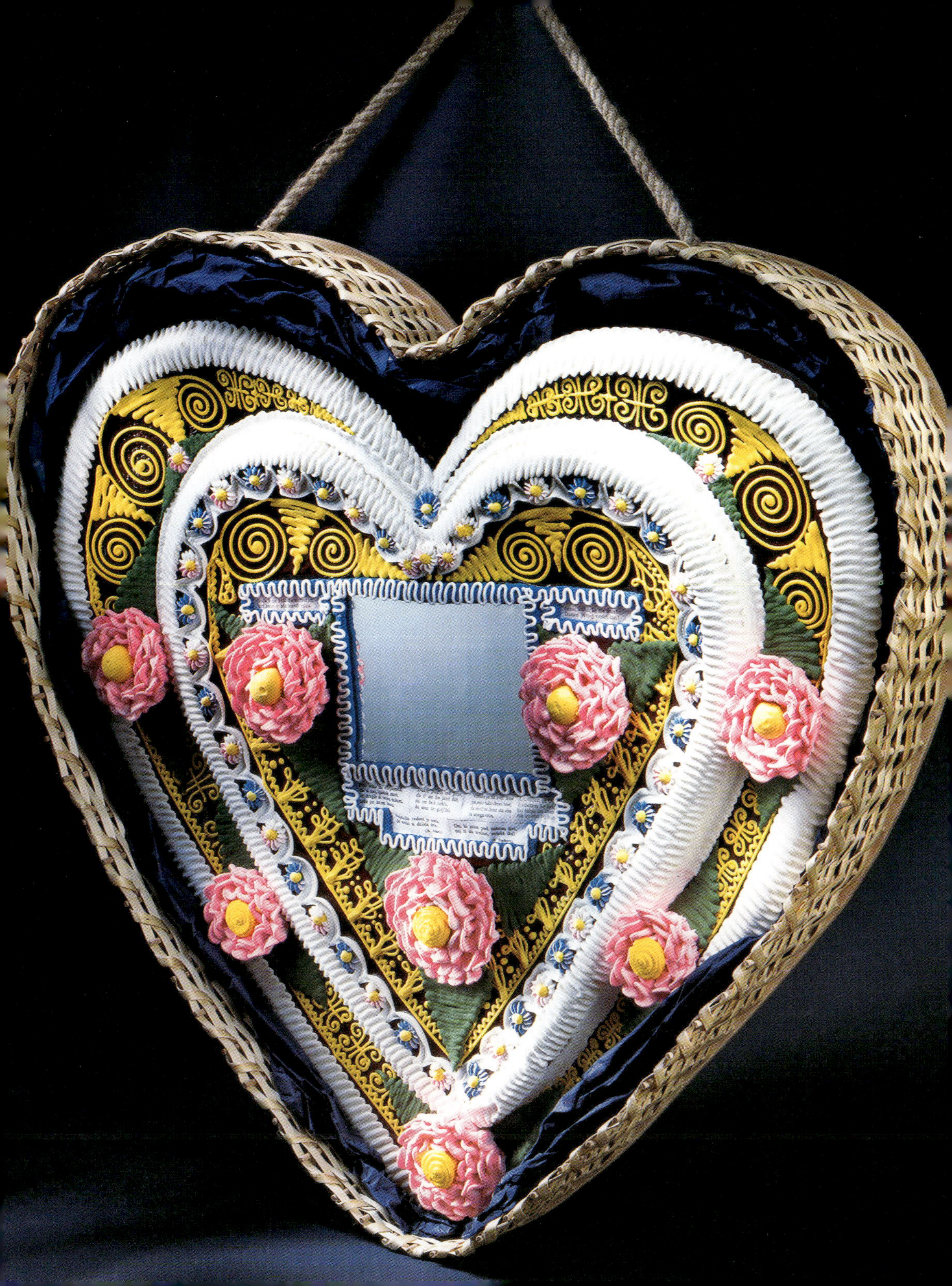

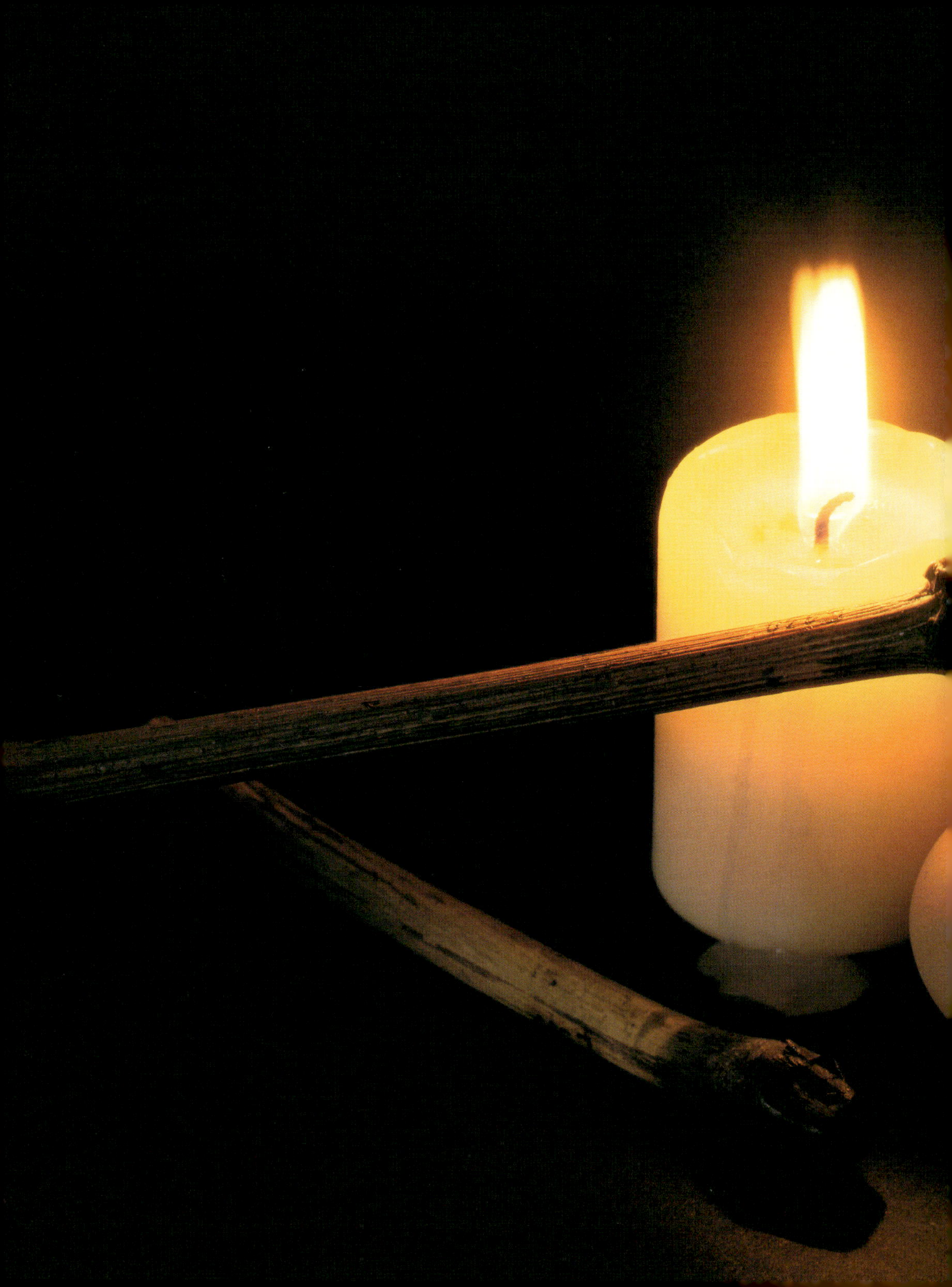

Natural Images of Fertility

Spring after spring, Nature awakens. Many centuries and millennia ago, people interpreted this annual rebirth in their own ways, creating their own world of symbols. One such symbol is the egg, an image of fertility and a symbol of the source of new life in spring. Christianity associated this ancient Indo-European symbol with the Resurrection of Christ . . .

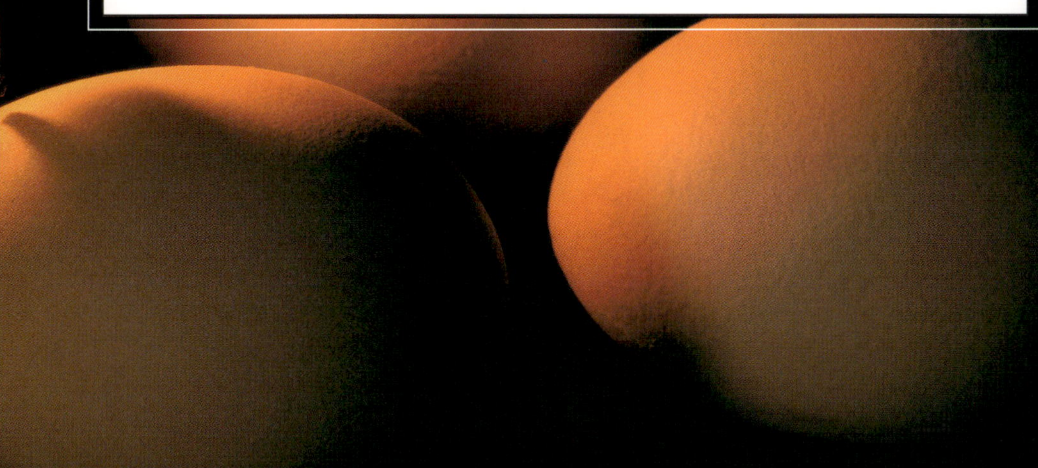

WITH THE POINT OF A KNIFE ►

Another equally old method of decorating Easter eggs is scratching patterns and decorations onto a painted eggshell. This method of decoration is known in Prekmurje where the decorated eggs are called *remenke* or *remenice* and in Bela krajina where **MILENA STAREŠINIČ** from Ravnace pri Suhorju is especially known for the high quality and integrity of her work. In addition to chicken eggs, she also decorates quail, duck, and goose eggs with the scratching technique. Her products have often been praised and awarded prizes at various competitions for the most beautifully decorated Easter eggs that take place in Slovenia yearly. These eggs are distinguished not only by the exquisite drawing of individual ornaments but also for their graduated shading.

***PISANICE* OF BELA KRAJINA ▼**

The ancient custom of painting and decorating Easter eggs has been preserved in Prekmurje and Bela krajina. In this part of Slovenia, painted Easter eggs are called *pisanice.* The basic colours used to paint the decoration are black and red, and graphic images or drawings are created with a pen containing liquid wax. Drawing decorations with wax is based on covering the colours we do not wish to paint or cover over with darker ones. This resembles the batik technique used in Africa and Asia for painting and decorating fabrics. Careful planning is necessary for such ornamentation and, above all, knowledge regarding the order of covering coloured surfaces one after the other from the lightest natural colour of the eggshell to the darkest black or dark brown shades.

MIHAELA GREGORČIČ from Metlika creates outstanding painted *pisanice.*

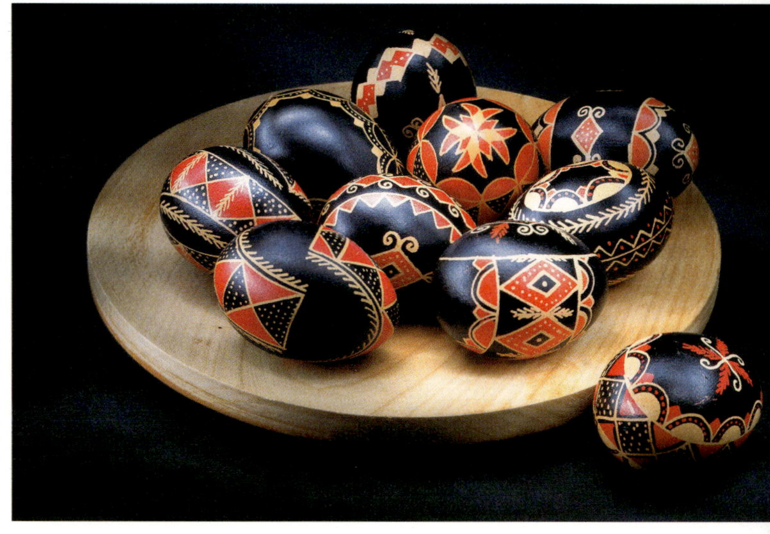

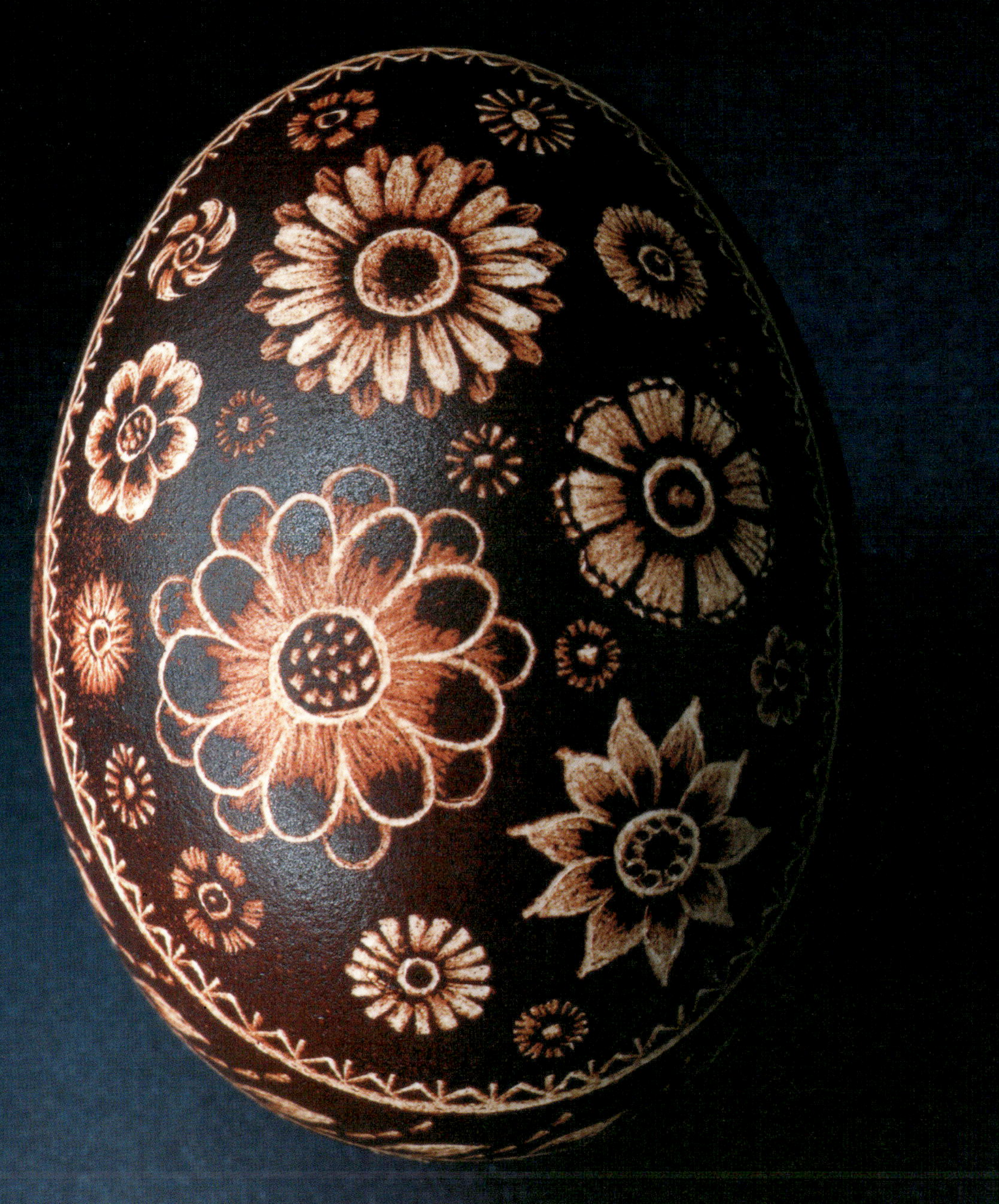

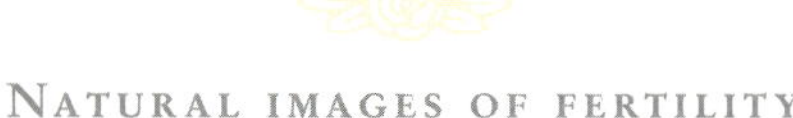

DRILLING 17,000 HOLES IN ONE EGG

Among decorated Easter eggs, we witness unique creative achievements as well. **FRANC GROM** from Vrhnika is the creator of the remarkable *vrhniški pirhi* ("Vrhnika Easter eggs"). To make these unique eggs, he first empties the eggs and then drills the shells with innumerable tiny holes (from 3,000 to 17,000!) in a disciplined rhythm of most various patterns, decorations, and inscriptions. The eggs thus become genuine lace masterpieces. For Grom's creations, not only is an exceptional personal working discipline important but also a feeling for rhythmically arranging ornaments and their parts along the universal natural shape of the eggshell. Naturally, Grom's masterpieces have exceeded their primary association with Easter and are frequently used as business or protocol gifts, as symbols of modern high quality creativity.

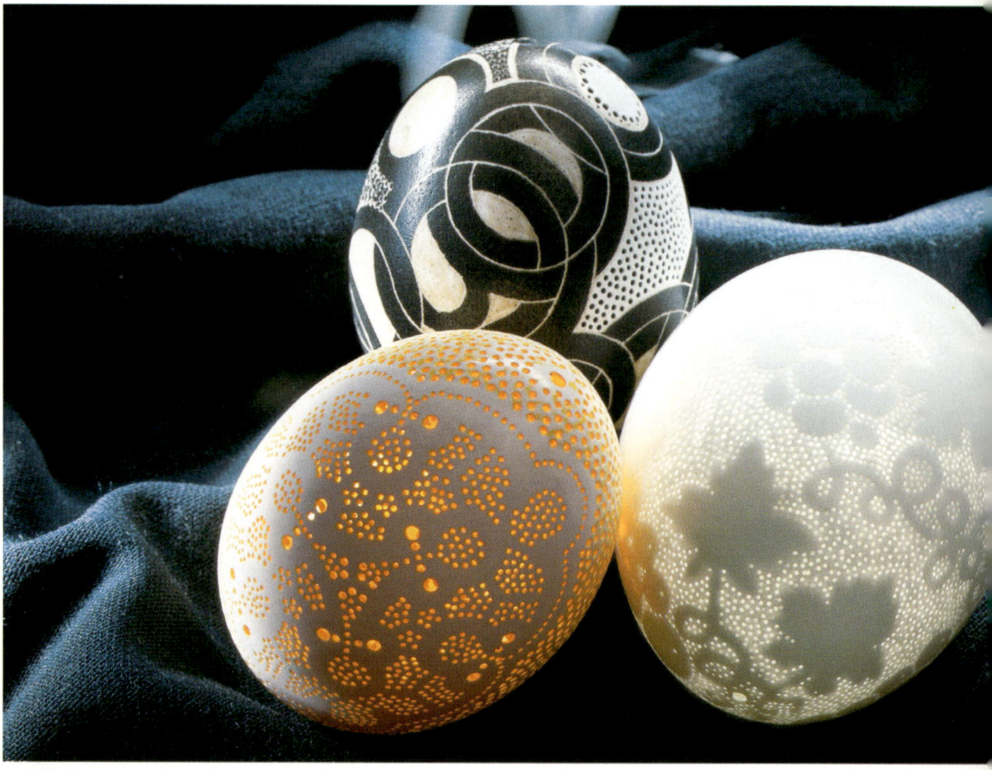

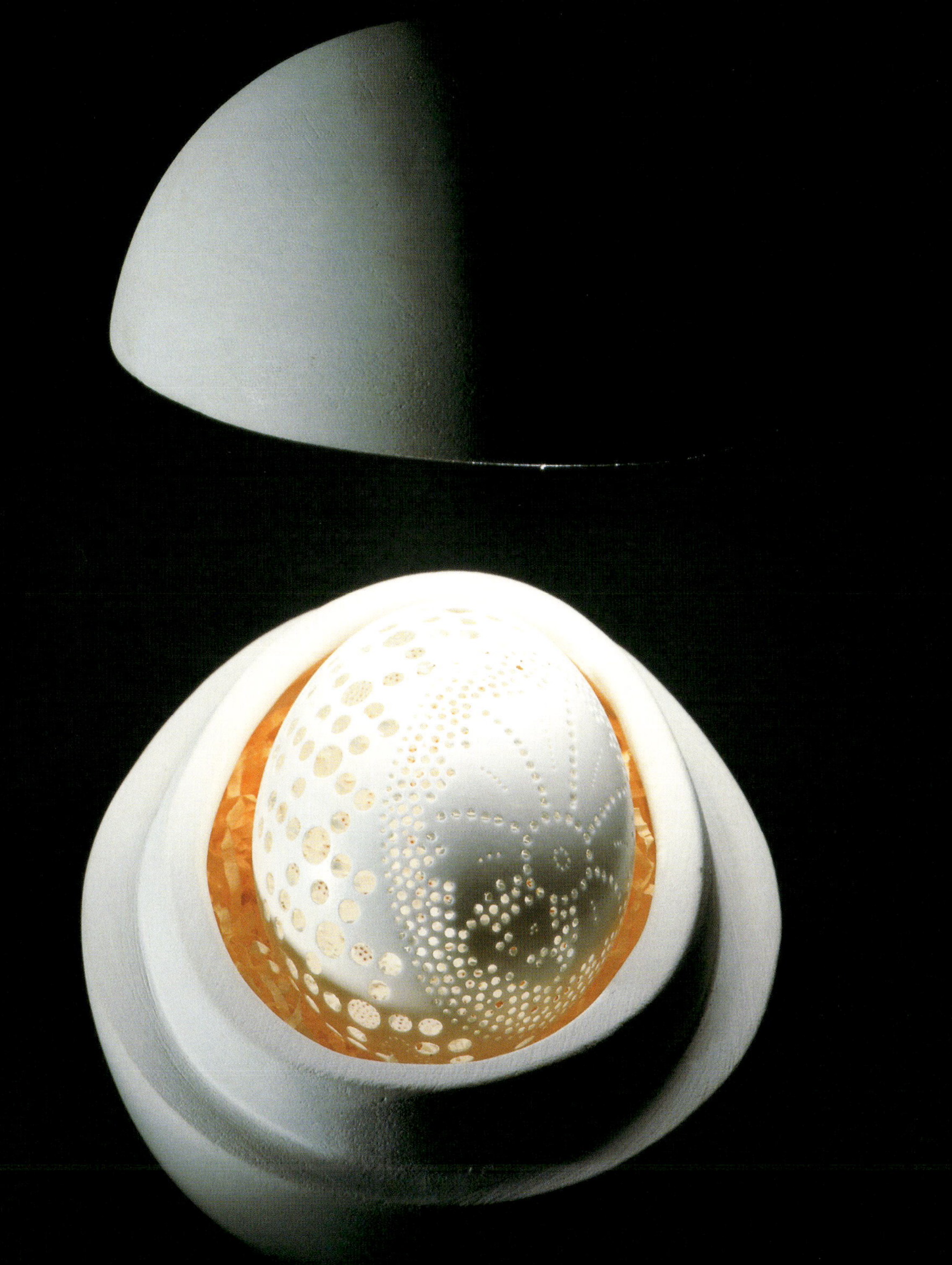

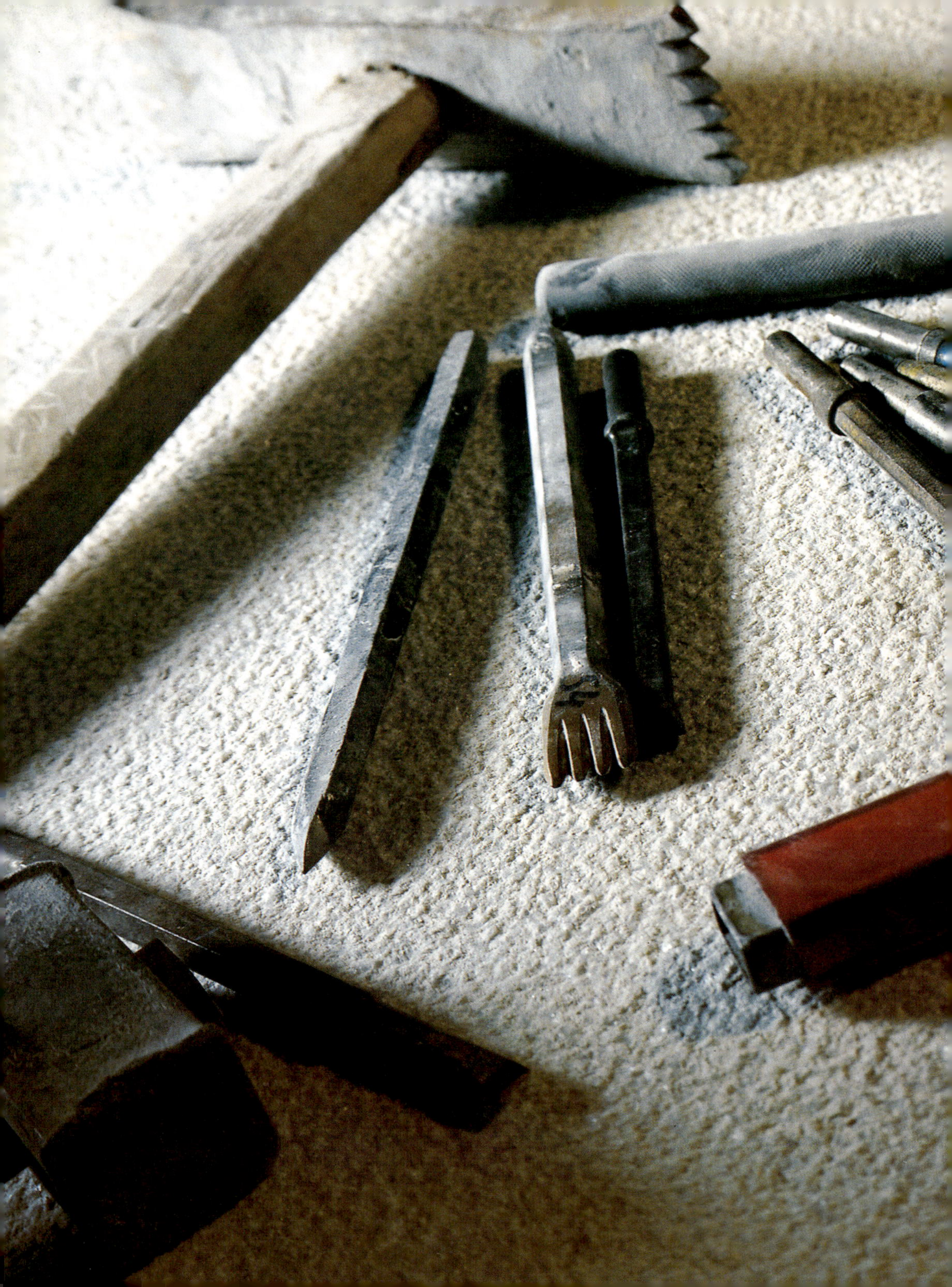

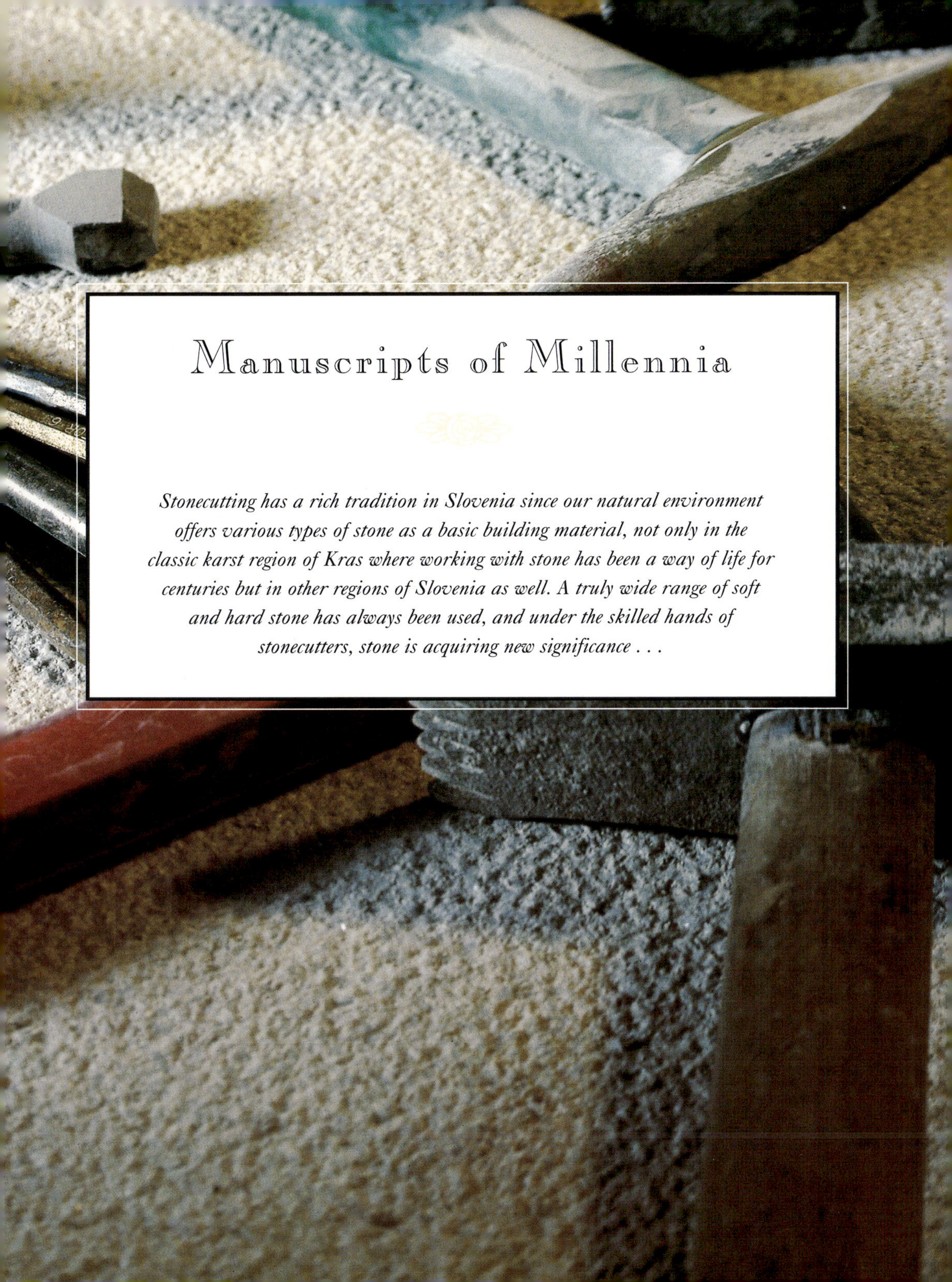

Manuscripts of Millennia

Stonecutting has a rich tradition in Slovenia since our natural environment offers various types of stone as a basic building material, not only in the classic karst region of Kras where working with stone has been a way of life for centuries but in other regions of Slovenia as well. A truly wide range of soft and hard stone has always been used, and under the skilled hands of stonecutters, stone is acquiring new significance . . .

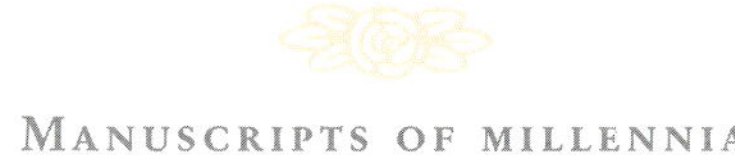

Utensils made from stone ►

In Primorska, the chiseled stone mortar was one of the most generally used aids for preparing food and a vessel at the same time. In it they ground herbs, prepared groats, etc. Due to their pure forms, mortars are now used primarily as decorative items, and we often find them employed as flowerpots. Today, carving mortars is a continuation of the traditional stonecutting that in the past was often a part of domestic handicraft skills and that with the development of a professional approach has achieved outstanding peaks of quality. One such peak is represented by the work of stonecutter **Zvonko Čehovin** from Ozeljan in the Vipava Valley.

A private quarry and top quality products ▼

The **Tavčar** stonecutting company in Povirje near Sežana is a modern firm that uses karst limestone from its own quarry. Working with professional modern approaches, the stonecutters employed here produce the most varied details in dressed stone, diverse building elements, and unique products including wells, pillars and pilasters, door portals, balustrades, etc. Many unique commissioned items are done entirely by hand by these skilled Kras stonecutters.

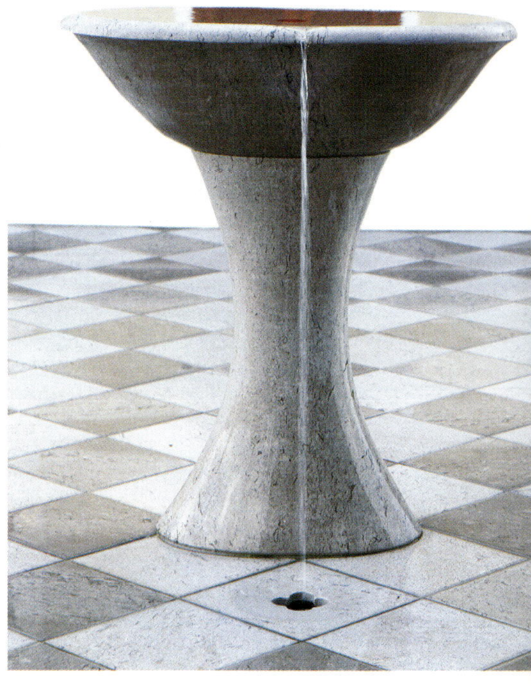

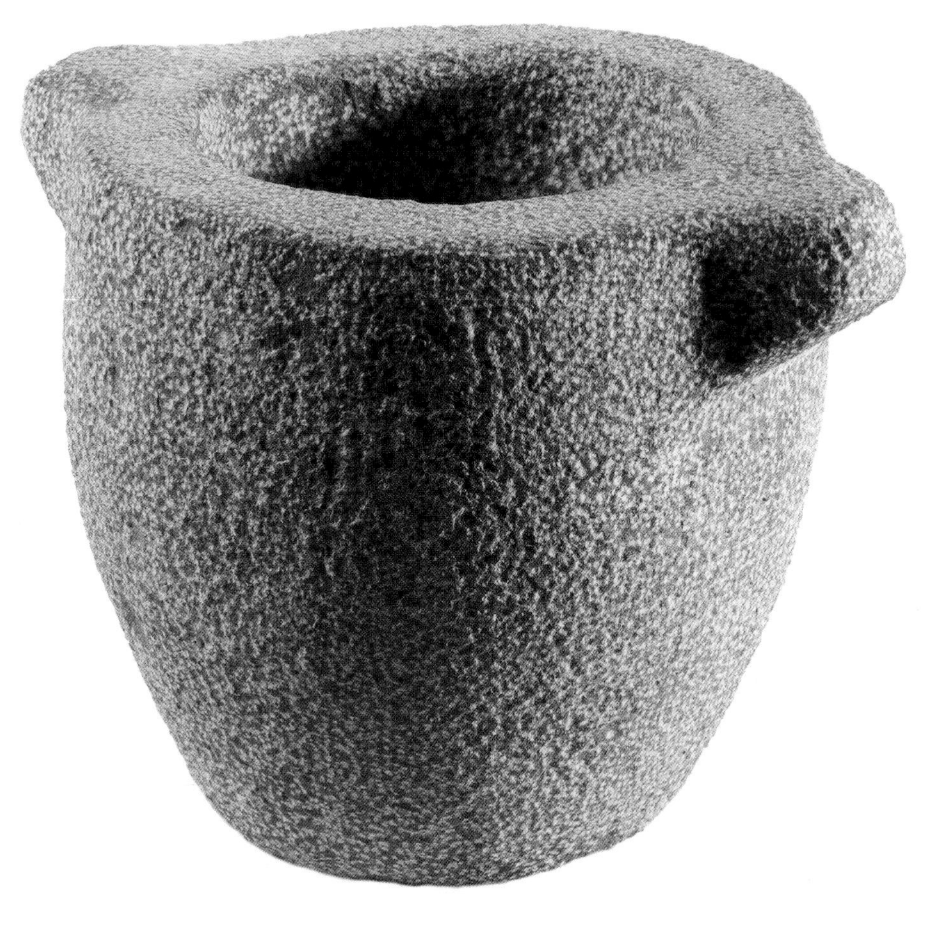

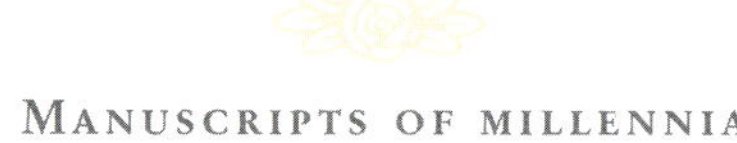

PAVEL GULIČ, THE EPITOME OF KRAS STONECUTTING ►
Although it may sound a bit romantic, we have to admit that even top quality modern technology using the most varied, even computer-guided machines cannot replace the classical stonecutting manuscript, that is, the manual sculpting of products and various stonecutting details. It is only through the touch of the hand that these items acquire their characteristic readable charm, uniqueness of form, and overall splendour. The hands of the outstanding master Pavel Gulič from Kopriva in Kras know how to create everything that still remains out of reach of modern technology.

ON THE PATH TO SCULPTURE ▼
Modern communication and transportation have naturally made possible the greater import of various types of stone from all over the world, and it is possible to perceive fashion trends in stonecutting as stonecutters have responded to customers' wishes. However, Slovene stonecutters and their clients can find a quite varied palette of colour, form, and structure in our native stone, and stonecutter **JOŽE GAVEZ** from Bilje pri Renčah uses Kras and Soča stone as his basic material.

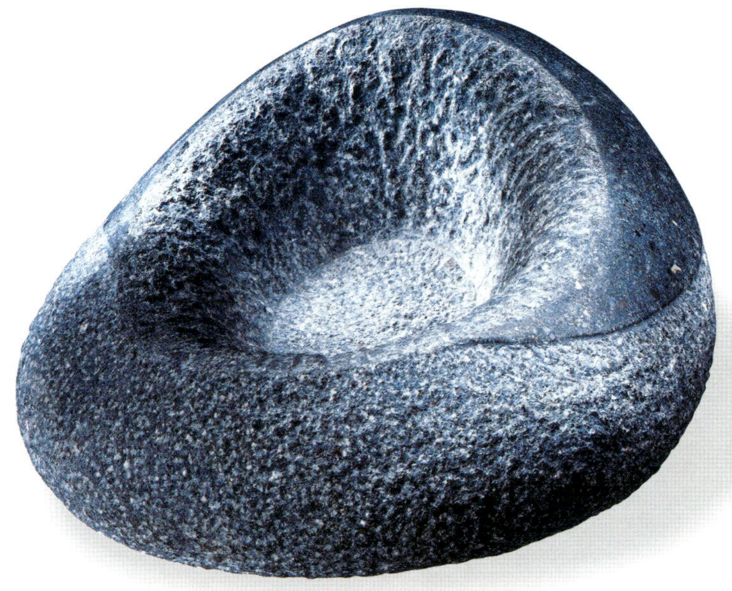

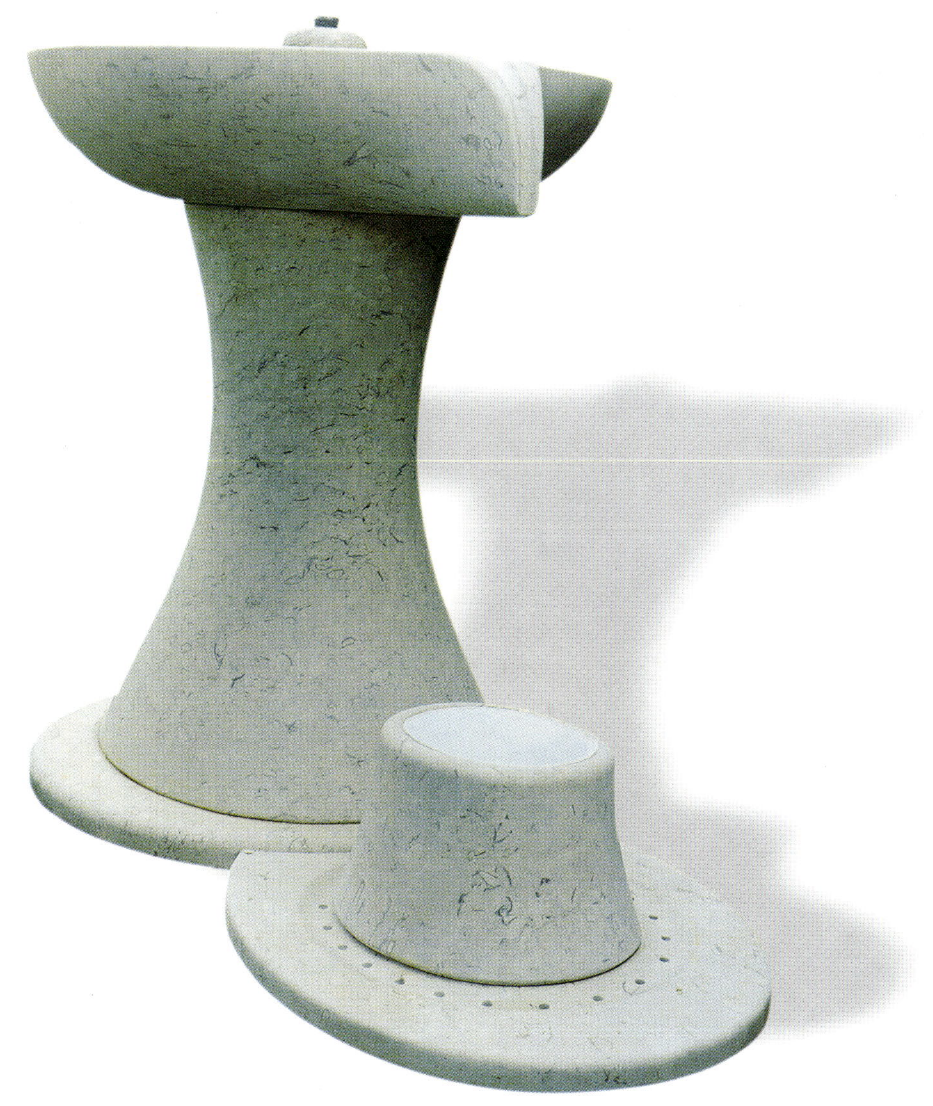

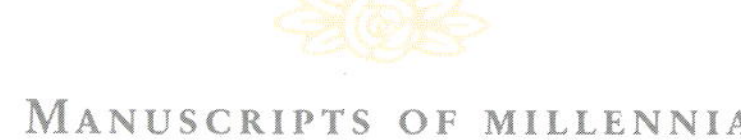

GREAT CONCERN FOR THE FUTURE OF STONECUTTING SKILLS

Despite the rich heritage and local skills, interest in the stonecutting profession began to decline among the young after World War II. In recent years, the situation has improved somewhat, largely due to the efforts of the Slovene crafts association to encourage the trade and the personal endeavours of **BORIS UDOVČ** from Naklo near Kranj, one of Slovenia's leading masters of stonecutting. His workshop undertakes the most demanding stonecutting orders and participates in renovating national heritage buildings and producing replicas. The workshop is continuing the outstanding work of several leading stonecutting workshops in Slovenia from the period between the two World Wars.

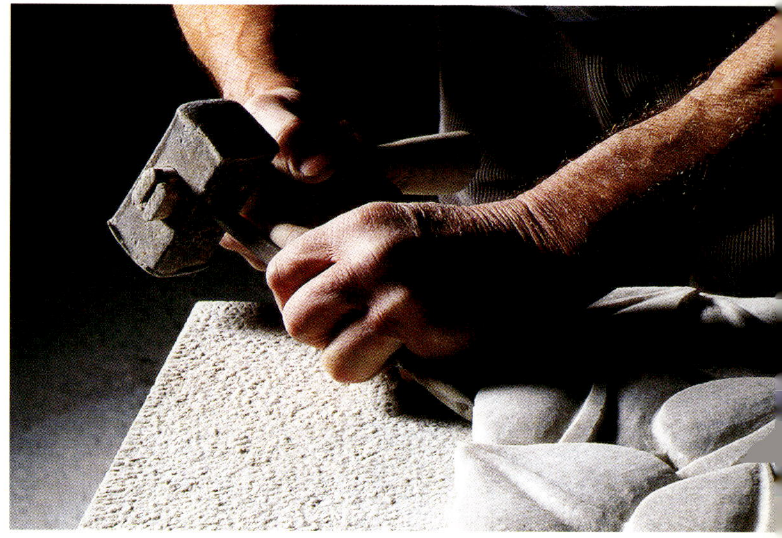

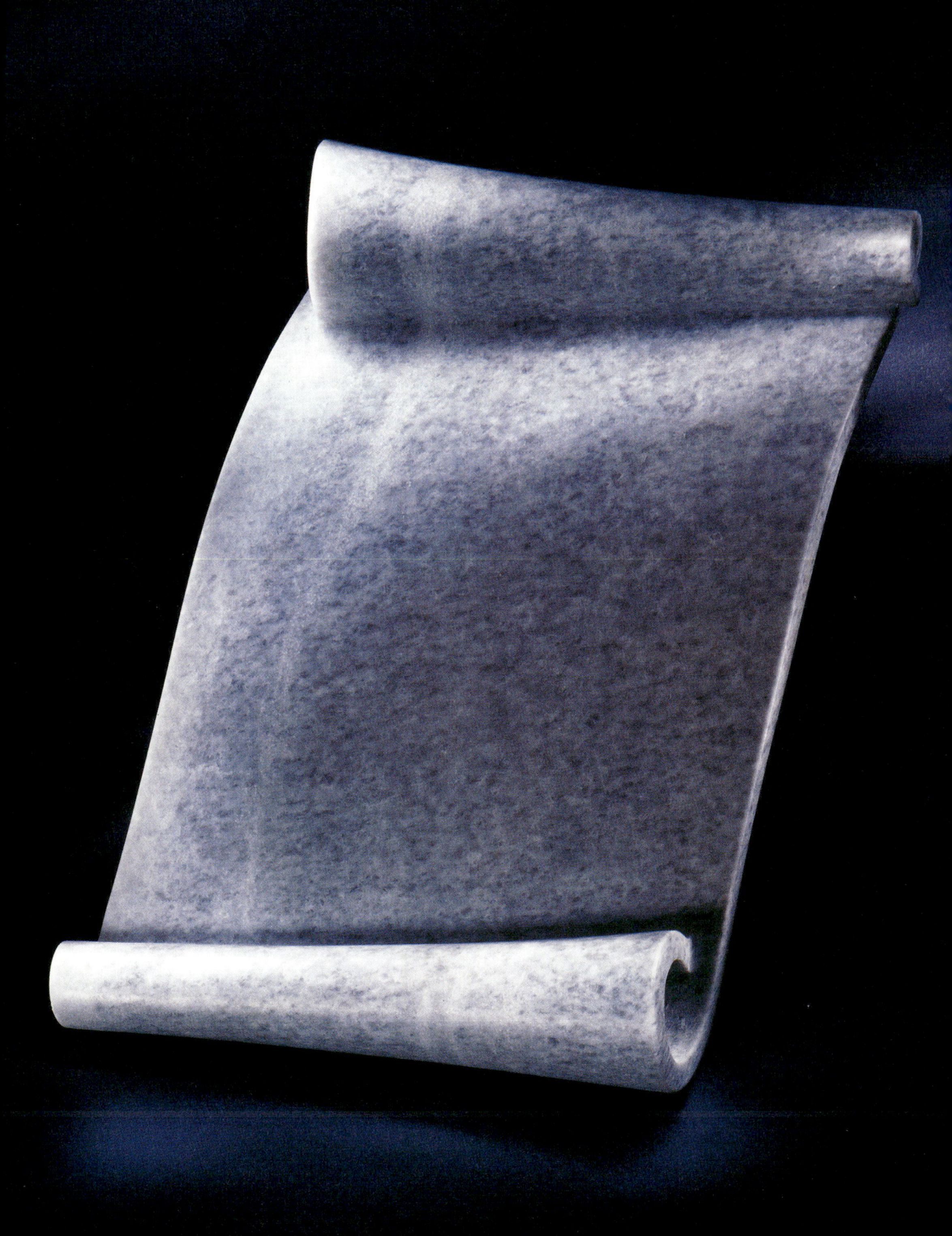

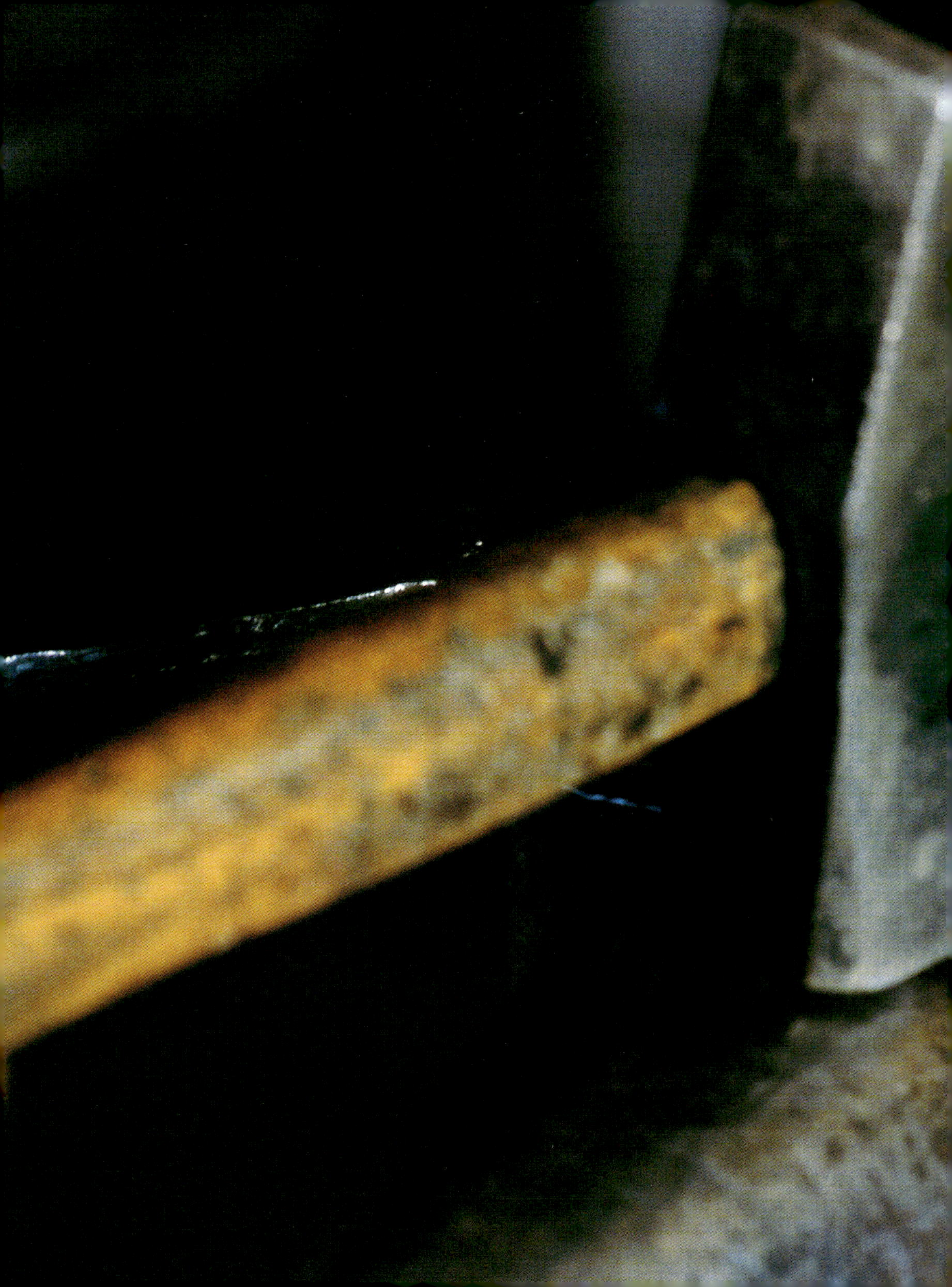

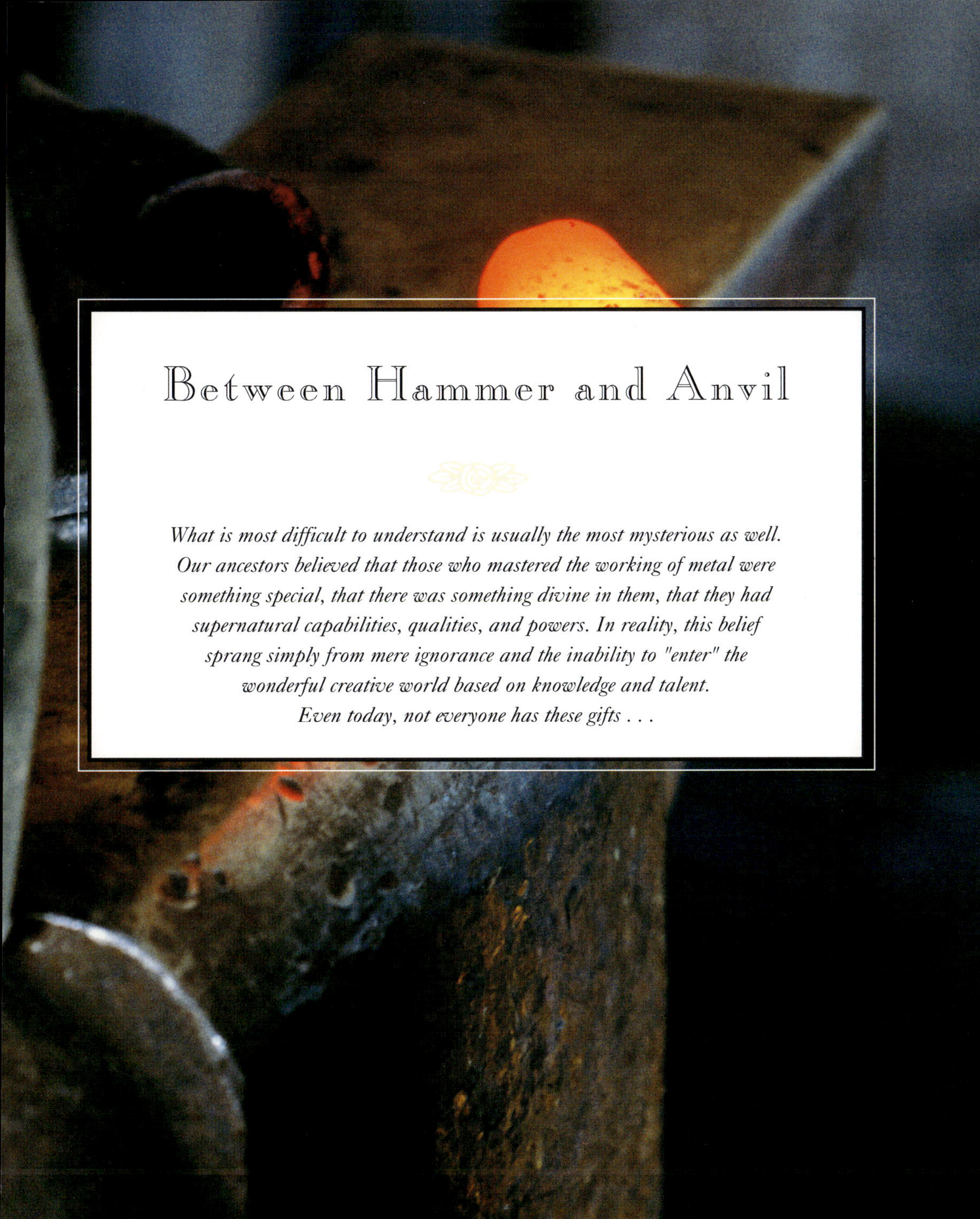

Between Hammer and Anvil

What is most difficult to understand is usually the most mysterious as well. Our ancestors believed that those who mastered the working of metal were something special, that there was something divine in them, that they had supernatural capabilities, qualities, and powers. In reality, this belief sprang simply from mere ignorance and the inability to "enter" the wonderful creative world based on knowledge and talent. Even today, not everyone has these gifts . . .

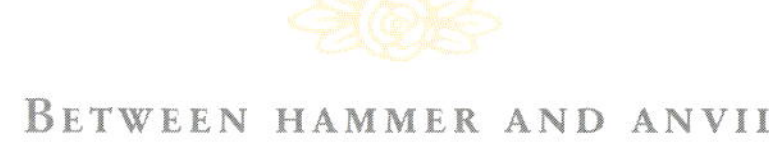

Forging skills and a natural talent for design ►

Modern Slovene artistic metalwork boasts masterpieces in the work of **Miha Krištof** from Vinarje near Maribor. His creativity is truly outstanding, ranging from unique original pieces to wrought-iron replicas needed for the restoration of heritage buildings. Although he belongs to the younger or middle generation of Slovene blacksmiths, he has received many awards for his original creations. Several years ago, his crucifix and two candlesticks won a competition to furnish an altar in one of Rome's basilicas. For the Pope's visit to Slovenia, Krištof forged a crucifix in the form of a living vine, uniting the centuries-old blacksmithing tradition with fundamental Christian symbolism and the most recognizable feature of Slovenia's winegrowing regions.

Exploring new directions in artistic metalwork ▼

Like all fields of handicraft, metalwork requires continuing development and a search for new creative possibilities. Mere repetitions of historical memory can lead to a somewhat stereotype "museology" in which both production and products quite quickly lose all the dynamic characteristics of creative restlessness. Blacksmith **Vlado Zupančič** creates on a path between traditional artistic metalwork and new explorations. His products are distinguished by their remarkable precision while many influences from our blacksmith heritage are still evident in their design and overall artistic appearance. He is successfully exploring and developing his own personal expression in the vital artistic and cultural environment of Slovenj Gradec.

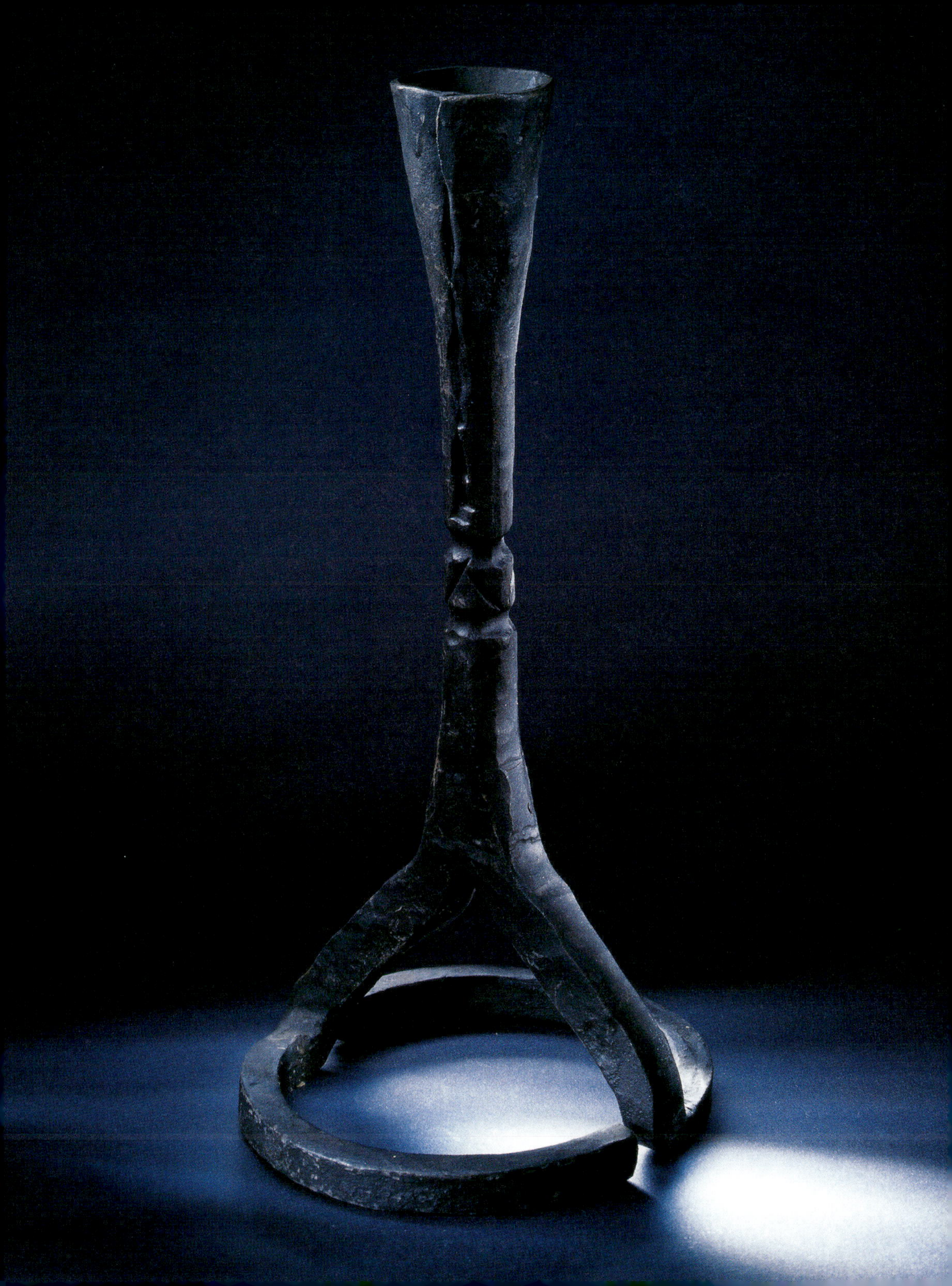

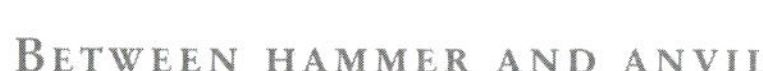

Every real man carries a pocket knife! ►

In the mountainous parts of western Slovenia around Čepovan and Lokovec, the local blacksmith trade was once highly developed, but **Jože Rijavec** is now the only person continuing the rich tradition of Lokovec blacksmithing, famed particularly in the 19th century for the production of knives, drills, and nails. Even today, local people like to recount how Empress Maria Theresa ordered twenty million nails for the needs of the Austrian army from their smithies. Even though this story may be no more than the fruit of local folklore, it still reflects a highly developed blacksmithing trade without which the story could not exist. Typical items forged by this master include a curved knife for pruning vines and manual wood drills.

Cheese knives of foremost design ▼

At his father's workshop in Škofja Loka, industrial designer **Jure Miklavc** crafted these cheese knives made from stainless steel and cherry wood. Regarding these items, we should first mention the exemplary cooperation in the family between design technology and execution (production). The basic question to be solved in designing the knives was how to connect the different parts in an artistic, esthetic whole, in other words, how to create a harmonious dialogue between blade and handle while considering two different materials that offered various design possibilities.

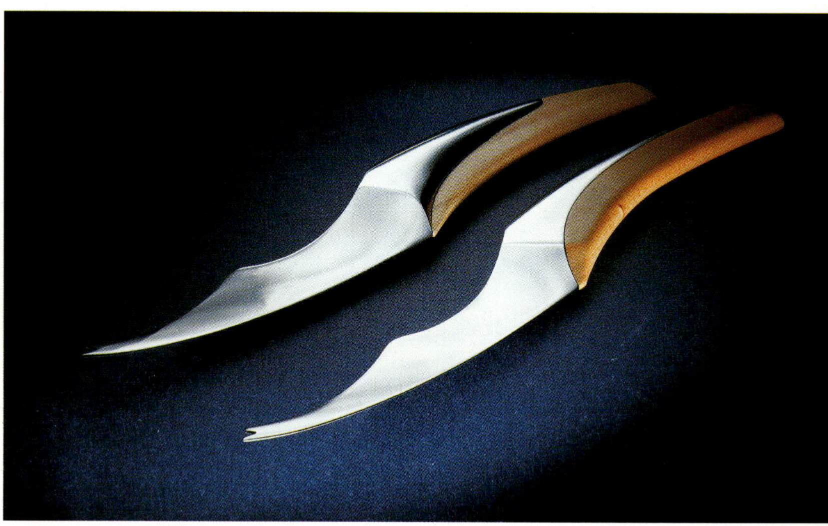

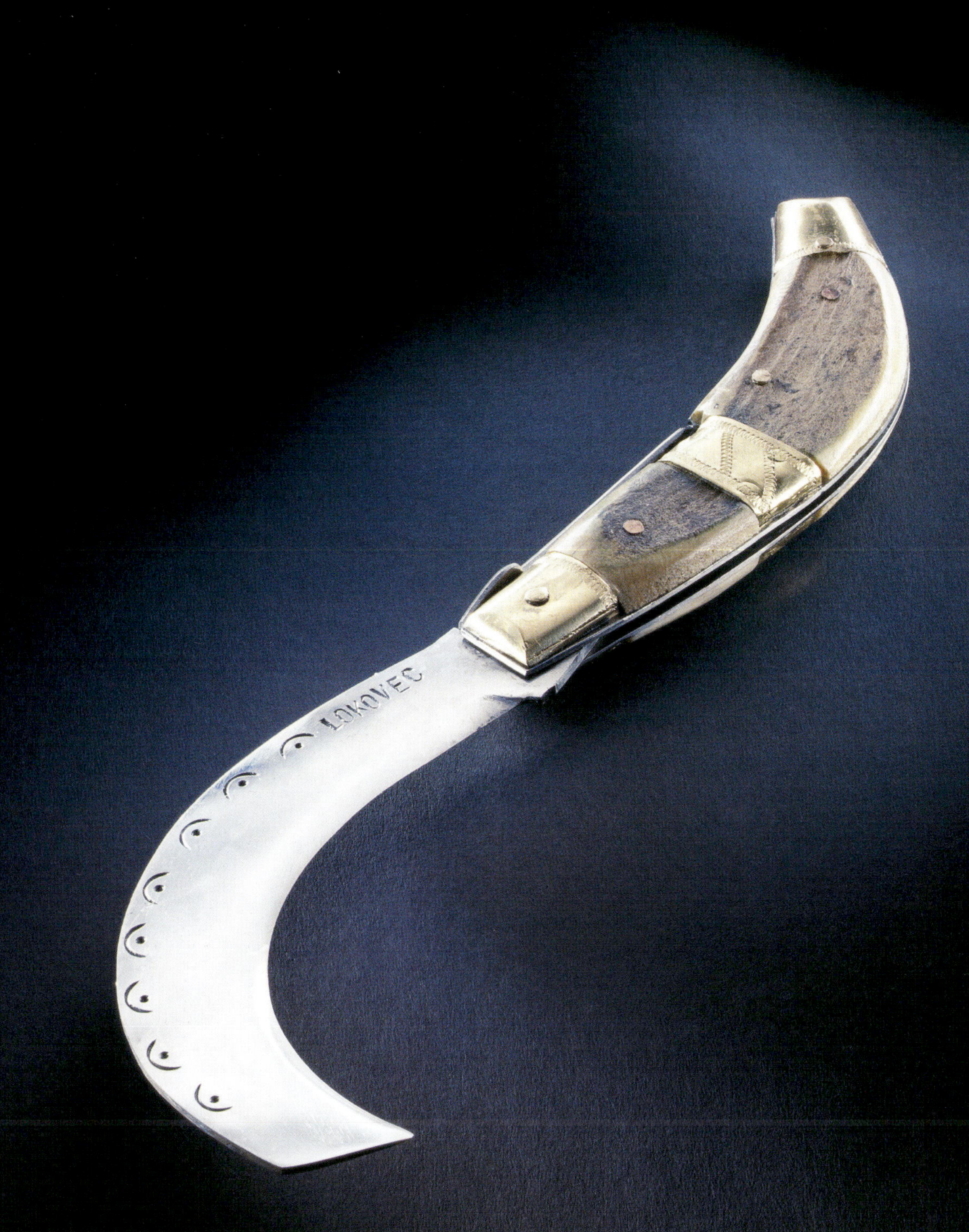
LOKOVEC

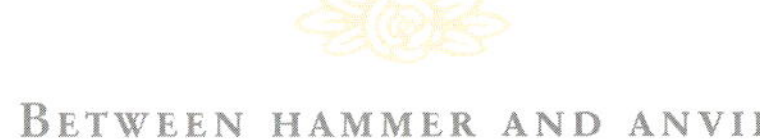

GUNSMITHING – THE TRADITION AND SYNTHESIS OF VARIOUS SKILLS ►

MILAN ŠTEH from Kamnik pod Krimom near Ljubljana is one of Slovenia's leading gunsmiths. His workshop carries on the tradition of top quality Slovene gunsmithing achievements from the Middle Ages when Ferlach in Austria was a major center of this activity. Later, Ljubljana, Maribor, and Kranj also became important gunsmithing centers, and following World War I, an eminent gunsmithing school began operating in Ljubljana. The foremost gunsmithing skills are found in the Šteh workshop, including not only forging "mysteries" and skills but also various machining work and metalworking. Metal parts are engraved by hand, while the gunstocks are carved with typical hunting motifs.

A RICH FAMILY TRADITION ▼

Metalsmithing ranks among the handicrafts in Slovenia that have a rich family tradition, and several famous names dominated and still dominate this field. Metalsmithing has a very old tradition. In the Middle Ages, making practical and decorative objects was initially part of the goldsmith's trade, but over time various branches employing copper, brass, and other metals grew independent and became separate handicrafts. Their "classic" works are marked by the names of three families: Žmuc, Pirnat, and Pezdirc. That metalsmithing is distinguished by outstanding creativity is proven by the work of **VLADIMIR PEZDIRC**, one of Slovenia's leading designers.

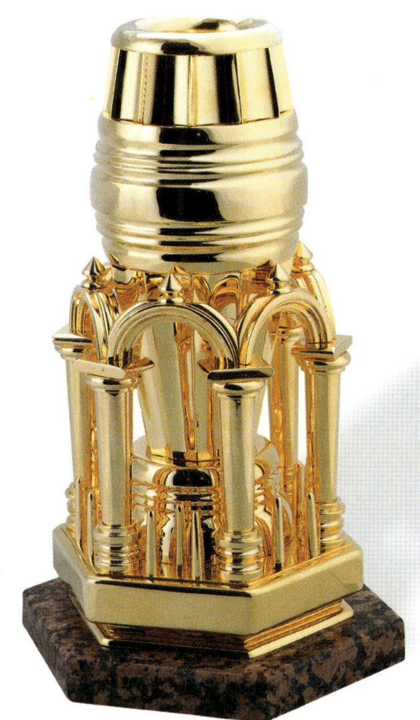

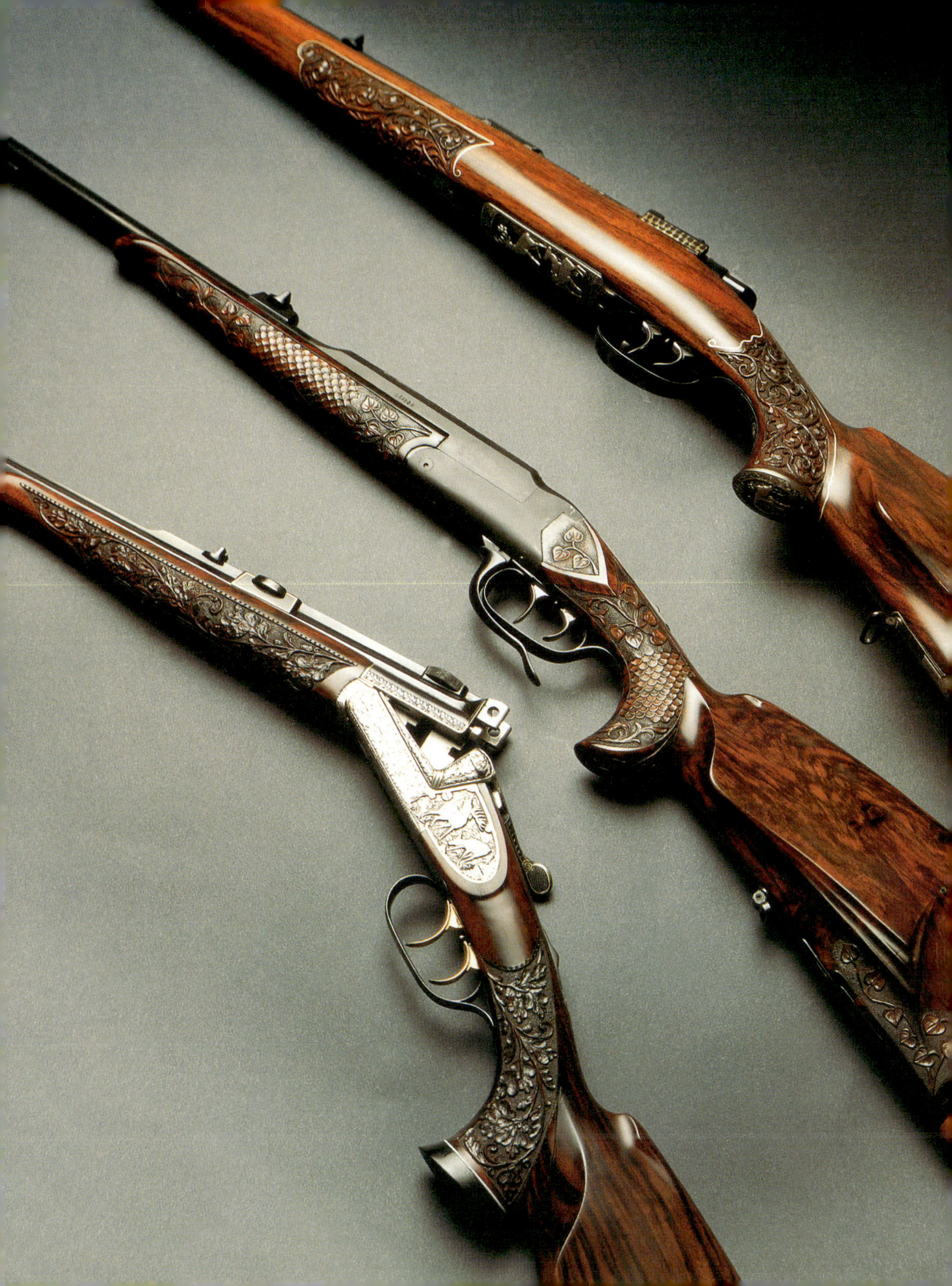

Collaboration with architect Jože Plečnik ►

Like other top Slovene metalsmiths, the **Žmuc** family of Ljubljana can boast of collaborating with the eminent architect Jože Plečnik (1872–1957). It was Plečnik's unwavering demand for precision and perfection in production and design that brought Slovene metalsmiths and other craftsmen to rank among the world's best.

From sacral vessels to chandeliers ▼

The development of metalsmithing from the goldsmith trade is linked to the basic materials used by metalsmiths to manufacture various vessels and furnishings for liturgical and secular purposes and for the interior and exterior furnishings of rooms and buildings. The basic materials are primarily nonferrous metals, but often precious and semi-precious stones, glass, natural stone worked by a stonecutter, various types of wood, and other materials are used to create harmonious designs. Thus, the products of all the foremost metalsmiths, including the **Pirnat** workshop, are actually a synthesis of the work of various handicraft masters.

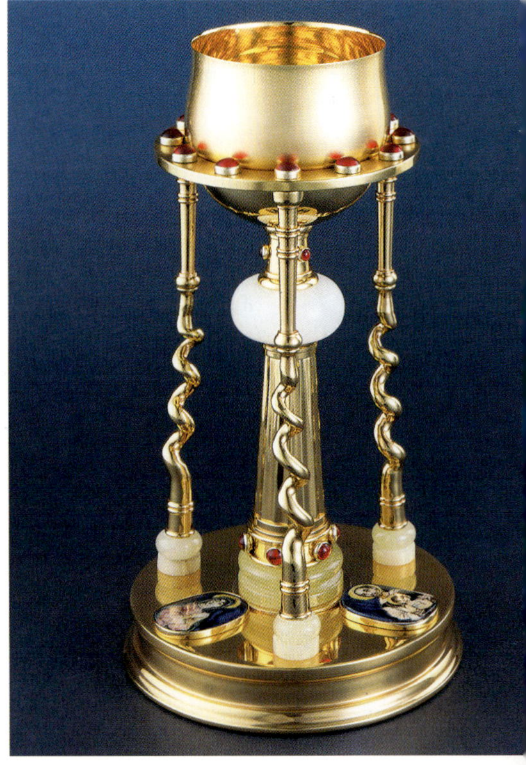

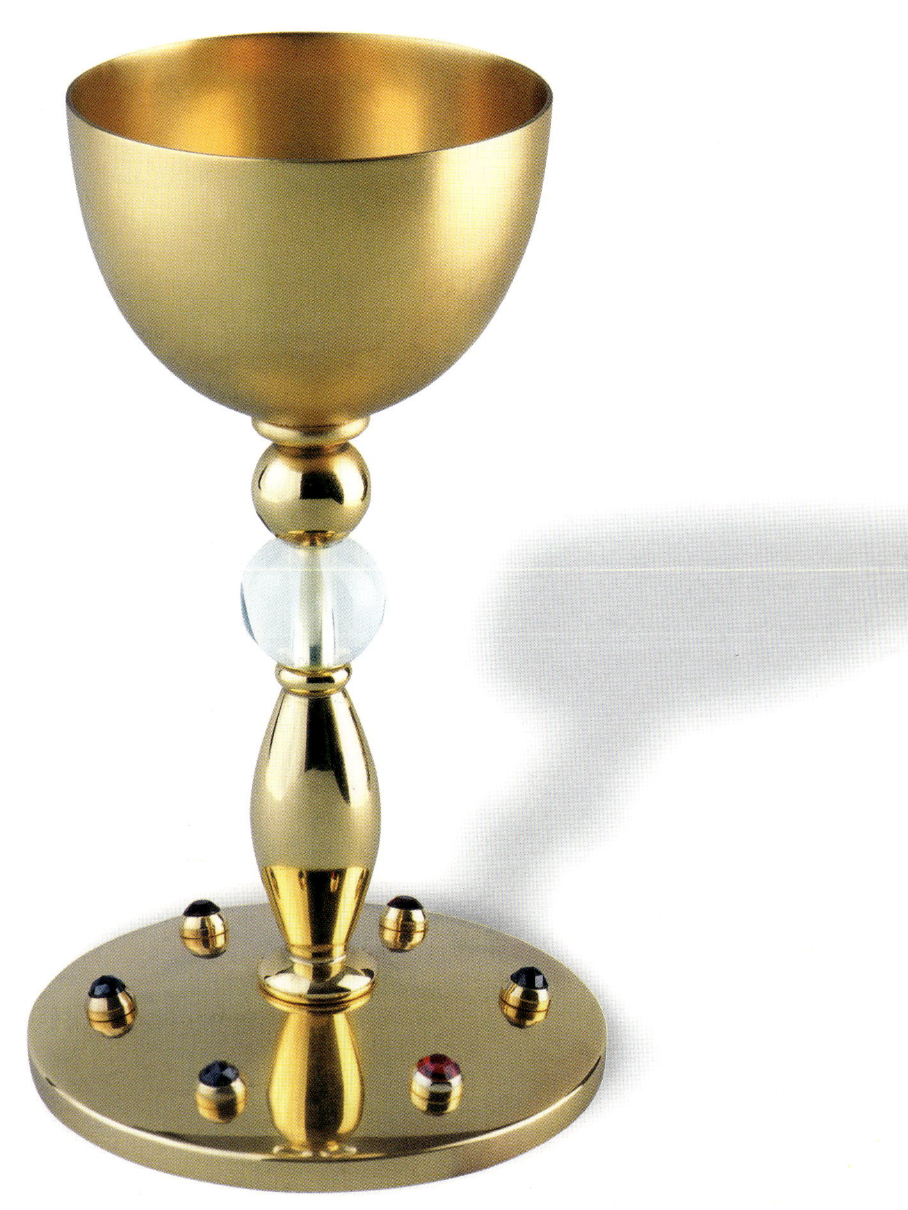

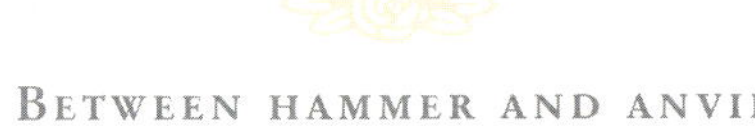

Miša Jelnikar, the First Lady of Slovene jewellery ►
The manually forged and shaped silver jewellery of Miša Jelnikar has long been among the most recognizable trademarks worldwide in this field of Slovene design. The artist graduated from the School of Design in Ljubljana and continued her studies in London. Several decades ago, she established herself at home and abroad with a distinctive, recognizable, and personal design style that is evident in the exceptionally pure shapes of her bracelets, earrings, rings, pendants, and decorative pins. Her jewellery truly allows the people who wear it to express their individuality.

Metals linked to new materials ▼
The young designer **Romi Bukovec** from Medvode makes jewellery from various materials, particularly from metals and modern resins. More important, however, is her conception of jewellery, which transcends the classical framework and the classical understanding of wearing it. Jewellery is a companion to the body as a whole. The artist's solutions become signs and markers, created so to speak for the entire body and its numerous parts at the same time. We can no longer talk merely about an adornment but rather about an equal companionship and the joint creation of an individual's persona that emphasizes above the qualities of communication, that is, its open or closed nature. It is oriented toward human beings, their interior worlds and their response to the outer world.

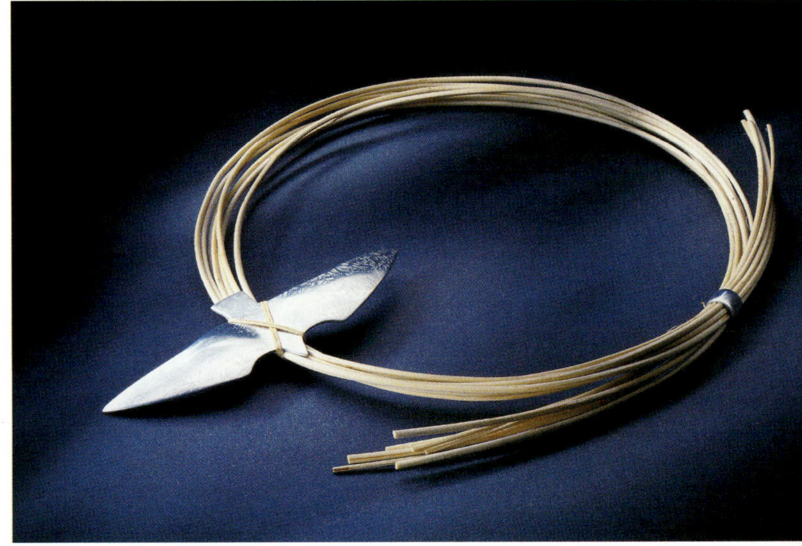

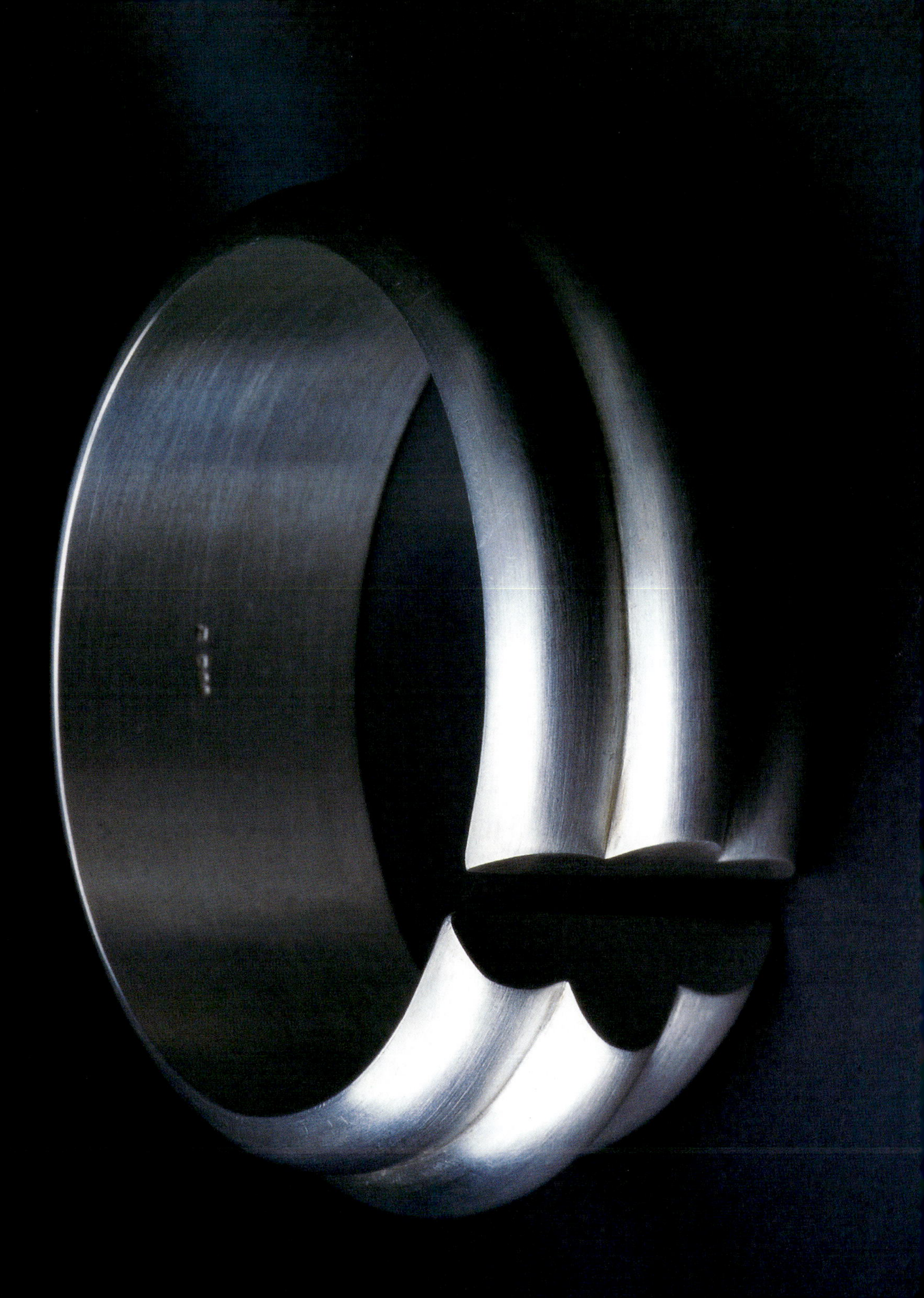

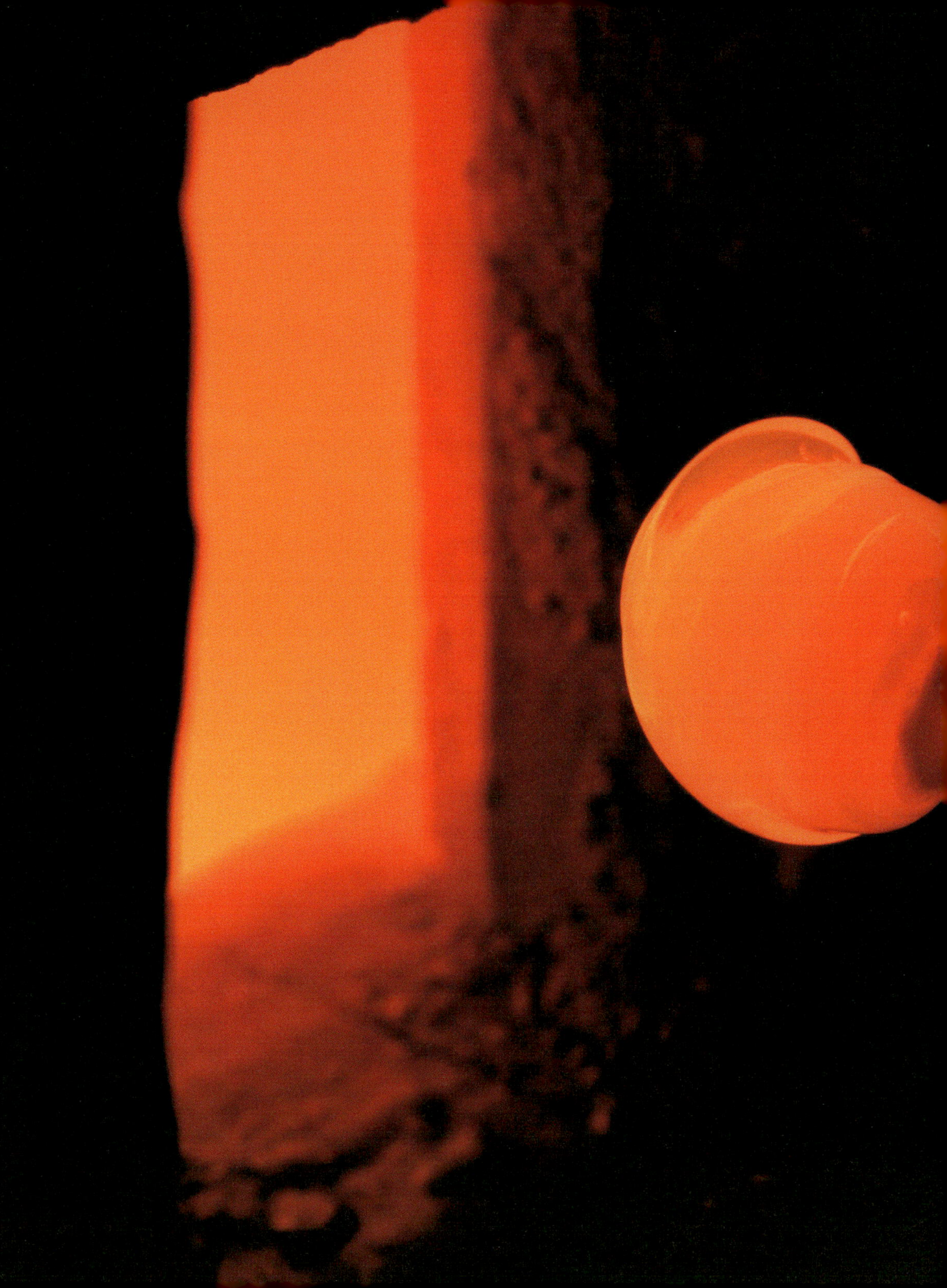

Fragile Eternity

Slovenia had excellent natural conditions for the development of glassmaking. The first glassworks appeared in the 16th century, and there is not sufficient firm evidence to prove the existence of more ancient production. The greatest number of glassworks were established between the end of the 17th century and the middle of the 19th century in heavily forested regions where settlements for glaziers and glassblowers were set up as well. Modern Slovene glassmaking is one of the best examples of the cooperation between foremost designers and the executors of their ideas, the glaziers and glassblowers.

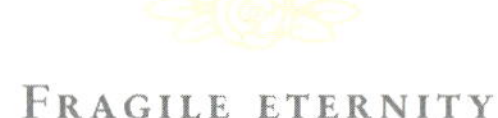

THE TECHNOLOGICAL HERITAGE, A STARTING POINT FOR MODERN DESIGN ►

PETER OGRIN from Ljubljana belongs to the youngest generation of Slovene designers trying to establish their recognizable design expression on the basis of exploring our heritage. As a starting point, he chose the technology of bubbled glass so typical of the popular traditional two-liter *Štefani* wine flasks and created a series of glasses and other drinking and table glassware. His collection is a continuation of the heritage and at the same time a step toward the recognizable identity of Slovene glass. It is therefore not surprising that after its first presentation, the entire collection was included in the collection of the Slovene National Museum as a witness and a significant achievement of authentic Slovene glassmaking.

REPLICAS FROM THE FOREST *GLAŽUTE* ▼

Items made in the former forest glassworks or *glažute* are preserved in numerous museums and collections. The idea of producing replicas from this heritage only recently awakened among Slovene glaziers and glassblowers. The undoubted leader among them is **CIRIL ZOBEC** from Rogaška Slatina, the center of Slovenia's glassmaking industry. He makes replicas from the glassmaking heritage as well as producing modern glass items. Making replicas is not merely a matter of duplicating the original designs but also of studying specific old technologies and methods of glassblowing and shaping items that were developed in the past.

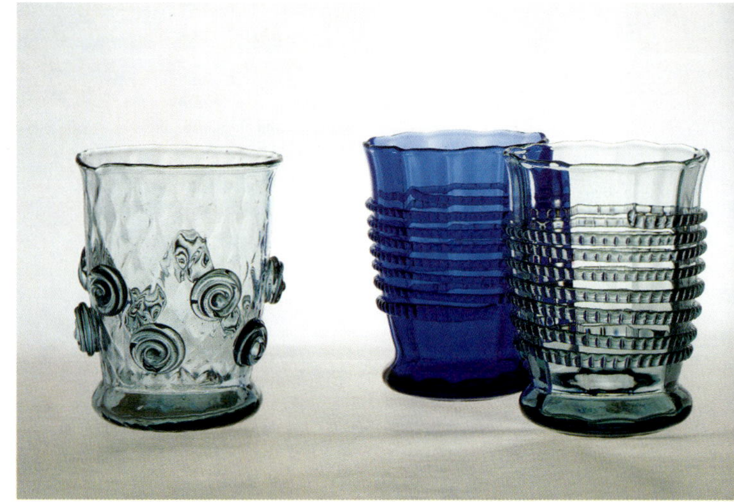

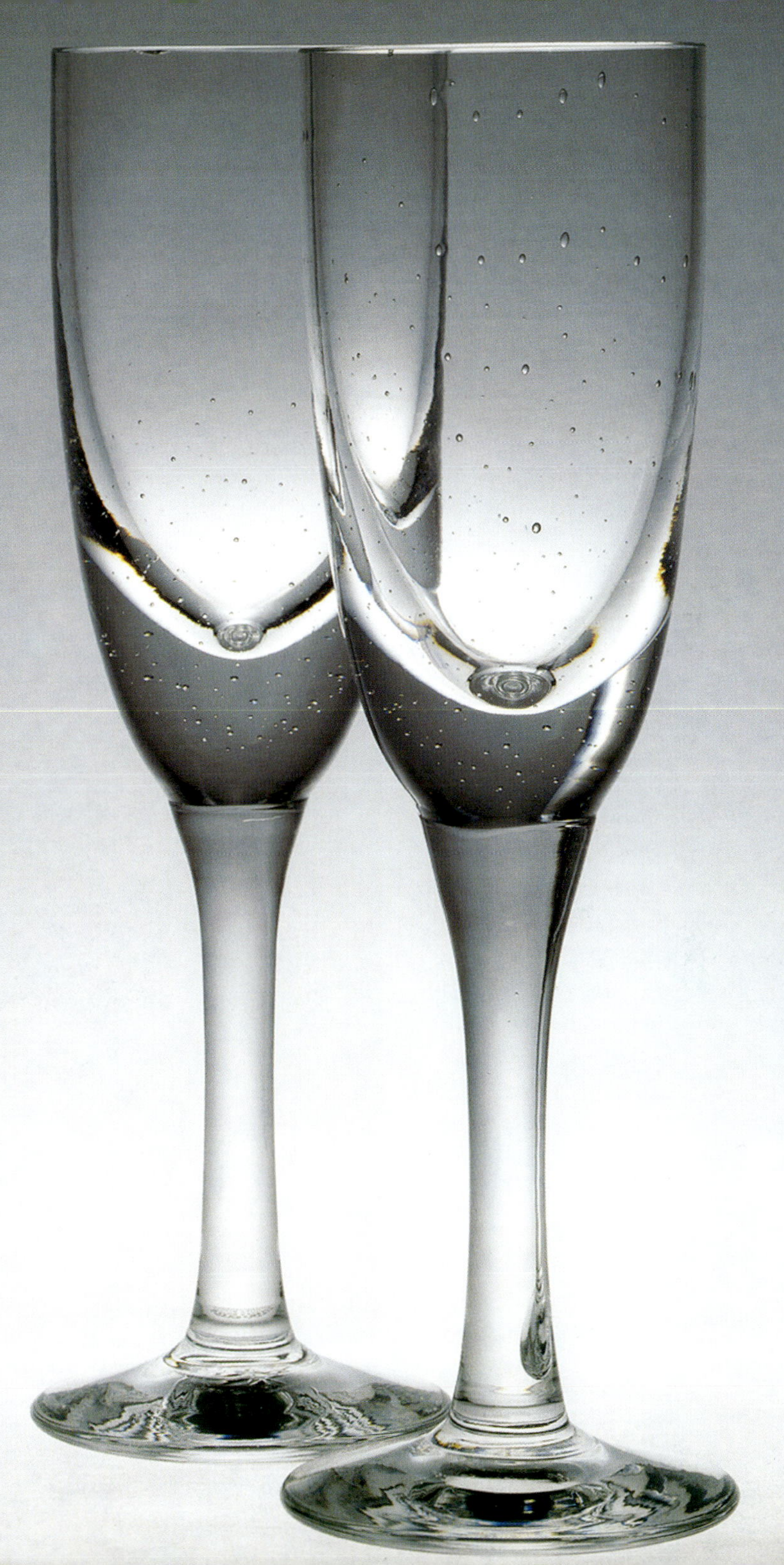

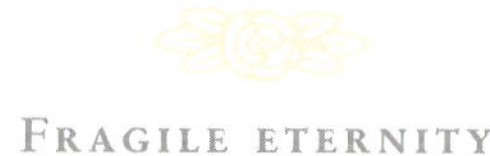

The decline of stained glass and the birth of etched glass ►

With the decline of stained-glass window production, a trend appeared in the Baroque period toward having ornamented and universally decorated light glass and thus glass etching developed. Etching glass uses mixtures of fluorine compounds that enable the creation of the most varied motifs, ornaments, and decorative effects on a glass surface. In Slovenia, the oldest preserved examples of etched glass are from Ljubljana and the period following the great earthquake of 1895. Glass etching thus became a means of expression that can be connected to the renovation of heritage buildings or can take completely modern artistic design directions. **Aleš Lombergar** from Ljubljana is the only master of this handicraft in Slovenia. While he creates completely new, modern decorative glass pieces, he is also the only master restoring and replicating the etched glass of our heritage buildings.

Light through drawings and fields of colour ▼

The production of stained-glass windows in Europe began in the 10th century and reached its peak in the 13th century when the greatest French cathedrals were built. Stained-glass windows were later used for decorating secular buildings and rooms as well. After the Baroque period, this handicraft suffered a decline and had to be revived in the 19th century. Slovenia's foremost master of making stained-glass windows is **Stojan Višnar** from Zasip near Bled. Many of the stained-glass windows from his workshop are based on the work of painter **Tomaž Perko**. Višnar's stained-glass windows adorn many public and private buildings and churches in Slovenia and abroad.

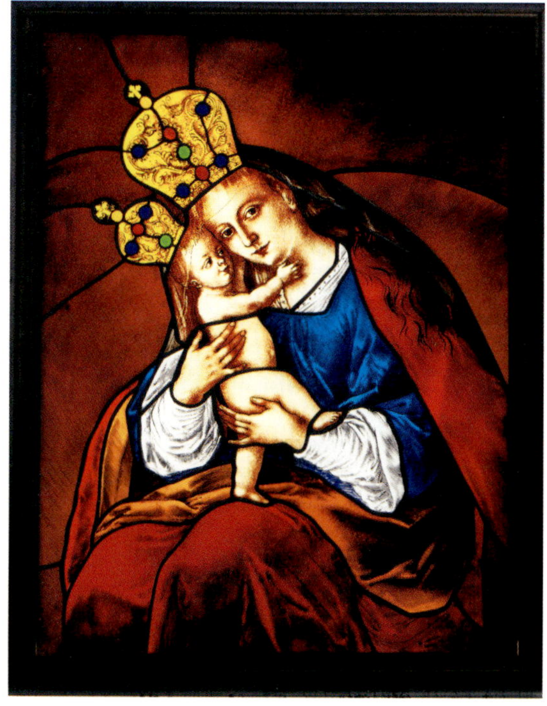

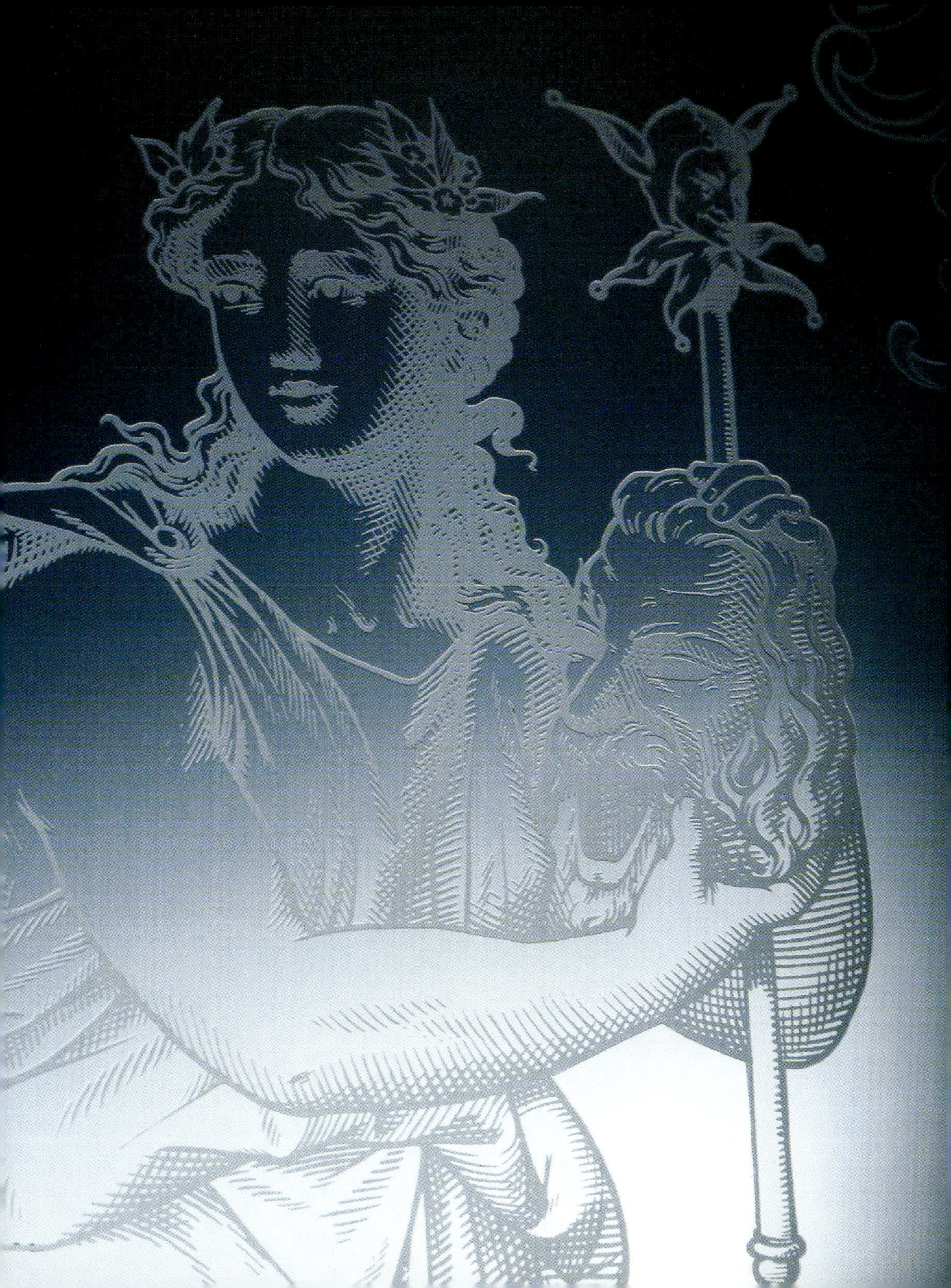

FROM FORMER INDUSTRIAL MASS PRODUCTION TO INDEPENDENT WORKSHOPS ►

The glassmaking industry in Rogaška Slatina developed with the establishment of independent glassmaking workshops that in the course of time began reaching into all fields of glass production. Recognized firms with their own trademarks appeared, one being the **SAJKO** workshop which makes product lines, unique pieces, and replicas of items made in the old forest glassworks. **FRANC SAJKO** and his son **MITJA** have promoted the family firm *Kreativ* with the trademark *Štajerska glažuta* ("Forest Glassworks of Štajerska") in memory of the formerly widespread glassmaking activity in the forests of Štajerska.

UNIQUE FORMS AND TOP QUALITY ENGRAVING ▼

One of the first peaks in glass design was achieved by designer and sculptress **LJUBICA KOČICA** from Rogaška Slatina. Her renowned unique products and design series have received many domestic and foreign awards. She has established her name through a distinctly personal style, creating unique works of art using a variety of design, technological, and artistic approaches. She creates not only with the basic shaping of a glass mass but also employs colour, engraving, and cutting, supplementing these with ceramic work to produce mostly sculptures and some unique decorative objects.

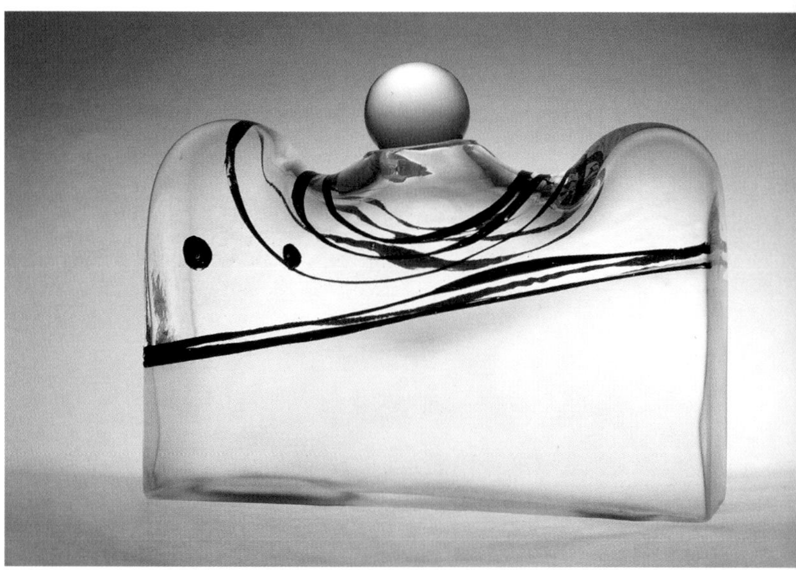

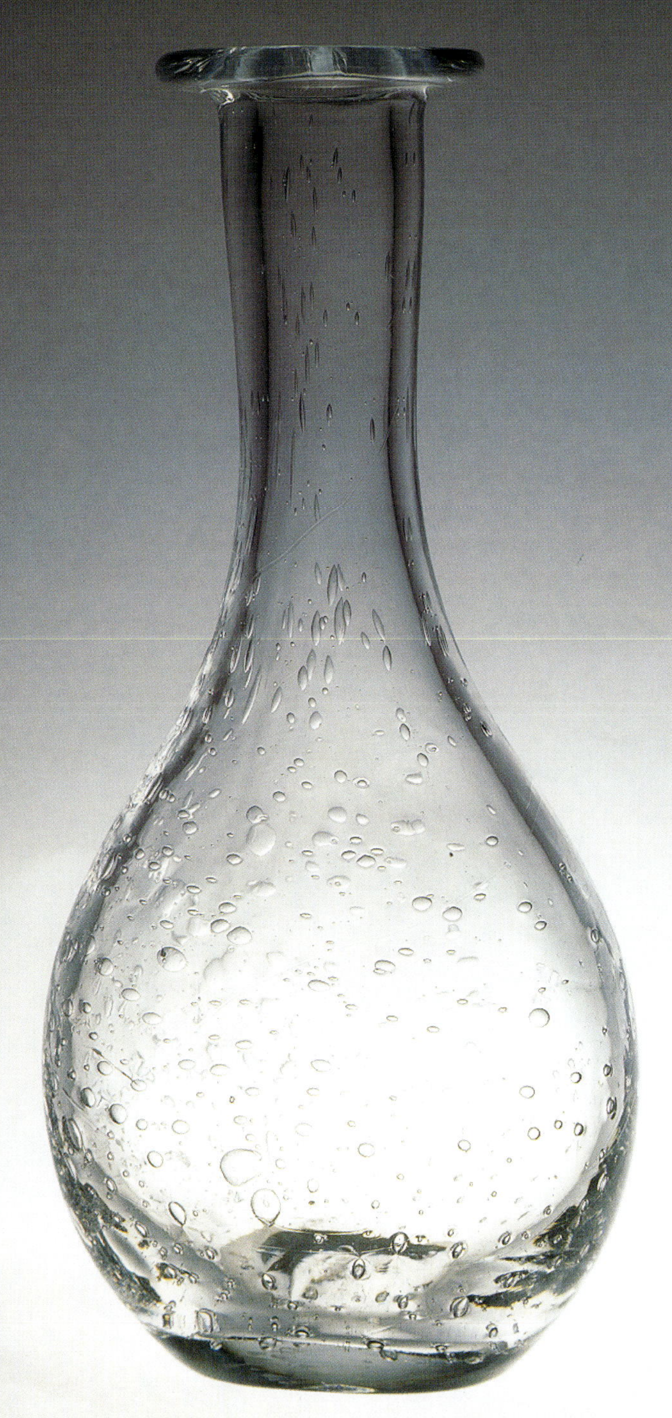

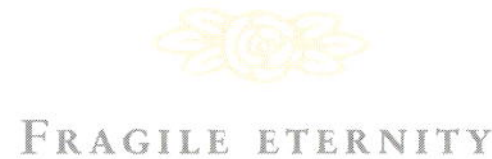

Imagination, cosmicness, and fluctuation ►

The young but world-renowned Slovene designer **Tanja Pak** was born into a glassmaking family in Rogaška Slatina. After graduating from the Department of Design at the Academy of Fine Arts of Ljubljana University, she continued her studies at London's Royal College of Art. Pak does not simply reiterate the heritage but instead uses it as a basis on which to build her creativity. Her glassmaking environment stimulated her creative imagination, and thus she has developed a range of technological and expressive possibilities. Her works are full of change and fluctuation; they are not static but rather convey the impression of being living changing forms. In this, she is guided by her fundamental conviction that glass itself is a "living" being.

Sculptures in glass ▼

The glasswork of designer **Barbara Dovečar** transcends basic functional forms to become sculpture. Especially interesting are the creations in which she combines glass and wrought iron, two extremely different materials, to create original artistic solutions. Glass becomes a powerful means of expression and at the same time a material for expressing special messages in the modern space.

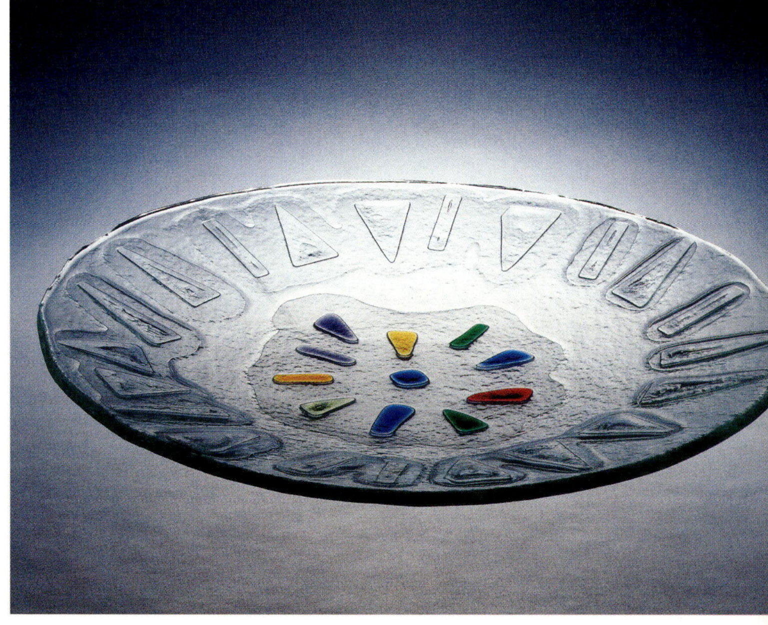

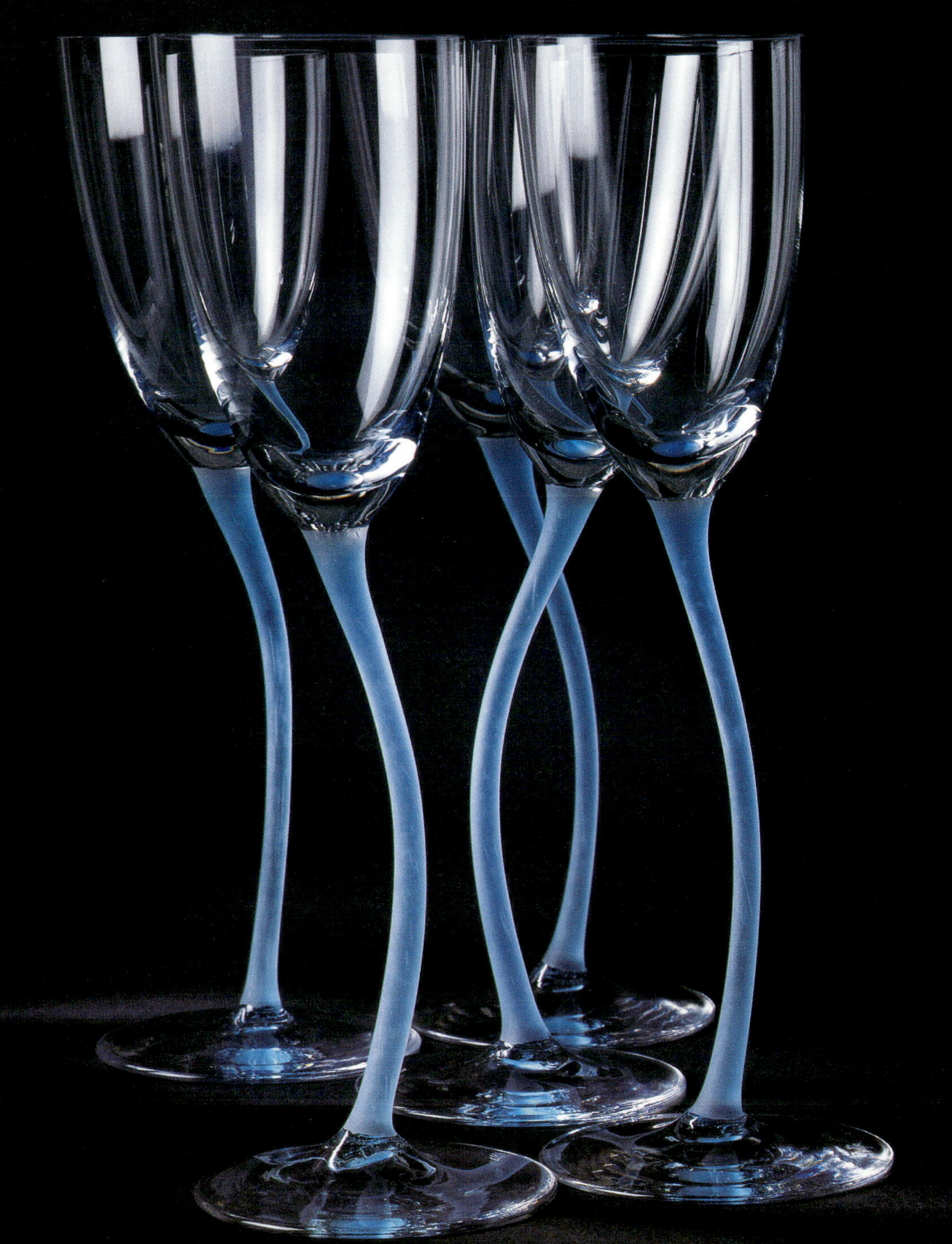

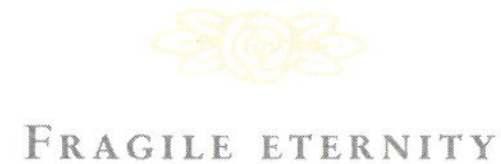

OSKAR KOGOJ'S *NATURE DESIGN* COLLECTION

The **GLASSMAKING SCHOOL** established in 1947 in Rogaška Slatina, Slovenia's main glassmaking center, not only carries out a training program but also produces outstanding glasswork products. Among other things, the school manufactures top quality glass items designed by the internationally recognized designer Oskar Kogoj, and in recent years, a large number of glasses and other glassware items have been added to Kogoj's *Nature Design* collection. Kogoj's designs are a synthesis of Slovenia's glassmaking heritage and the world of symbols, meanings, ancient worldviews, and modern mystical-philosophical horizons and consciousness. In his pieces, he incorporates elements from foreign cultures and explorations of the invisible but very significant energies that influence people's lives, relationships, communication, and the transfer of mental and creative currents.

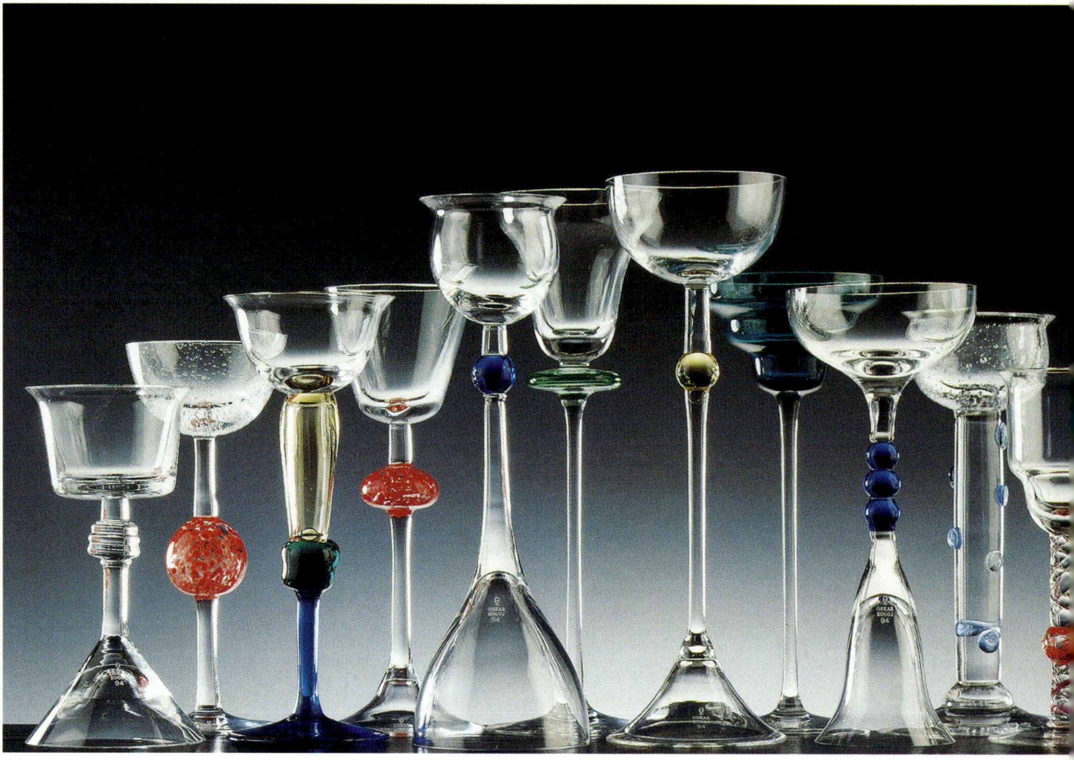

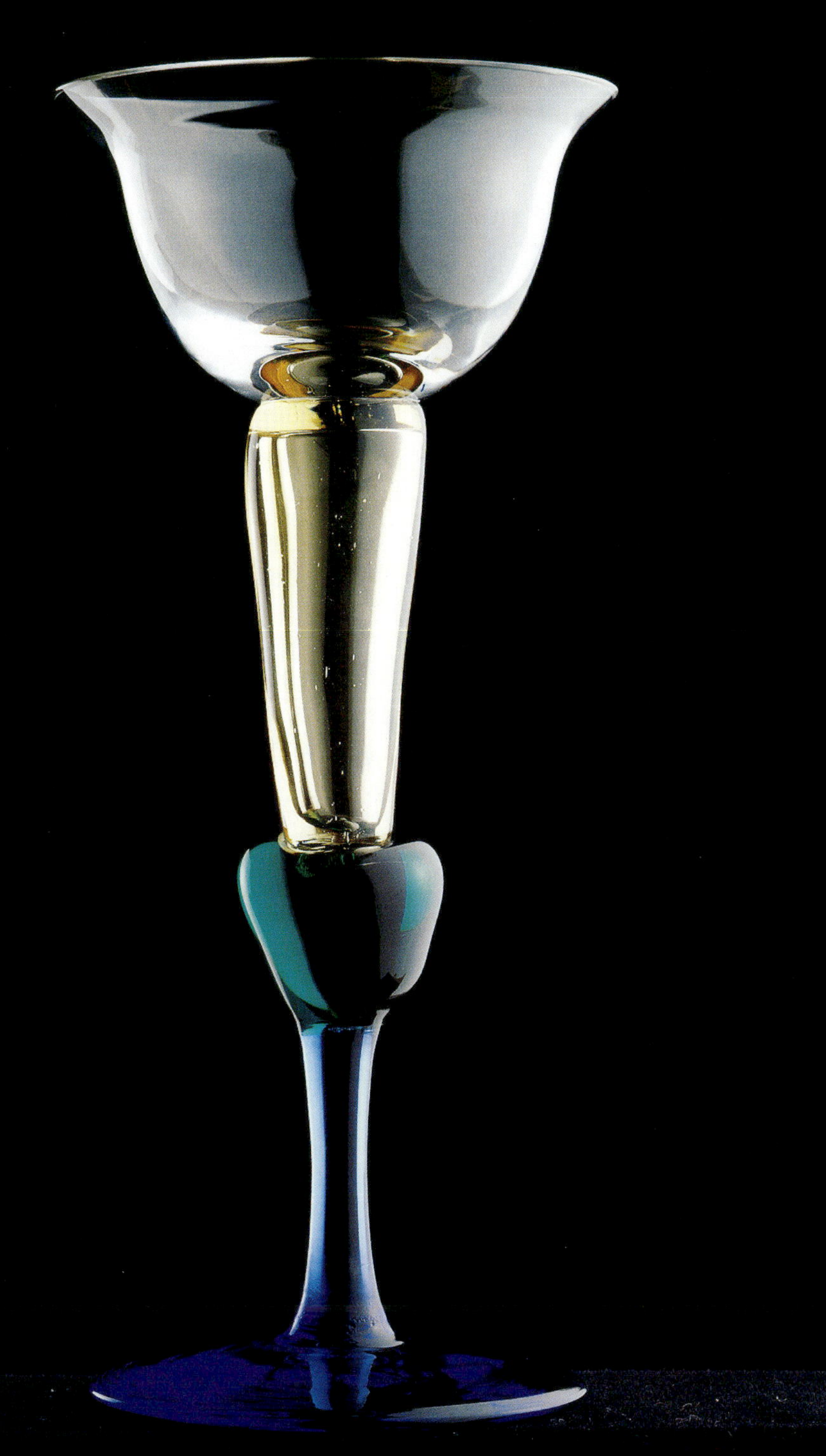

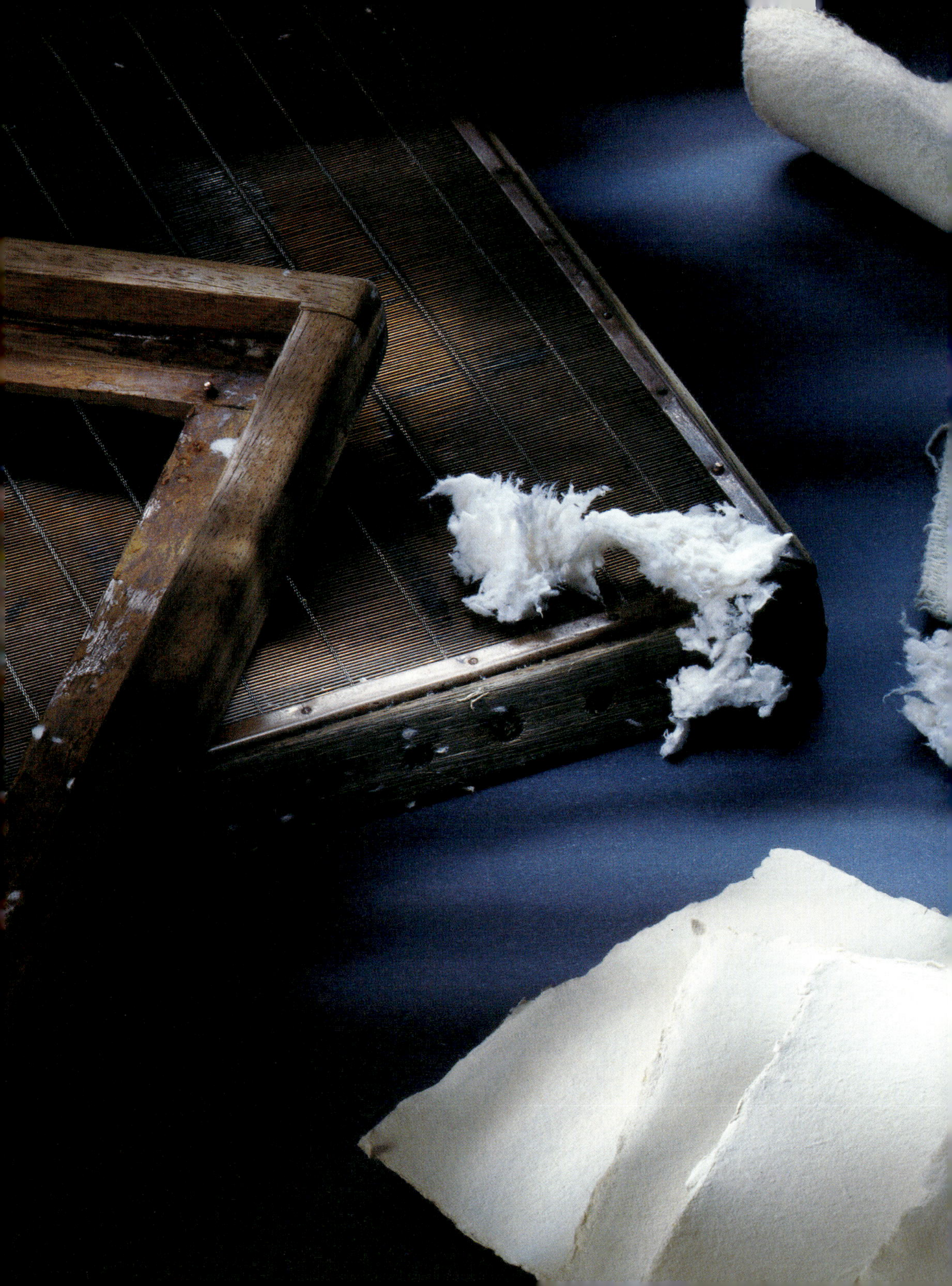

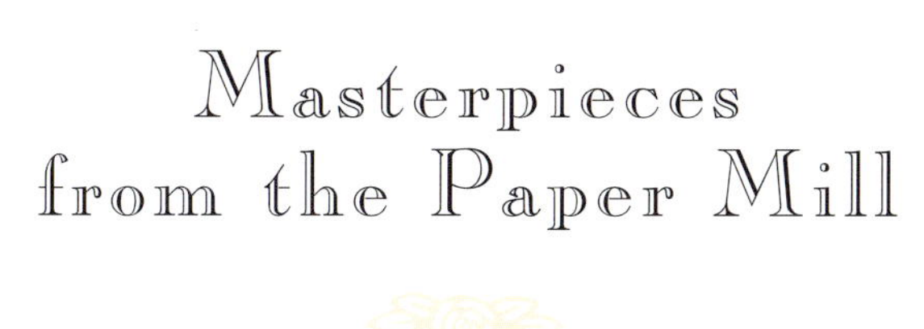

Masterpieces from the Paper Mill

The Chinese invented paper making more than 1900 years ago, and the Arabs introduced the process to Europe. Many paper mills once operated in Slovenia, but all collapsed with the exception of a mill in Fužine, a suburb of Ljubljana, that later grew into the large paper industry in nearby Vevče. Handmade paper from Fužine has been produced on the site of the original Vevče paper mill since 1579.

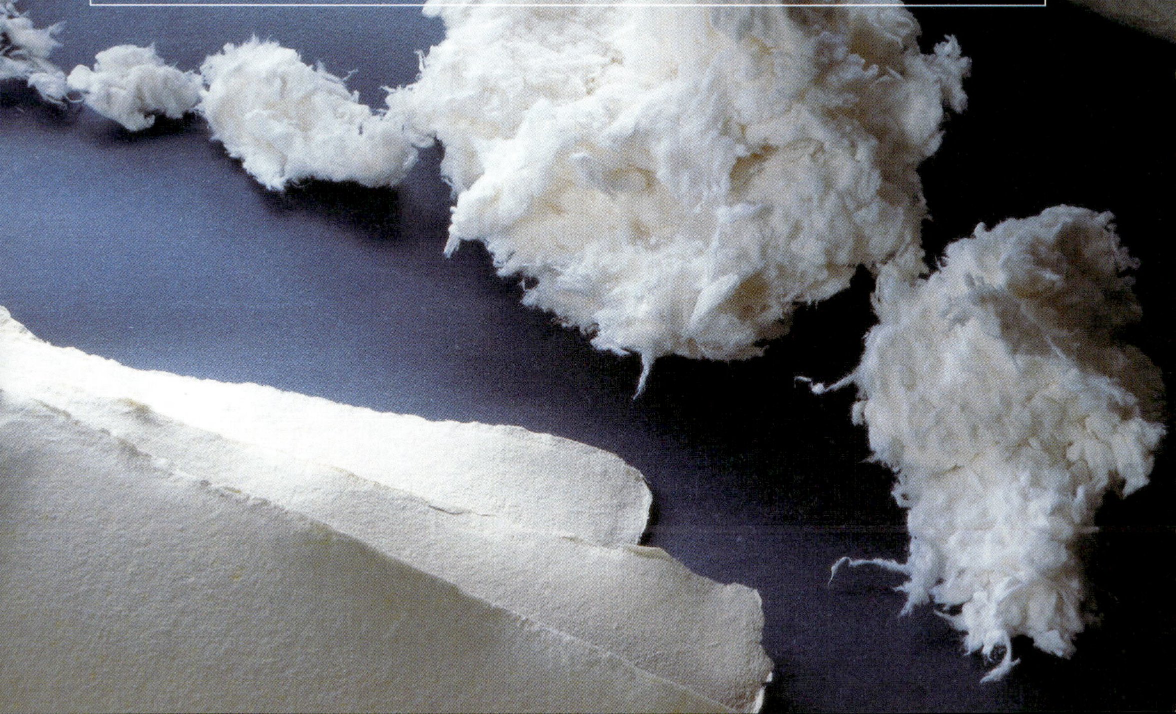

One of rare surviving manual procedures in Europe ►

The tradition of manual paper production in Vevče since 1579 has been preserved by the master workshop of **Jože Valant**. Handmade paper and the items made from it are the continuation of centuries of cultural development. Almost everything recorded in historical memory is preserved on paper. This gives handmade paper special value and significance whether it is used in its traditional role as a bearer of writing or as a creative and expressive material in various fields of design. Studying the history of paper, many details come to light that can offer starting points for new forms and new technological and artistic solutions. These possibilities are being discovered in Valant's workshop as well. Here they produce different kinds of paper using various materials offered by the natural environment, particularly the plant world, the world from which paper itself ultimately comes.

Flowers and love that do not fade ▼

Bridal wreaths and bouquets, corsages for the bride, groom, best man, and wedding guests, communion and confirmation decorations, and funeral bouquets and wreaths to accompany the deceased to their final rest are the most typical items traditionally made from paper. There are only a few regions in Slovenia where the mastery of this traditional craft survives. **Agneza Bezjak** from Ljutomer creates outstanding examples of this handicraft.

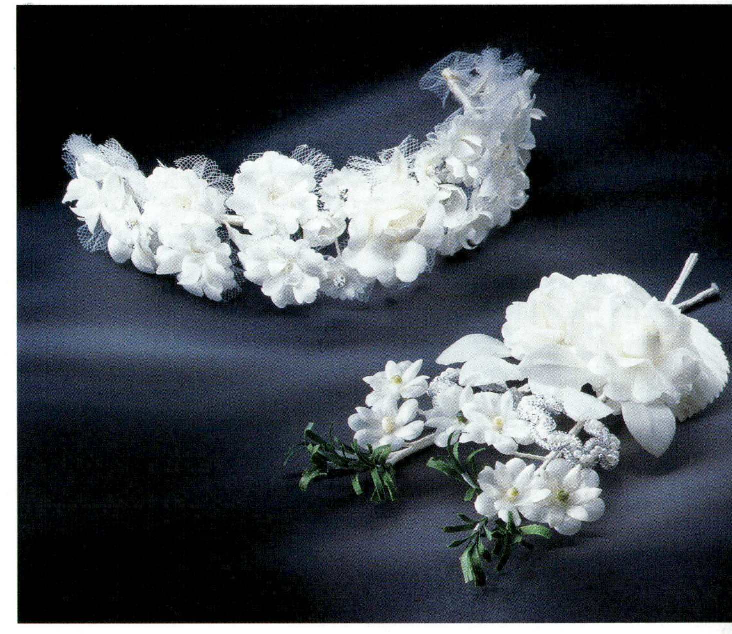

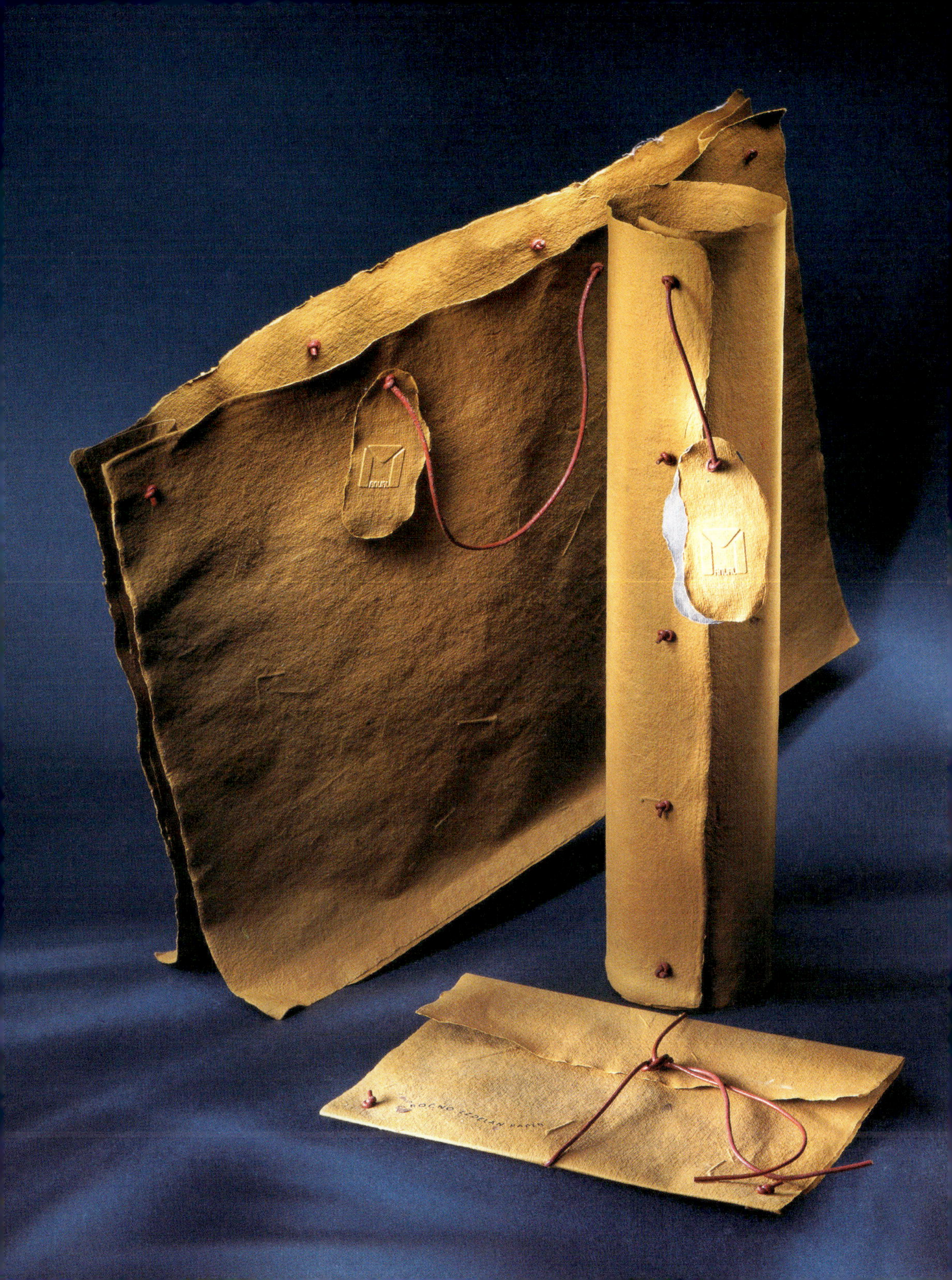

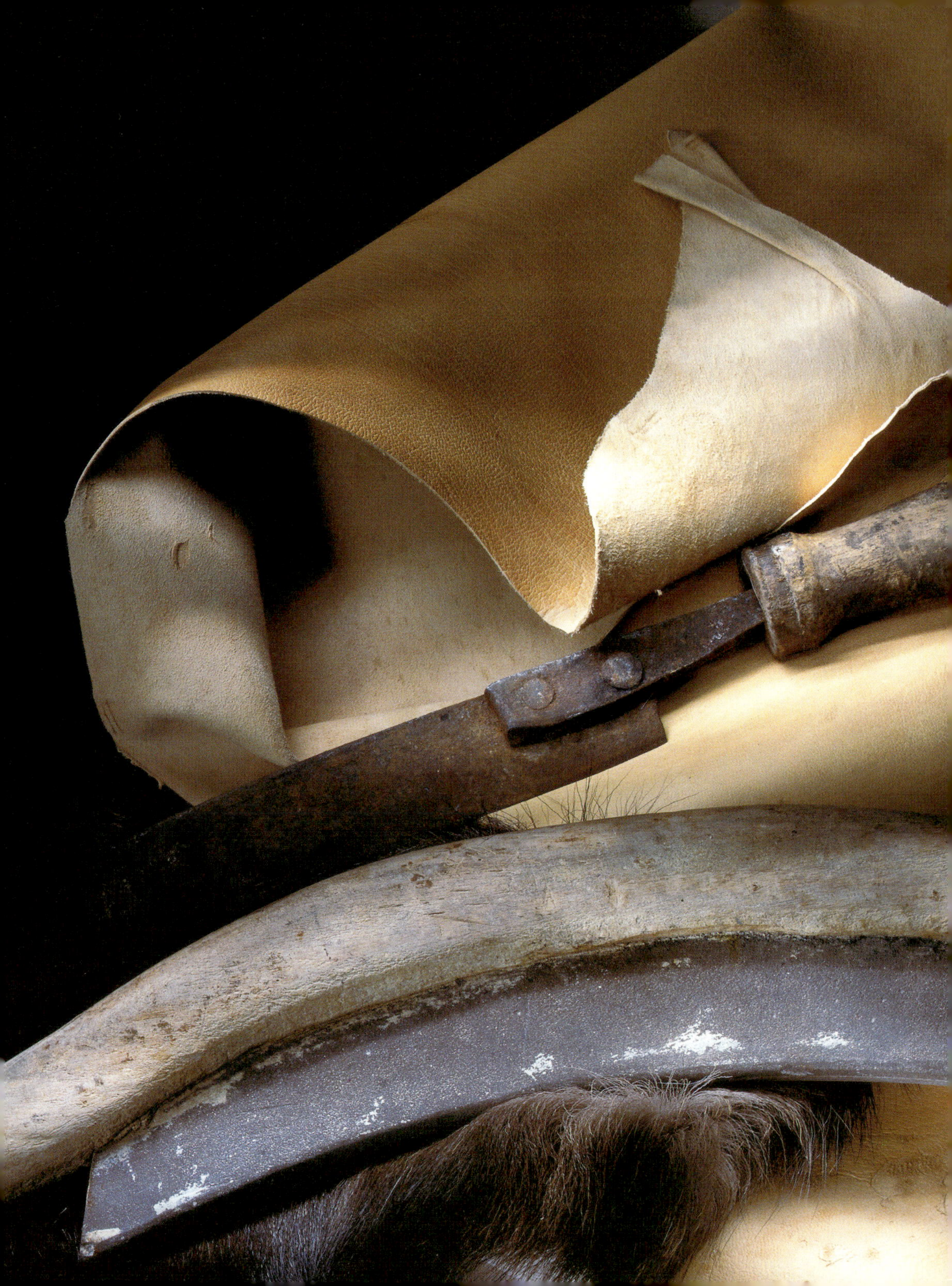

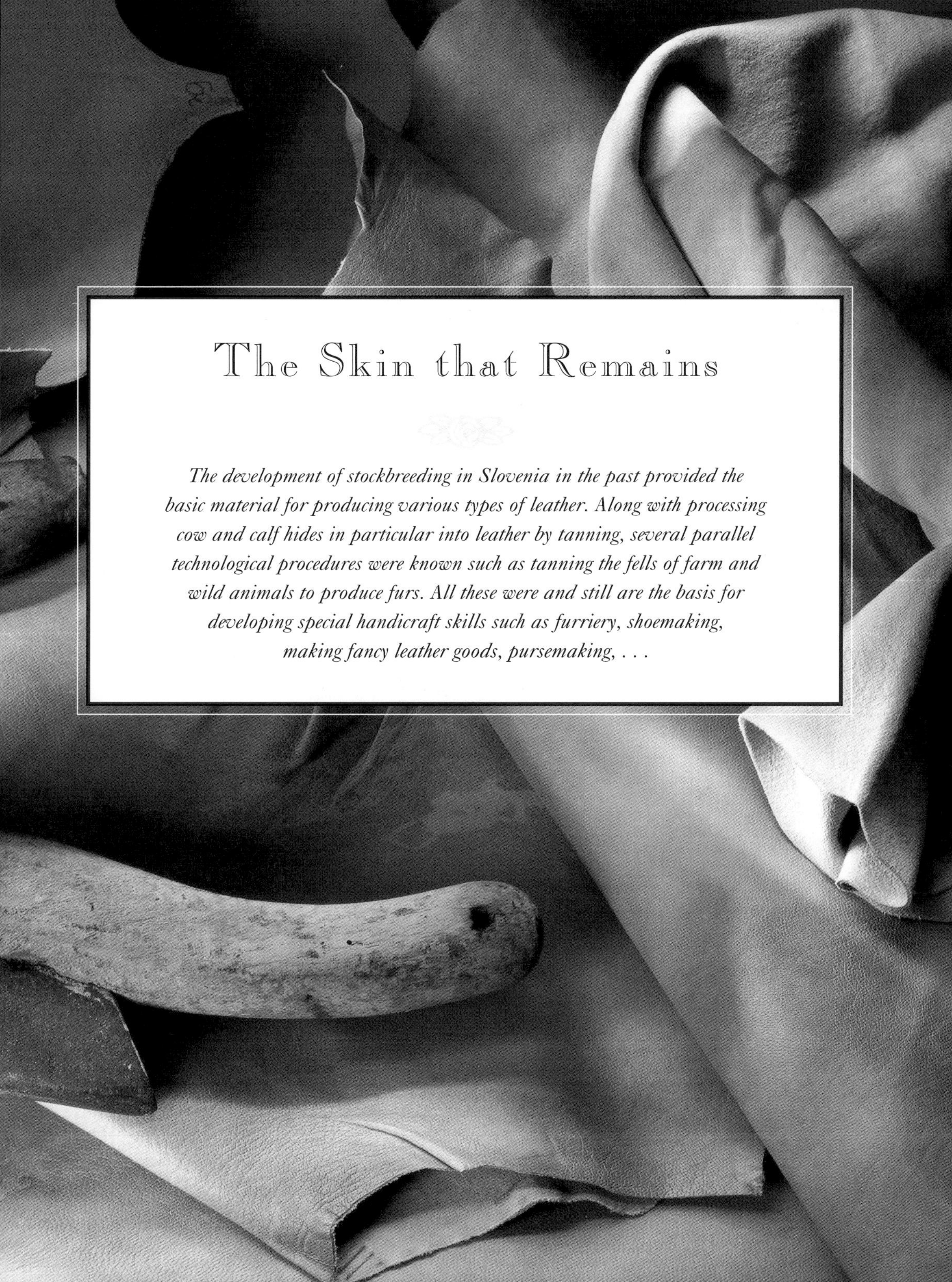

The Skin that Remains

The development of stockbreeding in Slovenia in the past provided the basic material for producing various types of leather. Along with processing cow and calf hides in particular into leather by tanning, several parallel technological procedures were known such as tanning the fells of farm and wild animals to produce furs. All these were and still are the basis for developing special handicraft skills such as furriery, shoemaking, making fancy leather goods, pursemaking, . . .

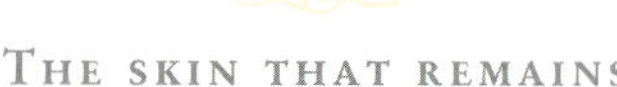

Slovenia's rich shoemaking tradition ►

The first records of shoemaking in Slovenia reach back to the Middle Ages. On this rich foundation, Tržič gradually developed into the largest shoemaking center in Slovenia, and modern shoemaking workshops operate in every major town. In Maribor, **Mario Herzog** designs and produces top quality custom footwear. His shoes are not only technological but also artistic masterpieces, a synthesis of handicraft skills employing all the classical shoemaking technologies. His shoes are truly unique since they are custom-made for each individual customer. They are the finest union of past experience and future human needs that this handicraft branch has achieved in Slovenia.

Good old-fashioned and still healthy footwear ▼

The traditional slippers of Rateče in Gorenjska are called *rateški žoki.* These examples are made by **Anica Koprivnik**, who uses leather that is more than forty years old. This gives her slippers an appropriate firmness and durability, guaranteeing at the same time the primary quality of the domestic materials needed for production, leather and wool. Furthermore, her slippers have an extremely simple and pure design dimension even though they were created as a continuation of historical memory.

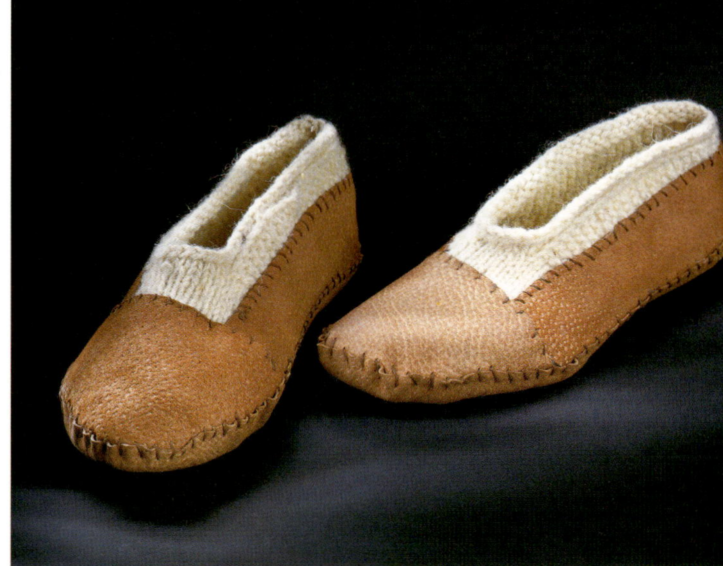

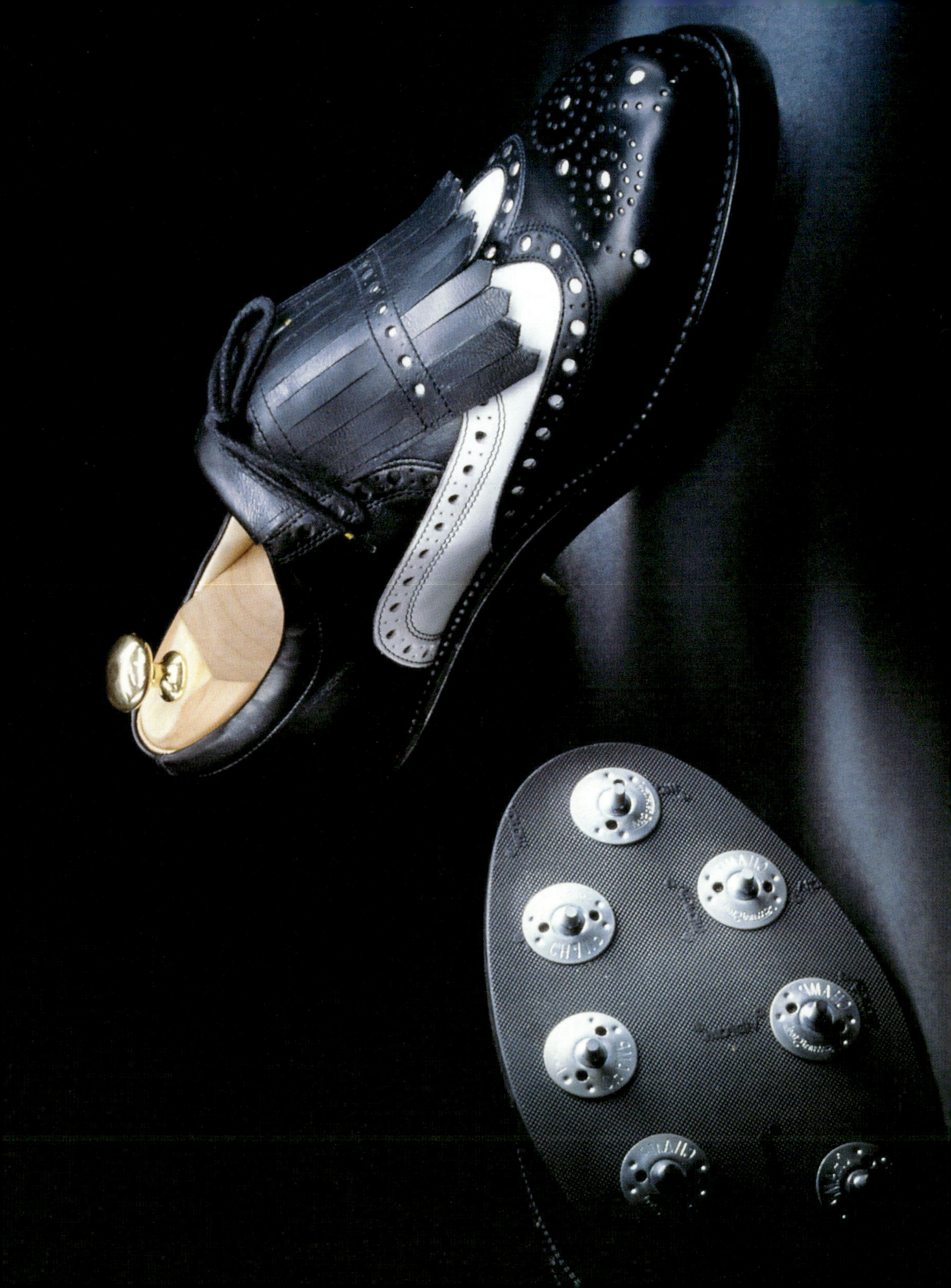

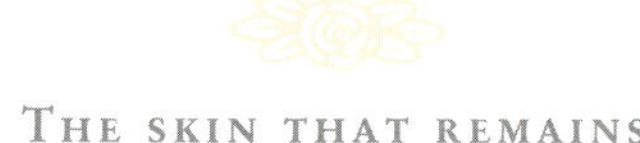

EXPLORING ORIGINAL FORMS WITH NATURAL MATERIALS ►

The manufacture of a wide range of fancy leather goods made from natural and artificial leather has a rich tradition in Slovenia, especially considering the technological experience and the palette of items produced and used centuries ago. Numerous workshops carry on this tradition, including the workshop of **VIKTOR BARLIČ** in Ljubljana's ancient city center.

***POLHOVKA*, A TYPICAL SLOVENE FUR CAP MADE OF DORMOUSE SKIN ▼**

Dormice once thrived in Slovenia's beech and oak forests, and since the dormice provided food (meat), medicine (dormouse tallow), and skins for the characteristic winter cap or *polhovka*, local people devised many ways of hunting them. Dormouse hunting was quite widespread in the distant past, and sources from the 17th century show that dormouse skins were exported in great quantities all the way to India. In recent times, the production of *polhovka* has fallen sharply, but this typical, predominantly men's winter headgear is still being made by some foremost furriery workshops such as the **EBER** workshop in Ljubljana.

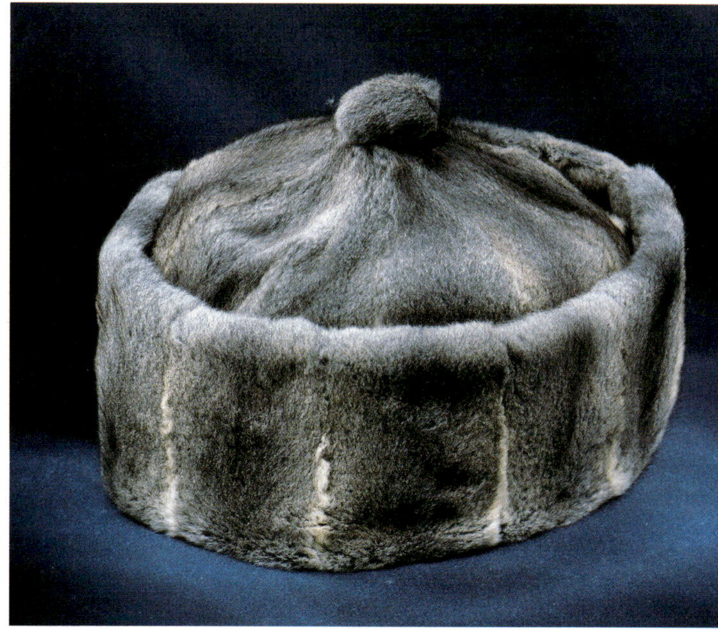

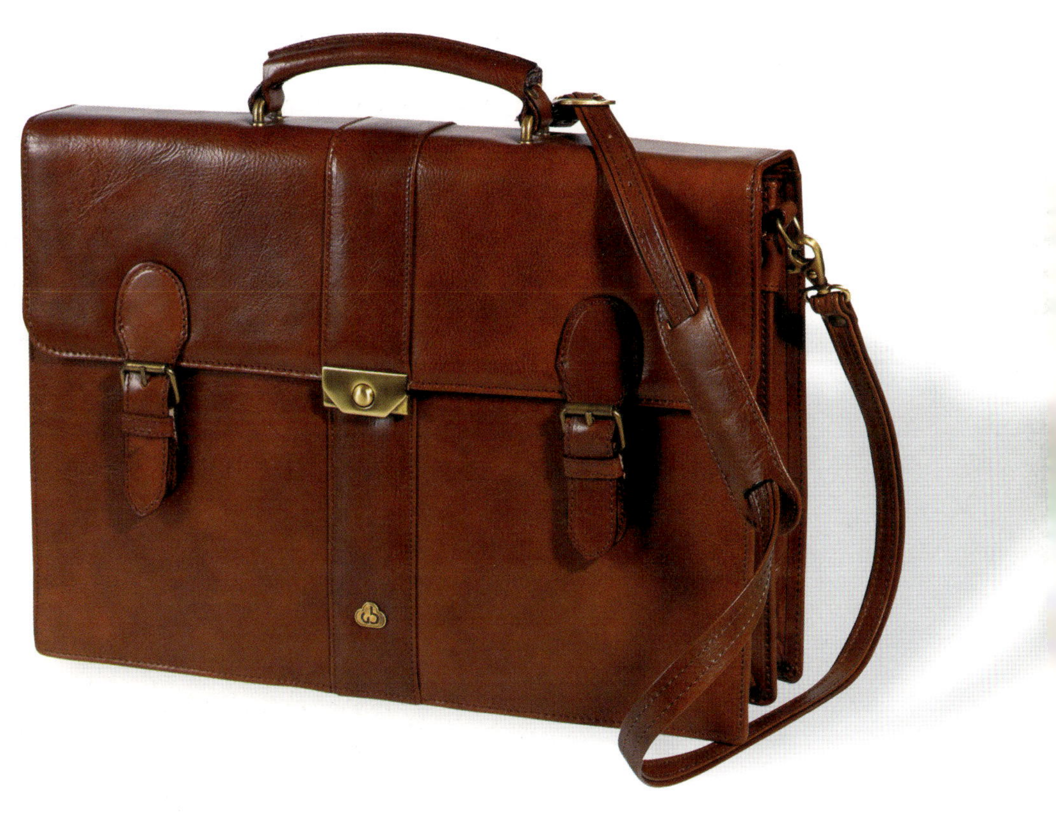

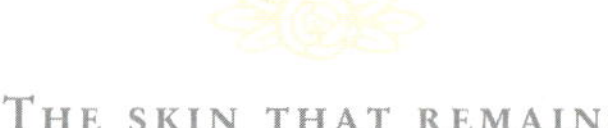

Marjeta Grošelj – the acme of purse design in international fashion ►

With the design of women's purses, Marjeta Grošelj has made her capital "G" an internationally recognized trademark. Her purses are distinguished by a quiet elegance that is always in fashion, unlike the garish results of fleeting fashion trends. Wearing her purses means having recognizable style and taste. This designer has built her work on a rich family tradition that reaches back to the period before World War II.

The foremost design of the *Lerota* trademark ▼

The *Lerota* workshop in Trzin has a sales gallery in Ljubljana offering fancy leather goods. Leather gives wallets, belts, purses, and vanity cases a unique charm that usually has two noble faces, the first when the product is still completely new and the second when time has impressed its seal through use.

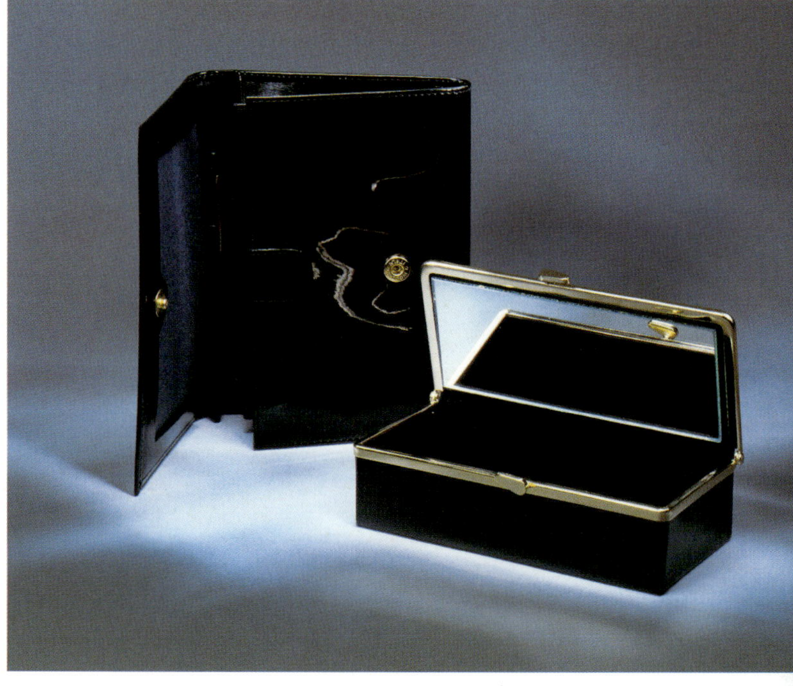

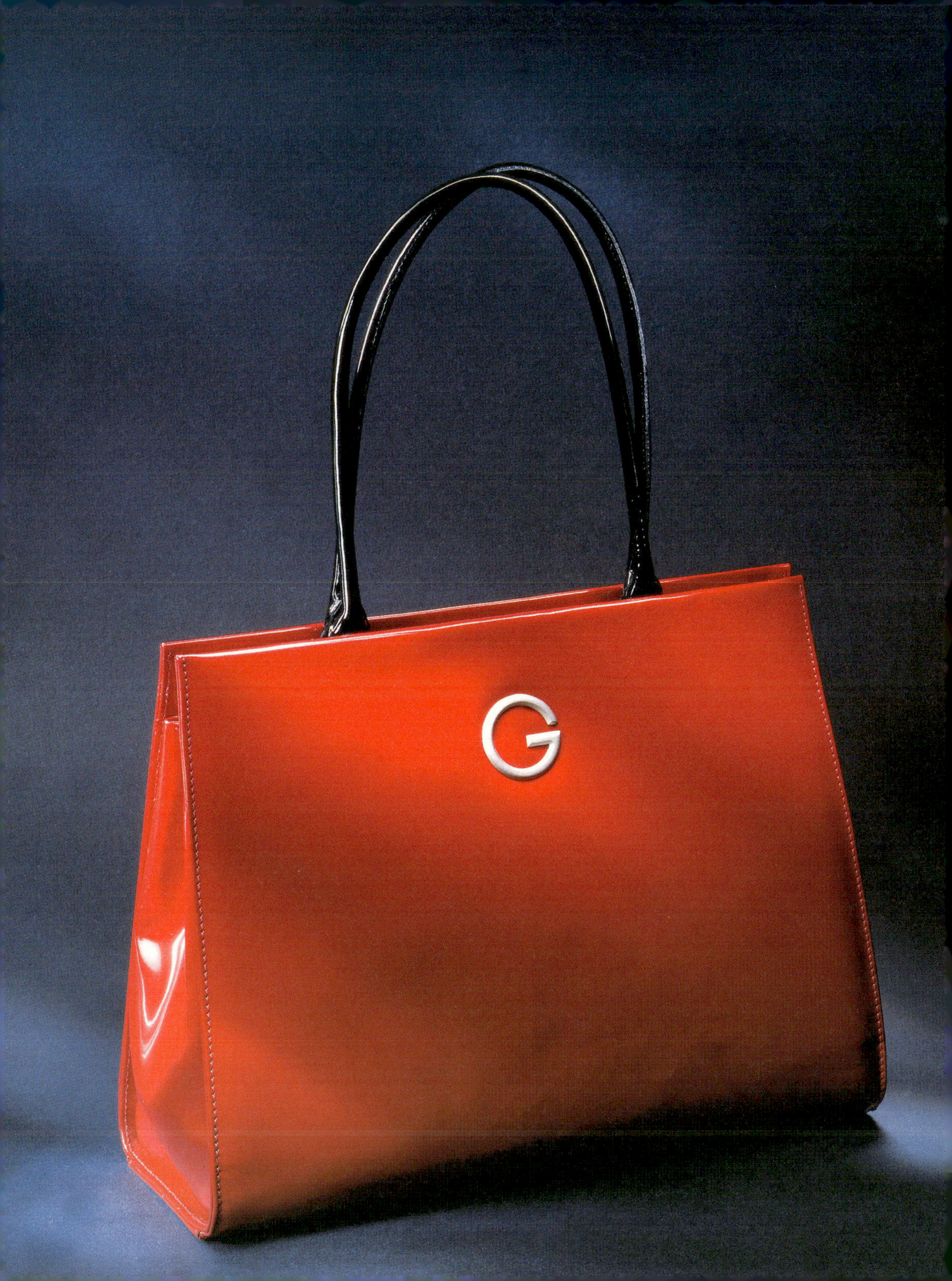

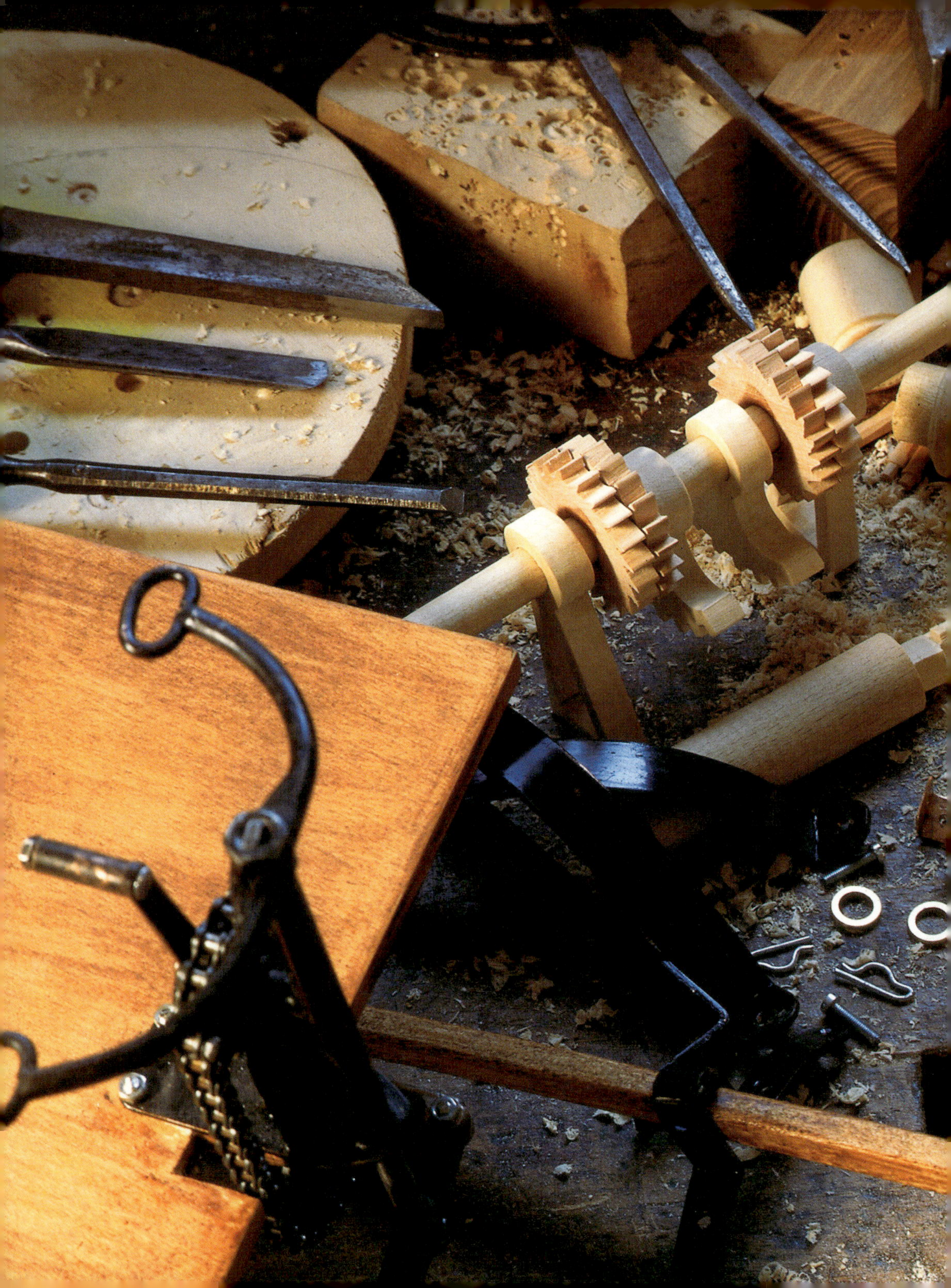

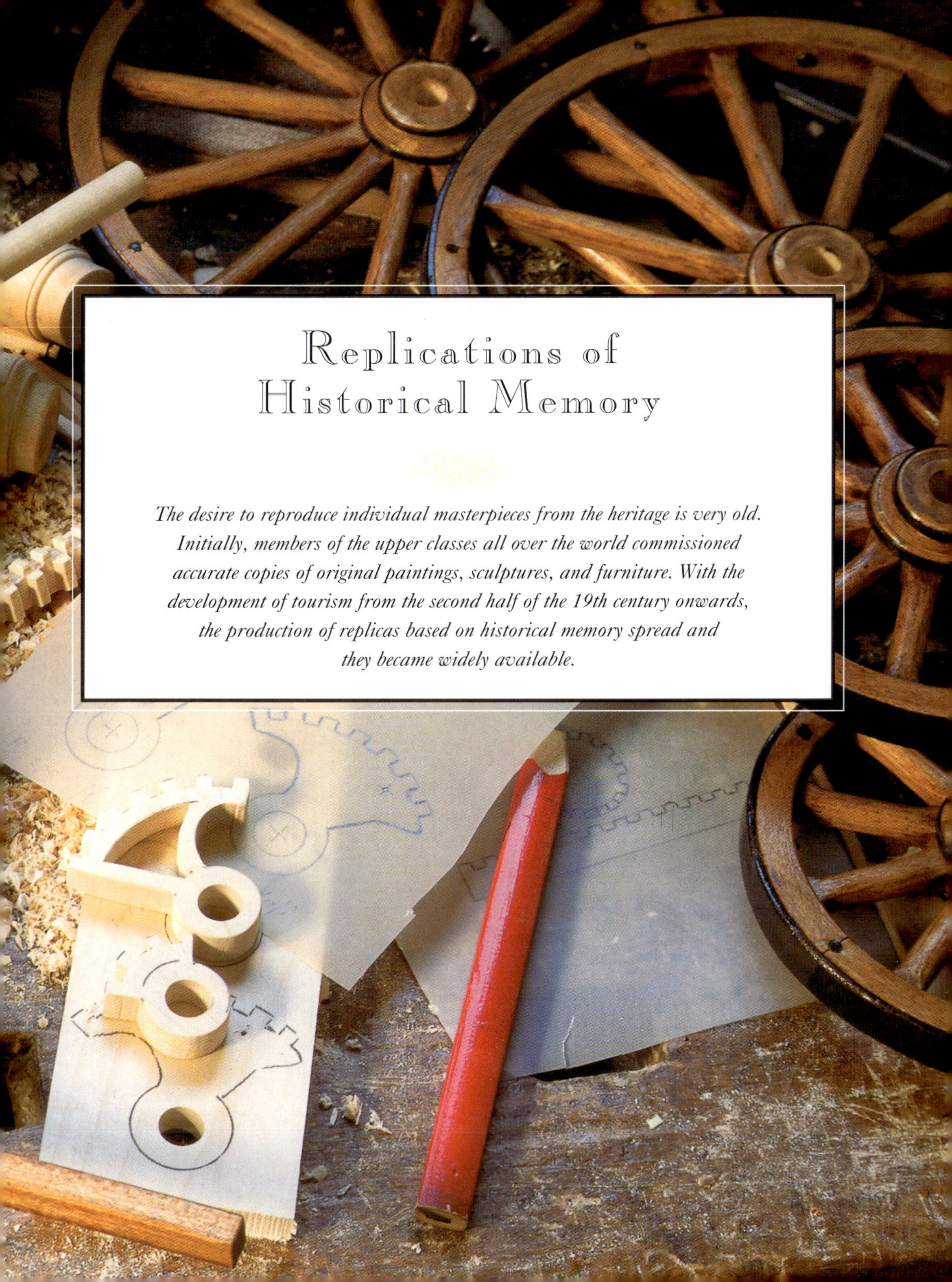

Replications of Historical Memory

The desire to reproduce individual masterpieces from the heritage is very old. Initially, members of the upper classes all over the world commissioned accurate copies of original paintings, sculptures, and furniture. With the development of tourism from the second half of the 19th century onwards, the production of replicas based on historical memory spread and they became widely available.

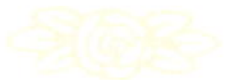

The modern image of an ancient carnival figure ►

Researchers believe that one of the oldest Lenten carnival figures in Slovenia is the *korant* from Ptujsko polje in northeastern Slovenia. Like all carnival masks, this one underwent many transformations until modern times when this carnival figure became the motif for many new relationships and meanings. Making the *korant* mask and the entire fur costume was traditionally the domain of individuals at home, but today we have handicraft workshops that make *korant* masks and outfit to order. The workshop of **Marko Klinc** in Spuhlja near Ptuj makes outstanding examples.

A gallery of folk philosophy and religious consciousness ▼

The Slovene heritage boasts a specialty known nowhere else in the world. With the development of apiculture in many parts of Slovene territory in the middle of the 18th century, the front panels of the individual beehives that comprised beehouses were painted with secular and religious scenes. This phenomenon reached its peak in the 19th century and began to wane in the 20th century. The proper replication of these masterpieces of Slovene folk art, a very widespread handicraft, requires an absolute and consistent respect for the originals stored in museums and numerous private collections. *Panjske končnice* (beehive panels) accurately duplicating such originals are made by **Darja Klevišar** from Ljubljana.

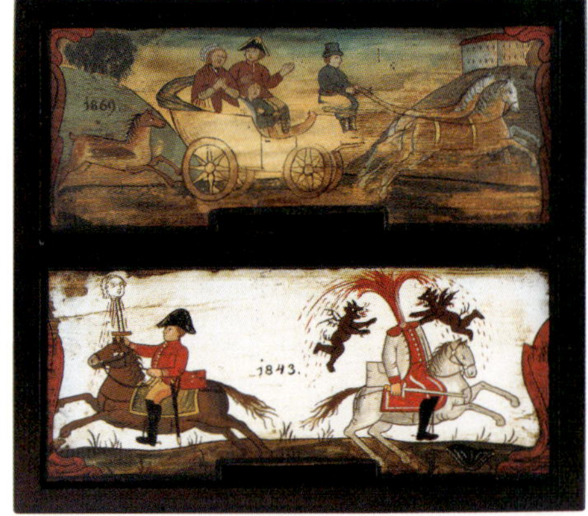

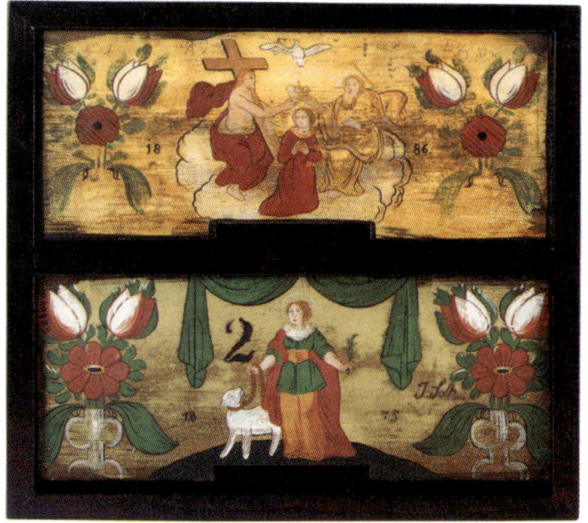

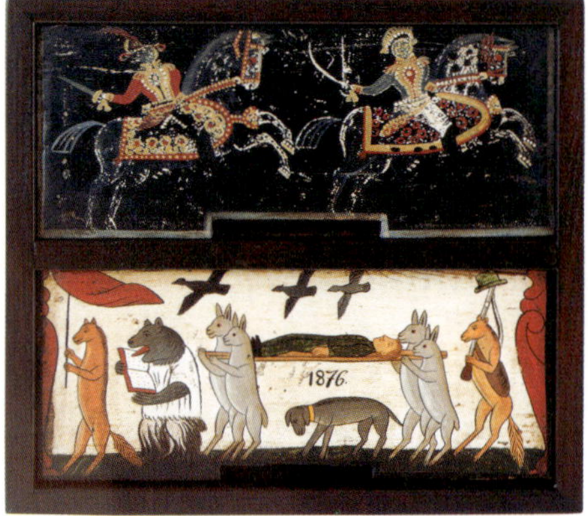

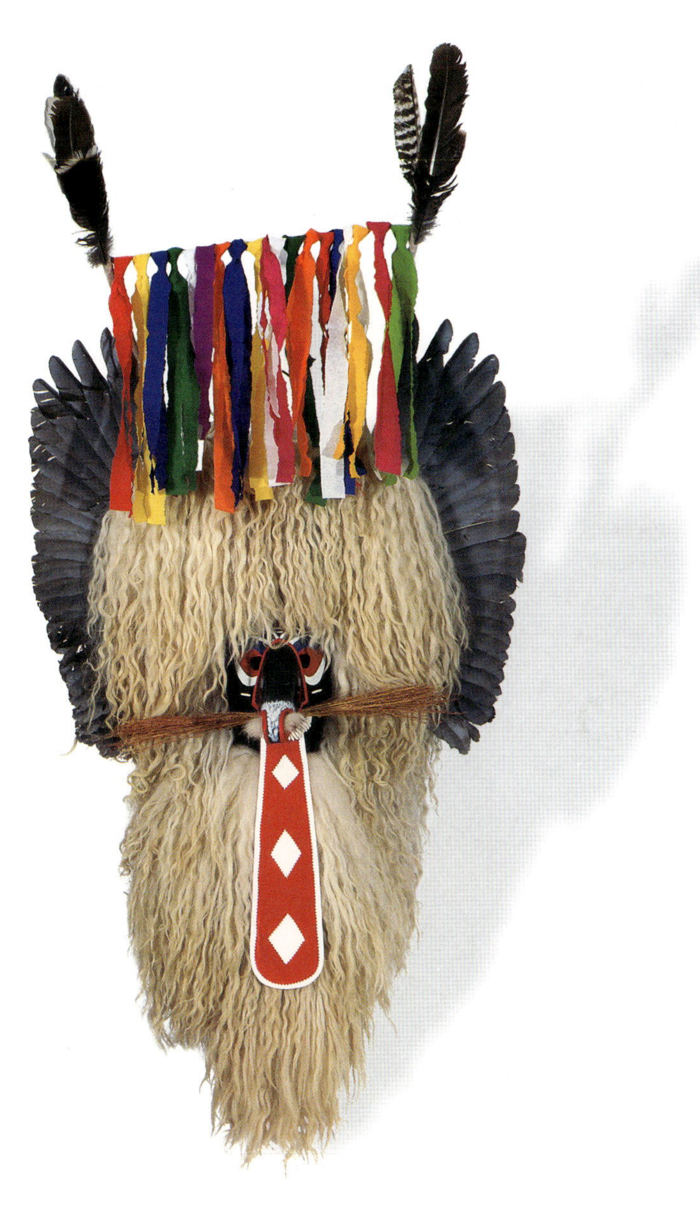

Reminders of a popular artistic culture of the 18th and 19th century ►
For paintings on glass, a smooth glass surface is only the base for an artistic creation whose mirror image is painted from a sketch on paper to the back or under side of a glass pane. During the 18th and 19th centuries, genuine centers developed in Central Europe where paintings were done on glass, mostly with religious motifs. Peddlers carried them abroad to sell as decorations for the interiors of homes, churches, and chapels. In those times they were a part of the popular artistic horizon. Today, **Ivan** and **Irena Jurjevič** from Ljubljana have excellently developed the superior artistic skills and the mastery of the numerous technical details required to replicate original works.

Replicas of painted furniture and folk art ▼
Janko and **Zdenka Mlakar** from Ljubljana have created the most comprehensive workshop in Slovenia for producing replicas of the hand-painted furniture found primarily in the alpine world and other objects of folk art. Their workshop also manufactures replicas of the furniture that belonged to the upper classes in the past. Replicating heritage objects has a major benefit in that it allows individual replicas to be available to everyone who enjoys enriching modern living with treasures from the historical memory while the originals remain in professional institutions such as museums or in their original cultural settings.

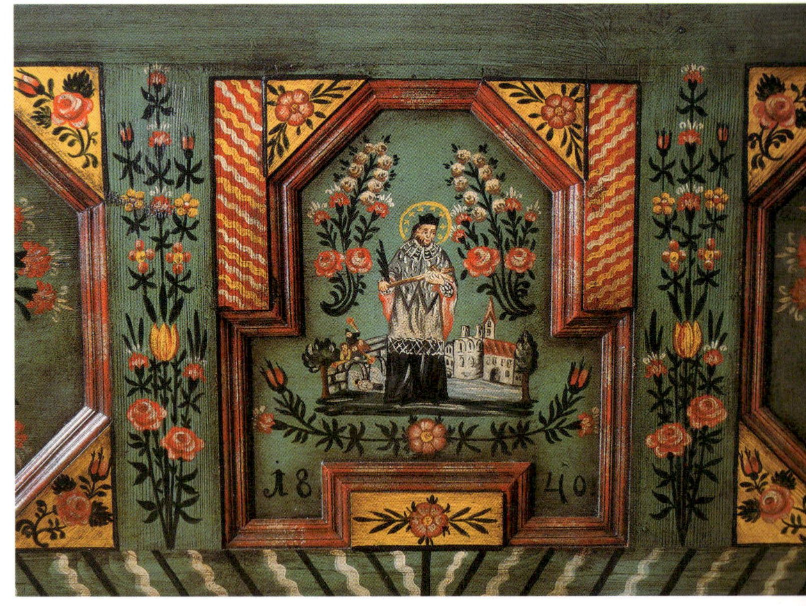

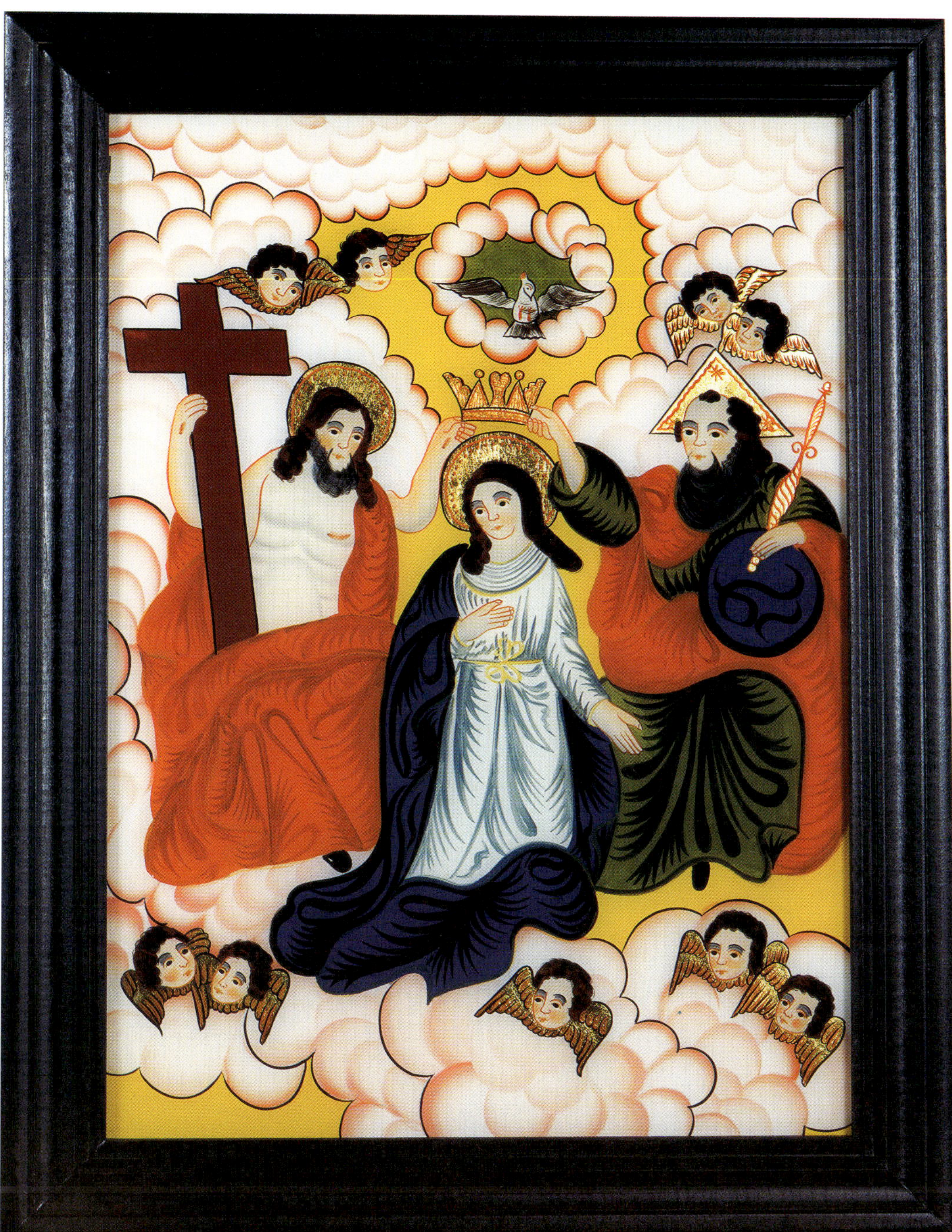

Panpipes and *trstenke* (syrinxes) ►

Darko Korošec from Ljubljana specializes in replicating traditional Slovene folk instruments. His instruments are not merely ornamental but distinctly useful since it is possible to play them, and in recent years they have often been used for music lessons in our schools. Although folklorists and ethnomusicologists have discovered and researched a veritable treasure trove of Slovene folk instruments, it is only recently that modern craftsmen decided to produce suitable replicas from the historical memory of Slovenia's music culture.

Rhythm has its heritage as well ▼

Vera Vardjan from Veliki Nerajec in Bela krajina produces a traditional rhythm instrument of Bela krajina and Prekmurje, the *gúdalo* or *lončeni* bajs. It is made from an earthenware pot with a pig's bladder stretched across the top. A reed stalk is stuck and sewn in the middle of this membrane. Rubbing the palm along the stalk creates vibrations that force a hollow sound from the membrane. While playing the *gúdalo*, the palm must be kept wet.

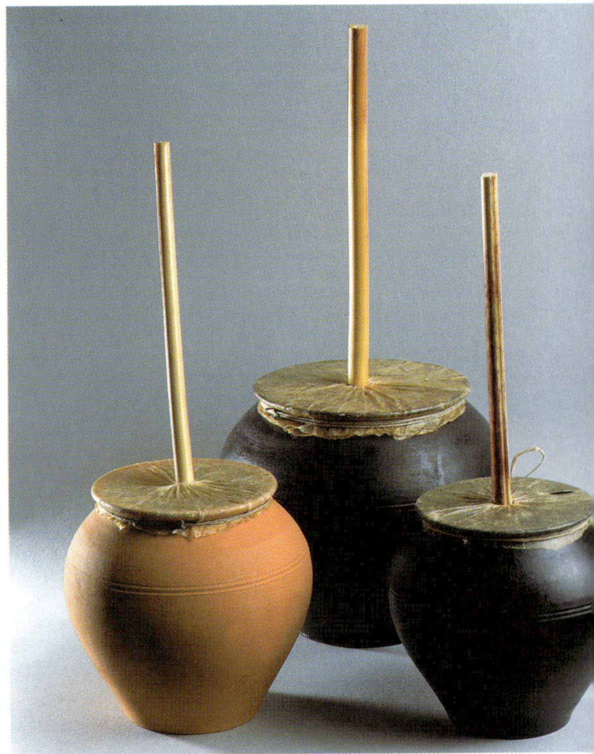

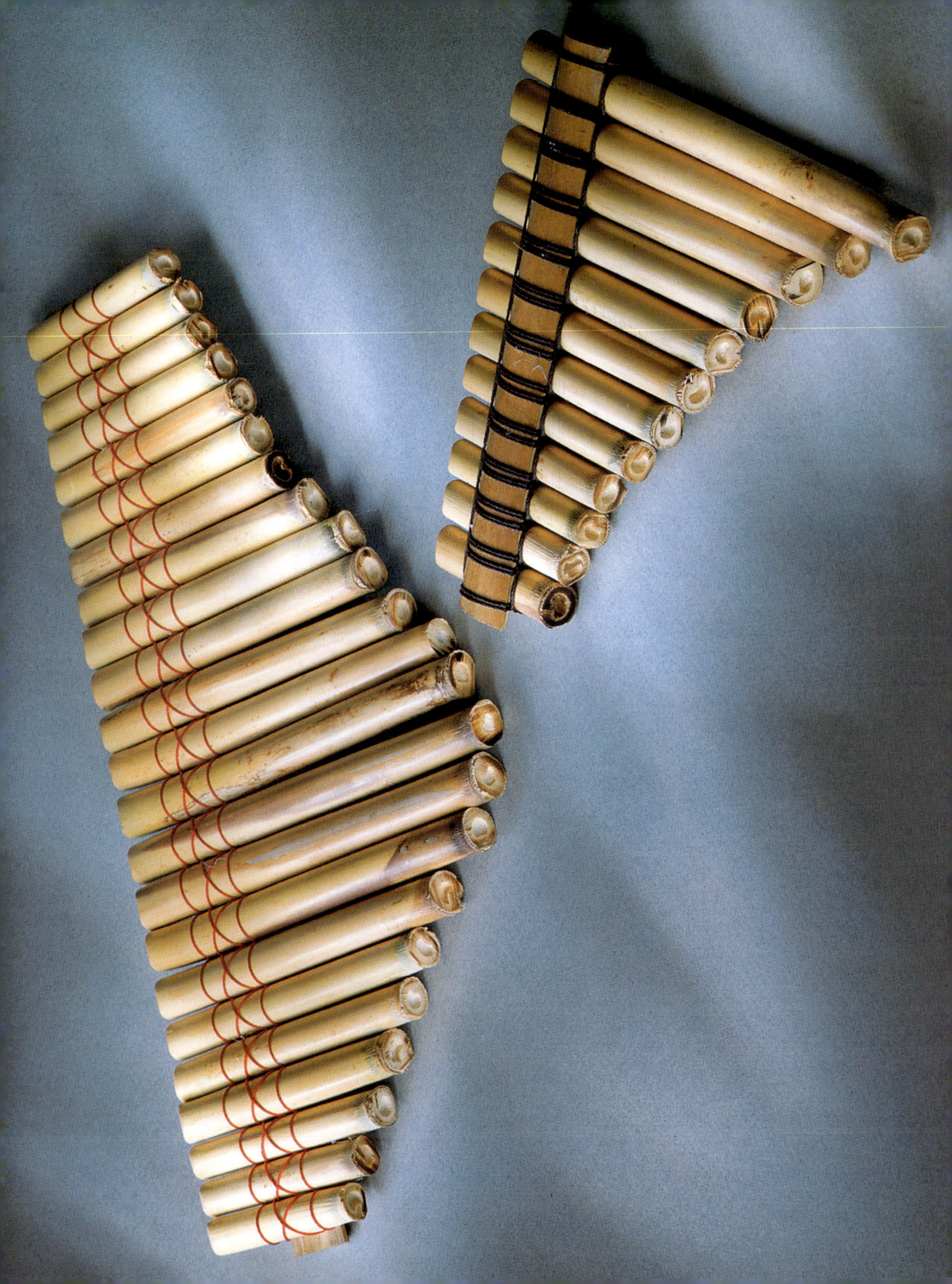

A RELATIVELY YOUNG BUT VERY POPULAR INSTRUMENT ►

Like elsewhere in Central Europe, the zither apparently only appeared in Slovenia in the 19th century. The zither became very popular, especially as an accompaniment to singing or for creating an atmosphere in inns and other similar public places. The master **JOŽE HOLCMAN** from Selnica on the Drava River carries on the tradition of producing this favourite instrument. His zithers are the result of the highest craftsmanship, and he has received many awards at exhibitions in Slovenia and abroad.

A RESEARCHER AND INNOVATOR ▼

Like the zither, the accordion is a relatively young but very popular instrument. There are many modern craftsmen producing either diatonic (*frajtonarice*) or piano accordions. The untiring innovator **VALENTIN ZUPAN** from Mengeš has achieved the highest mastery in synthesizing the various handicraft skills needed to produce an accordion. Today, Zupan´s accordions are ranked among the world's best. Their creator is constantly discovering and inventing new technological solutions to enhance the quality of their sound. The external appearance of his accordions has also become a distinguishing feature and a unique overall artistic image..

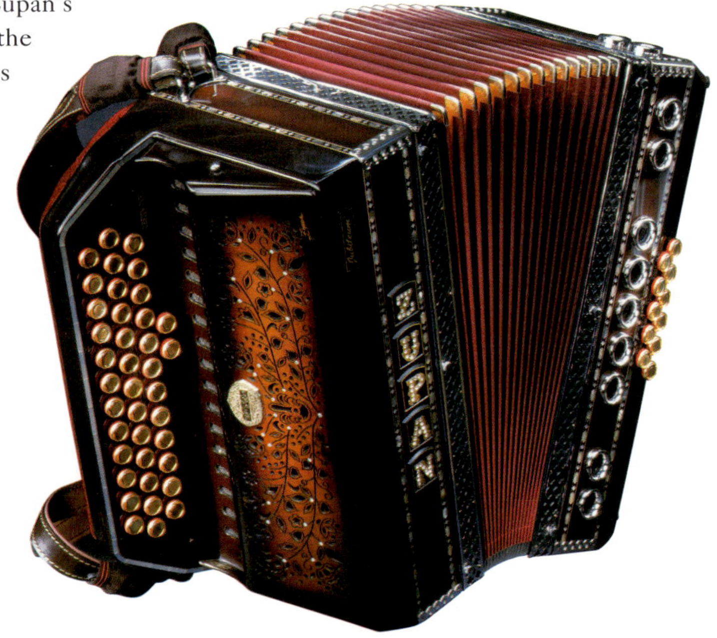

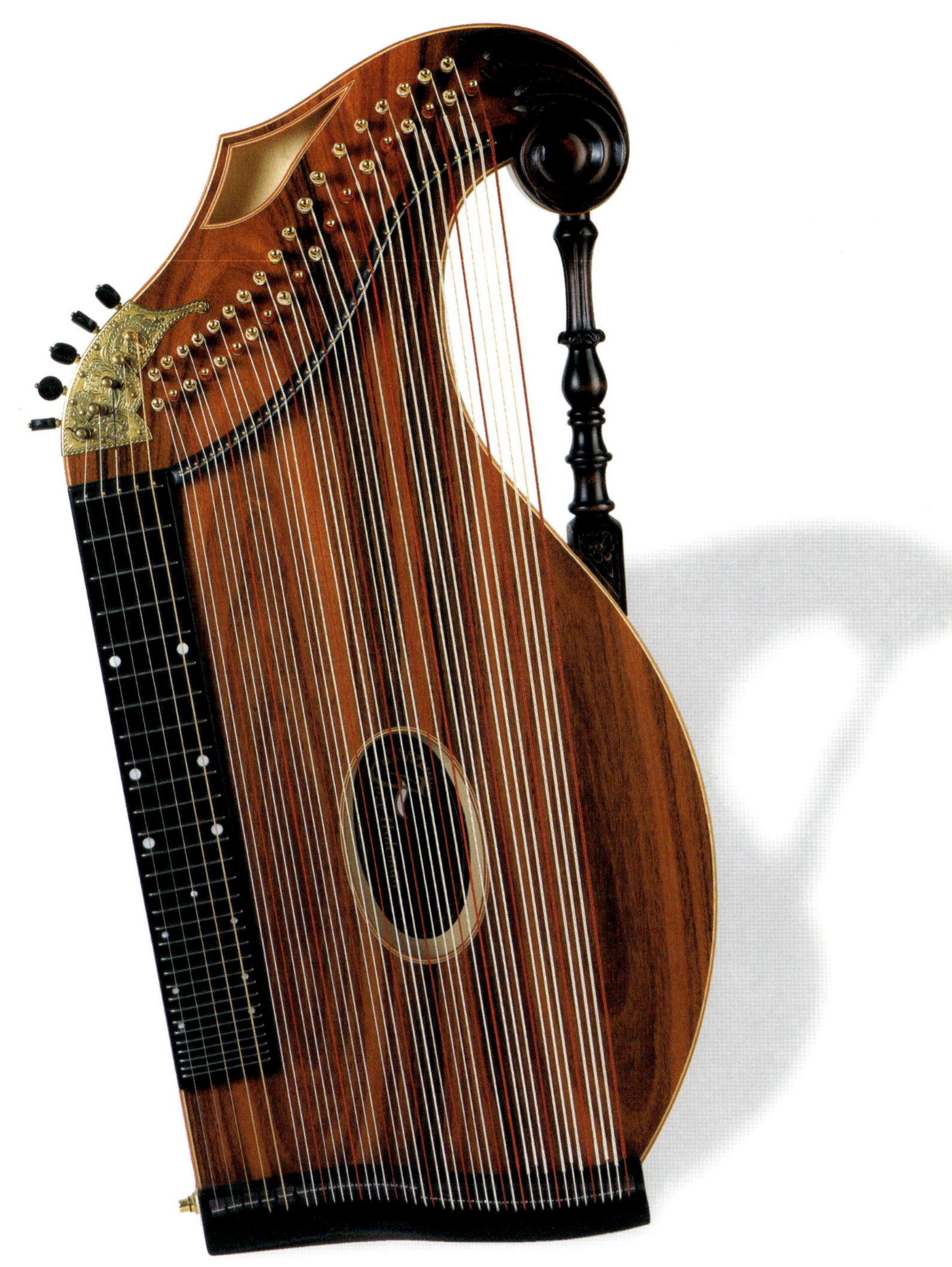

You can recognize a hunter by his buttons ►

Slovene hunters belong to a special fraternity with their own lifestyle, rituals, values, and moral standards and can be immediately recognized by their style of dress. A unique handicraft skill developed related to the hunter's uniform: the carving of figural and ornamental buttons from the horns of wild animals. Each button with its hunting motif is a distinctive *objet d'art* produced by the precise carving of bone and horn. **Boris Leskovic** from Ljubljana is a master of this handicraft.

A glimpse of the heritage through miniatures ▼

In Pliskovica na Krasu, **Dušan Žerjal** miniaturizes individual objects typical of past life in Slovenia's karst region such as the *žbrinca*, a round shoulder basket, models of karst households, and scenes from everyday life and work in the countryside. Every year, he sets up a Christmas crèche in the local church. The interesting thing about his crèche is that the entire miniaturized portrayal of the Nativity scene, including animals and people, is transferred to the karst setting. In essence, Žerjal's crèches are a commemoration of the environment and life characterized by the karst heritage.

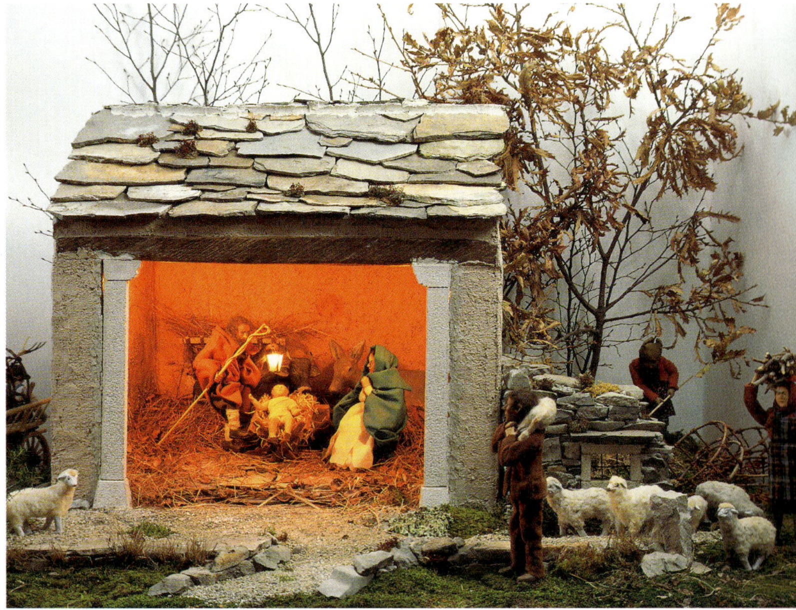

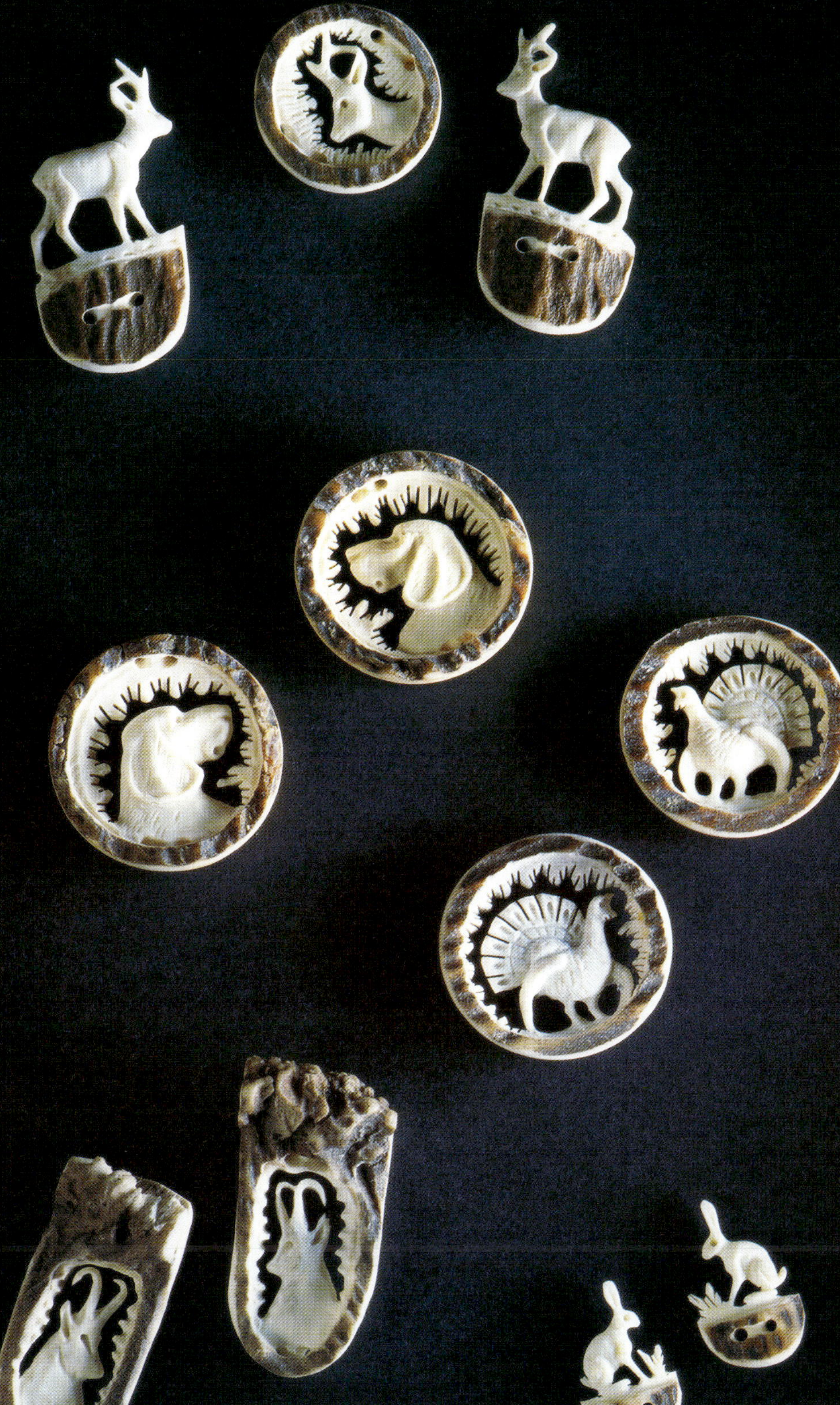

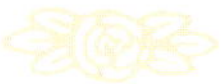

The accurate documentation of historical memory

The miniatures of **Janko Samsa** from Žirje near Sežana are in a class of their own. He produces the highest quality miniatures of handcarts and horse-drawn wagons from the Slovene heritage in a uniform scale of 1:6. All their features down to the smallest detail are miniaturized to this scale and correspond exactly to the originals. A special value of these "didactic" miniatures lies in their demonstration of the use and purpose of individual carts and wagons. Samsa's miniatures present the developmental and typological wealth of the cart and wagon heritage in Slovenia with all its regional variations and specialties.

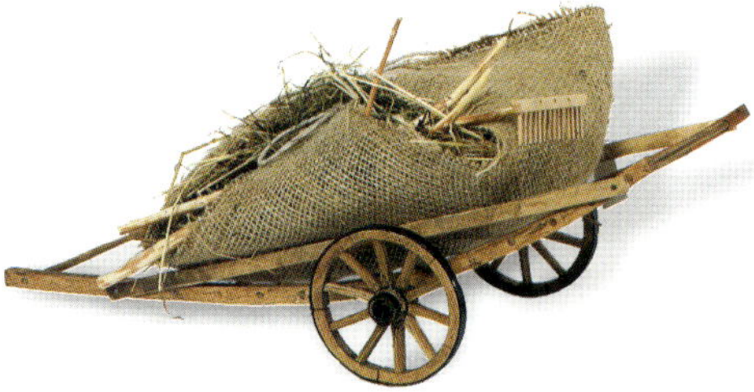

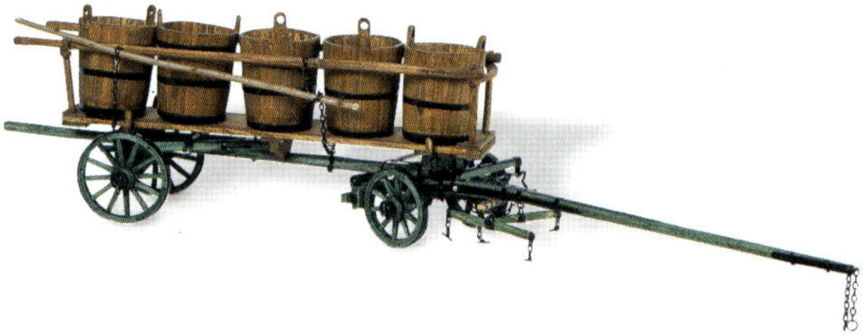

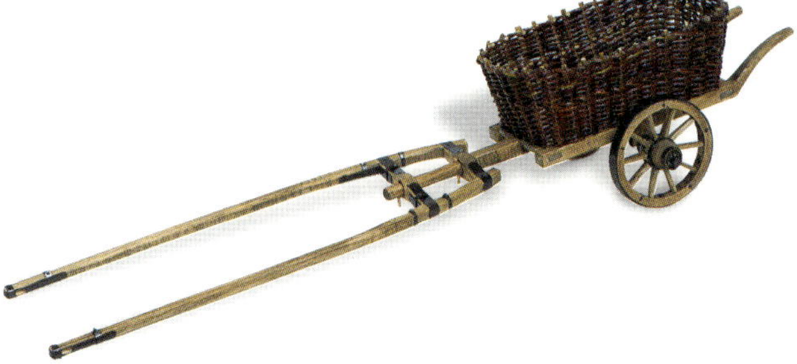

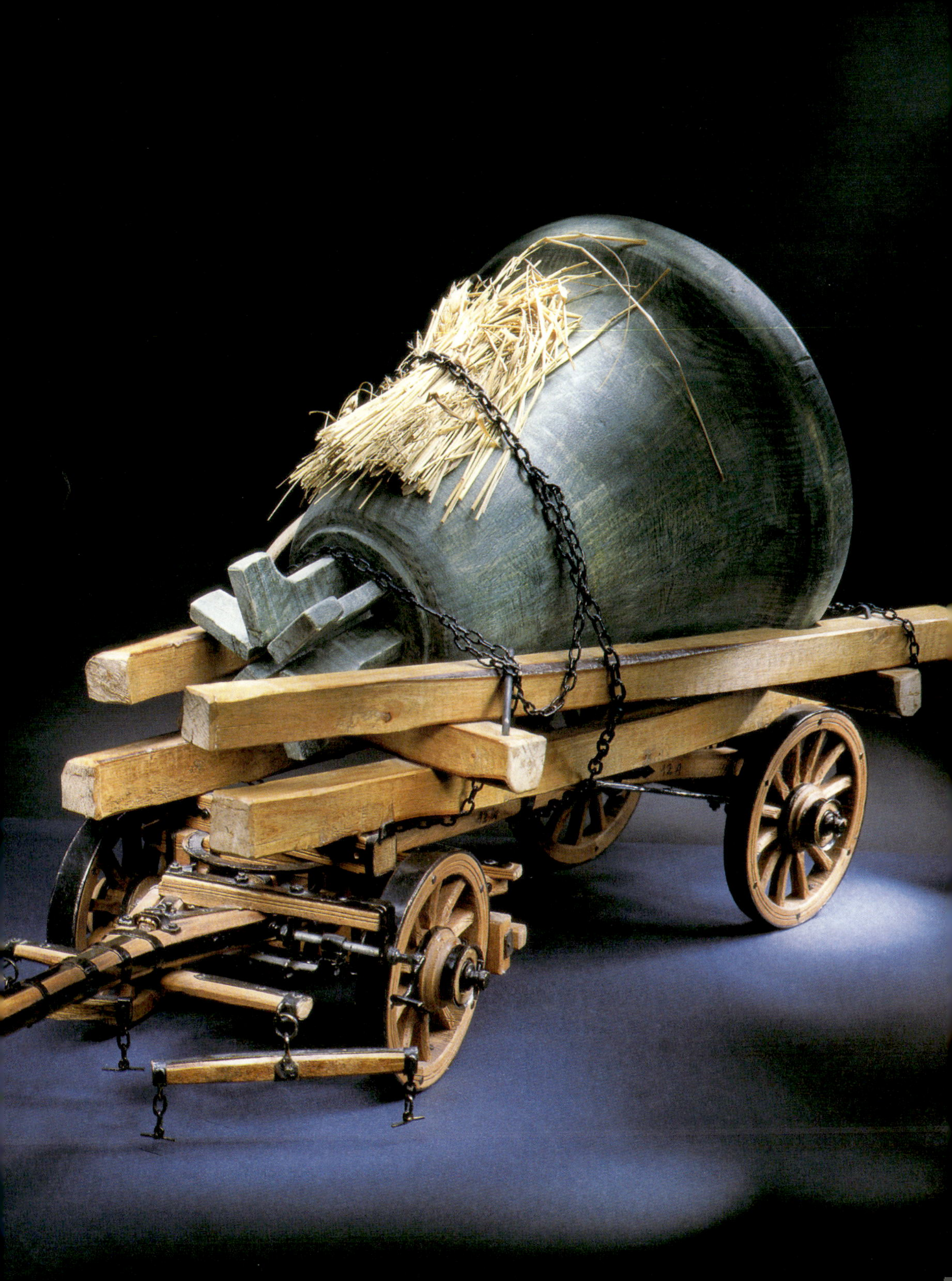

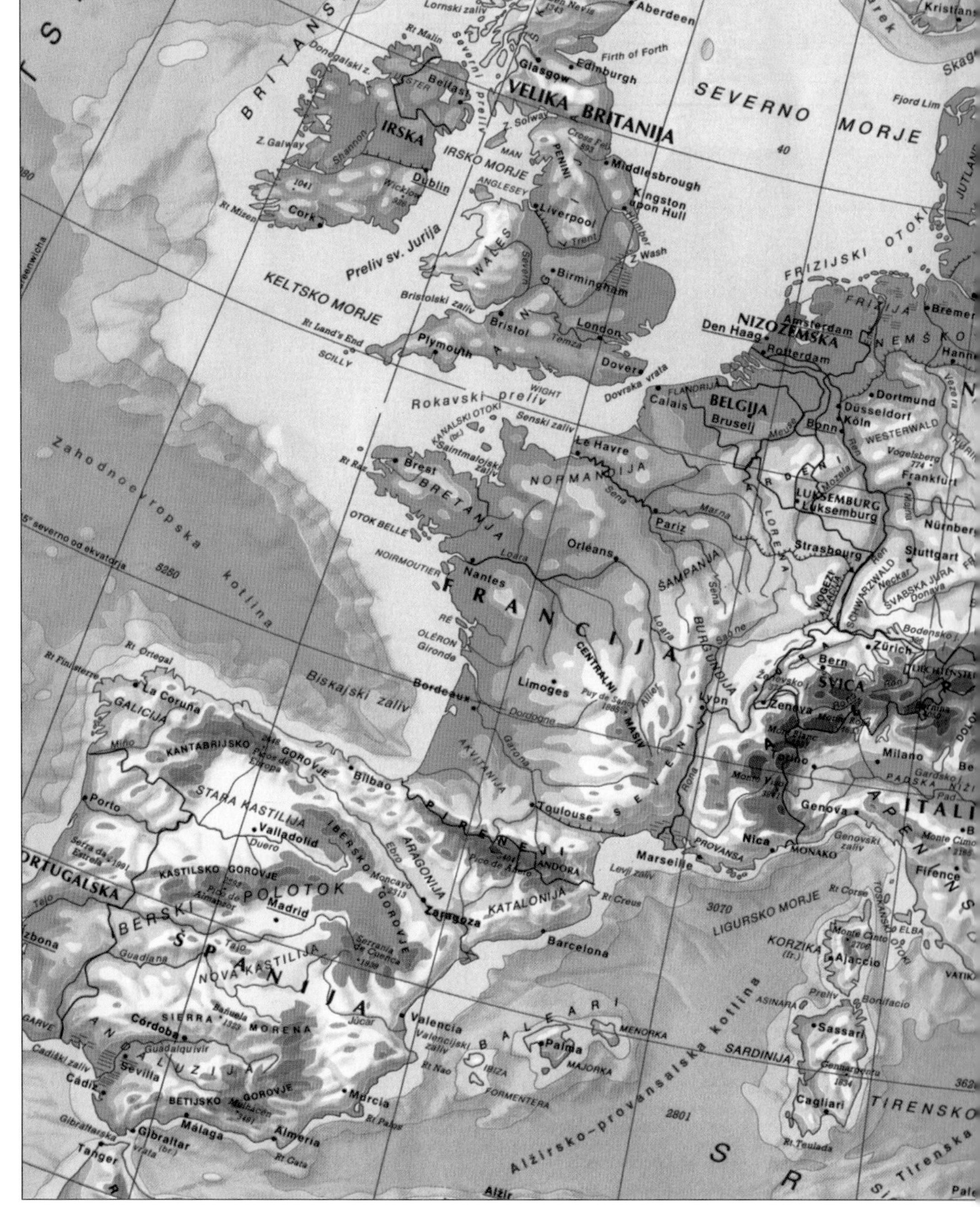

BRITANSKI
Lornski zaliv
Ben Nevis
Aberdeen
Rt Malin
Donegalski z.
Severni preliv
Glasgow
Edinburgh
Firth of Forth
Belfast
VELIKA BRITANIJA
SEVERNO MORJE
IRSKA
Z. Galway
Shannon
Z. Solway
MAN
IRSKO MORJE
PENINI
Middlesbrough
Dublin
ANGLESEY
Kingston upon Hull
Cork
Rt Mizen
Liverpool
Humber
Trent
Z. Wash
Preliv sv. Jurija
WALES
Birmingham
KELTSKO MORJE
Bristolski zaliv
Bristol
London
Temza
Rt Land's End
SCILLY
Plymouth
Dover
Dovrska vrata
WIGHT
Rokavski preliv
KANALSKI OTOKI
Senski zaliv
Saintmaloiški zaliv
Rt Raz
Brest
BRETANJA
Le Havre
NORMANDIJA
Sena
OTOK BELLE
NOIRMOUTIER
Nantes
Loara
Orléans
Pariz
Marna
FRANCIJA
RÉ
OLÉRON
Gironde
CENTRALNI MASIV
Limoges
Bordeaux
Dordogne
Garona
AKVITANIJA
Toulouse
SEVENI
Zahodnoevropska kotlina
Biskajski zaliv
Rt Ortegal
Rt Finisterre
La Coruña
GALICIJA
Miño
KANTABRIJSKO GOROVJE
Picos de Europa
Bilbao
Porto
STARA KASTILIJA
Valladolid
Duero
IBERSKO GOROVJE
Ebro
ARAGONIJA
PIRENEJI
ANDORA
Moncayo
PORTUGALSKA
KASTILSKO GOROVJE
Pico de Almanzor
IBERSKI POLOTOK
Madrid
Zaragoza
KATALONIJA
Barcelona
Lizbona
Tajo
Guadiana
ŠPANIJA
NOVA KASTILIJA
Serranía de Cuenca
SIERRA MORENA
Córdoba
Guadalquivir
ANDALUZIJA
Sevilla
Cádiz
Cadiški zaliv
BETIJSKO GOROVJE
Mulhacén
Málaga
Almeria
Murcia
Rt Palos
Rt Gata
Gibraltar
Gibraltarska vrata
Tanger
Valencia
Valencijski zaliv
Júcar
Rt Nao
BALEARI
IBIZA
FORMENTERA
Palma
MAJORKA
MENORKA
Alžir
Alžirsko-provansalska kotlina
Levji zaliv
Marseille
PROVANSA
Rona
Lyon
BURGUNDIJA
Saône
ŠAMPANJA
LORENA
Strasbourg
VOGEZI
ALZACIJA
ARDENI
Meuse
Mozela
LUKSEMBURG
Luksemburg
BELGIJA
Bruselj
FLANDRIJA
Calais
NIZOZEMSKA
Den Haag
Amsterdam
Rotterdam
FRIZIJSKI OTOKI
FRIZIJA
Bremen
NEMŠKO
Dortmund
Düsseldorf
Köln
Bonn
WESTERWALD
Vogelsberg
Frankfurt
Ren
Nürnberg
Stuttgart
SCHWARZWALD
Neckar
ŠVABSKA JURA
Donava
Bodensko j.
Zürich
Bern
ŠVICA
Ženeva
Mont Blanc
Torino
Monte Viso
Milano
PADSKA NIŽINA
Genova
Nica
MONAKO
Genovski zaliv
APENINI
ITALI
Firence
LIGURSKO MORJE
Rt Corse
KORZIKA (fr.)
Monte Cinto
Ajaccio
ELBA
TOSKANSKI OTOKI
Preliv Bonifacio
ASINARA
Sassari
SARDINIJA
Gennargentu
Cagliari
Rt Teulada
TIRENSKO
JUTLAND
Skagerak
Fjord Lim
Kristians
Greenwicha
45° severno od ekvatorja
SREDOZEMSKO

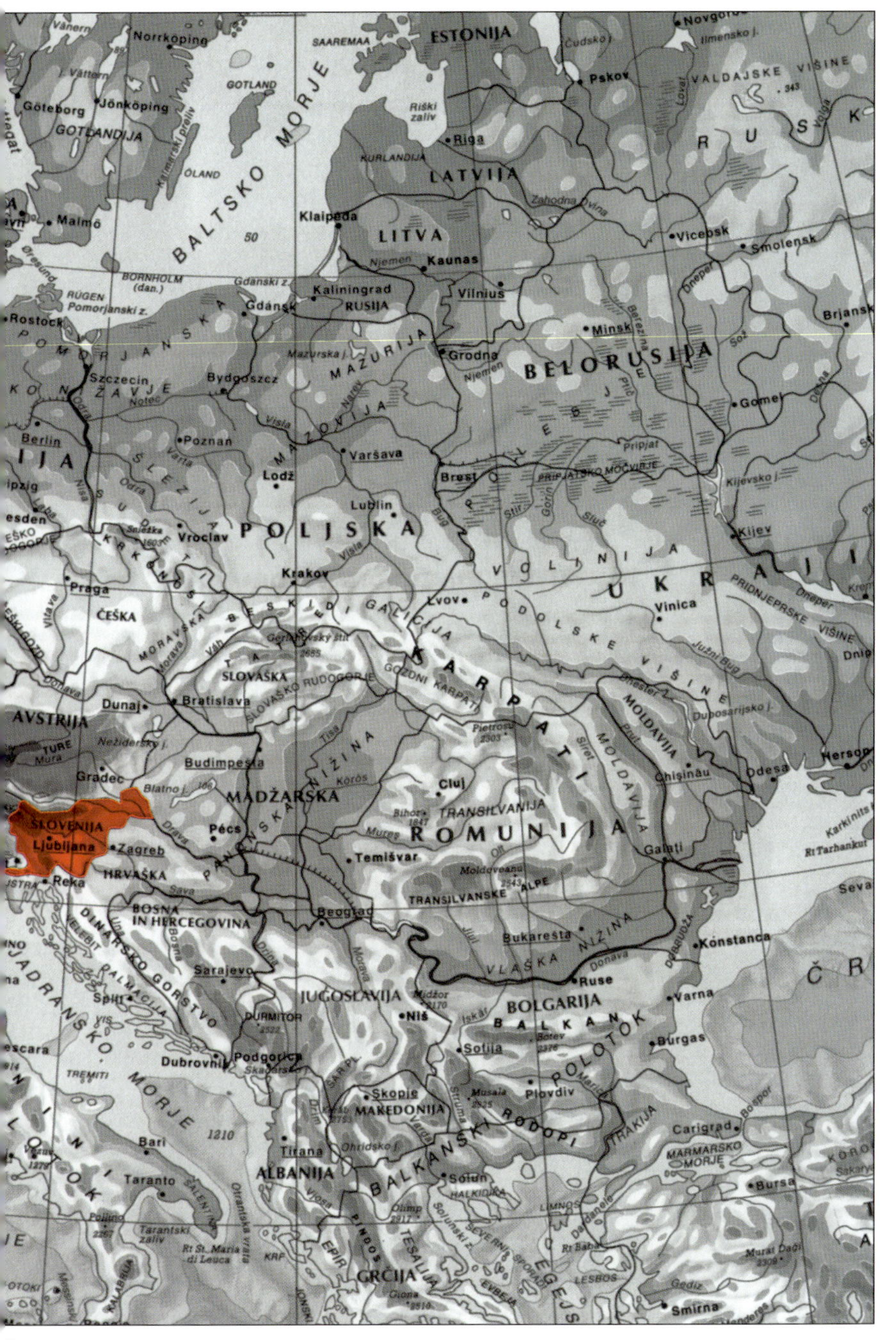

Slovenia, the Ring of Europe

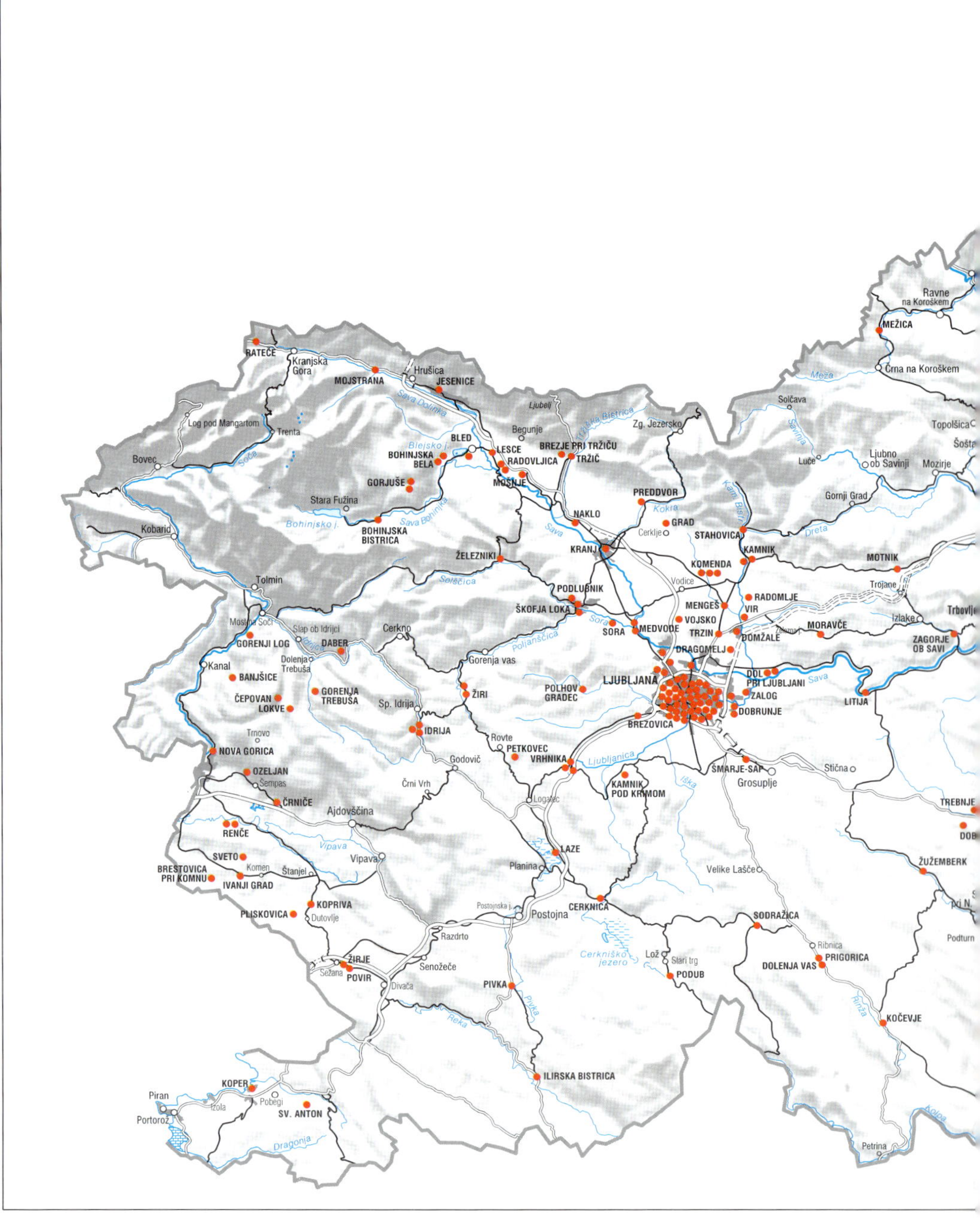

RATEČE
Kranjska Gora
MOJSTRANA
Hrušica
JESENICE
Ravne na Koroškem
MEŽICA
Črna na Koroškem
Meža
Solčava
Savinja
Topolšica
Šošt
Luče
Ljubno ob Savinji
Mozirje
Gornji Grad
Dreta
Log pod Mangartom
Trenta
Bovec
Soča
Sava Dolinka
Ljubelj
Tržiška Bistrica
Begunje
Zg. Jezersko
BLED
Blejsko j.
BOHINJSKA BELA
LESCE
RADOVLJICA
BREZJE PRI TRŽIČU
TRŽIČ
MOŠNJE
GORJUŠE
Stara Fužina
Bohinjsko j.
Sava Bohinjka
BOHINJSKA BISTRICA
PREDDVOR
Kokra
Kam. Bistrica
NAKLO
GRAD
Cerklje
STAHOVICA
Kobarid
Sava
KRANJ
KAMNIK
ŽELEZNIKI
KOMENDA
MOTNIK
Tolmin
Selščica
Vodice
PODLUBNIK
Trojane
RADOMLJE
MENGEŠ
VIR
ŠKOFJA LOKA
VOJSKO
Izlake
Trbovlje
Most na Soči
Slap ob Idrijci
Cerkno
Sora
SORA
MEDVODE
TRZIN
DOMŽALE
MORAVČE
GORENJI LOG
DABER
Idrijca
Poljanščica
DRAGOMELJ
ZAGORJE OB SAVI
Kanal
Dolenja Trebuša
Gorenja vas
LJUBLJANA
DOL PRI LJUBLJANI
BANJŠICE
Sava
ČEPOVAN
GORENJA TREBUŠA
ŽIRI
POLHOV GRADEC
ZALOG
LITIJA
LOKVE
Sp. Idrija
DOBRUNJE
Trnovo
IDRIJA
BREZOVICA
Rovte
NOVA GORICA
PETKOVEC
VRHNIKA
Godovič
Ljubljanica
ŠMARJE-SAP
Grosuplje
Stična
OZELJAN
Šempas
Črni Vrh
KAMNIK POD KRIMOM
Iška
ČRNIČE
Logatec
Ajdovščina
TREBNJE
RENČE
DOB
Vipava
LAZE
SVETO
Komen
Vipava
Planina
BRESTOVICA PRI KOMNU
Štanjel
Velike Lašče
ŽUŽEMBERK
IVANJI GRAD
KOPRIVA
Postojnska j.
Postojna
CERKNICA
PLISKOVICA
Dutovlje
SODRAŽICA
Razdrto
Ribnica
Cerkniško jezero
Lož
Stari trg
PRIGORICA
ŽIRJE
Senožeče
PODUB
DOLENJA VAS
Sežana
POVIR
Divača
PIVKA
Pivka
Reka
Rinža
KOČEVJE
ILIRSKA BISTRICA
KOPER
Piran
Izola
Pobegi
Portorož
SV. ANTON
Dragonja
Kolpa
Petrina
Podturn

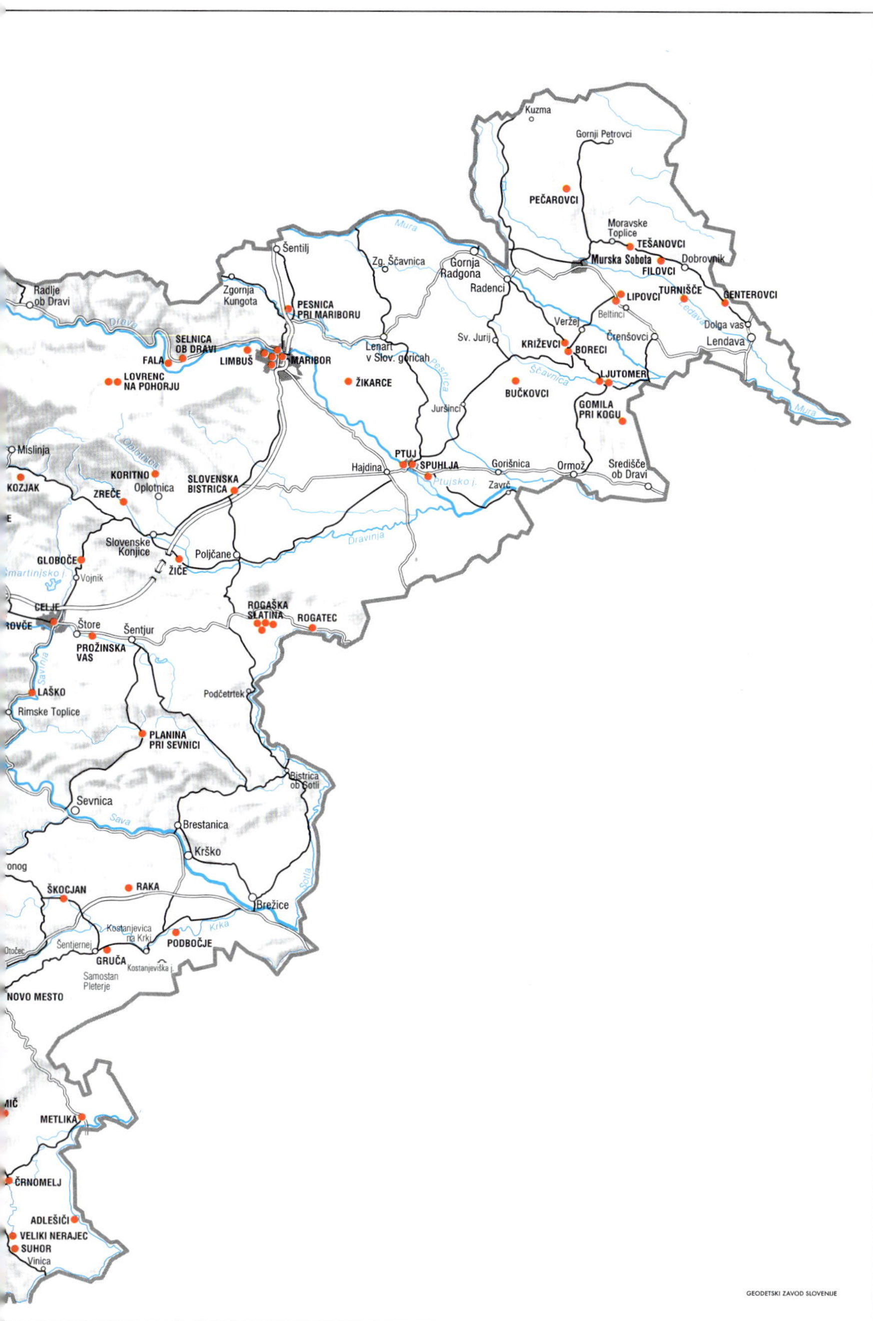

Locations of Slovene handicraft centers

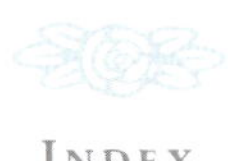

Index

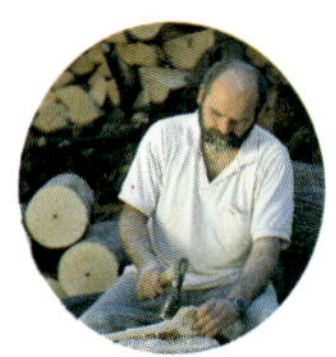

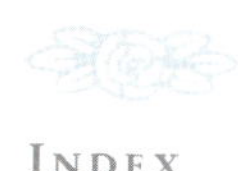

Index

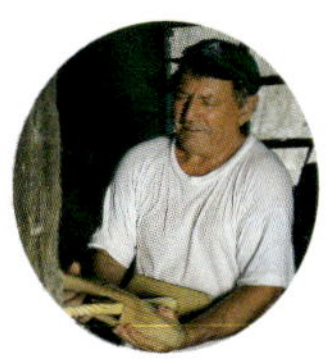

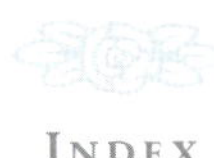

Index

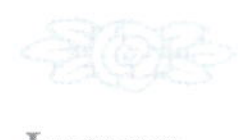

Index

Index

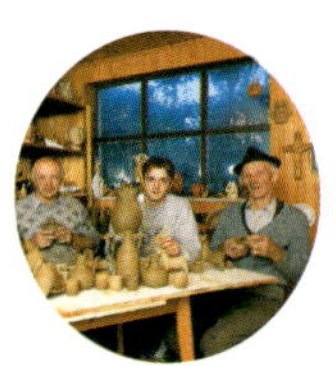

Index

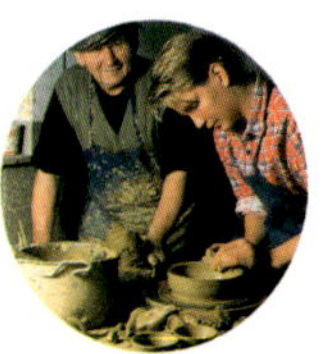

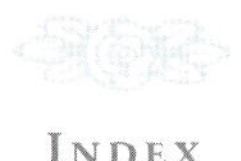

Index

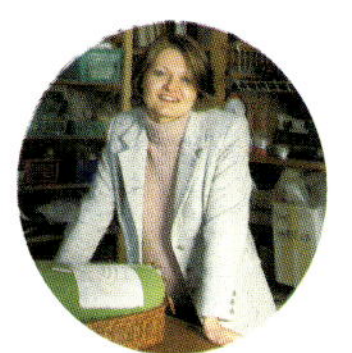

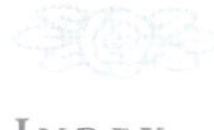
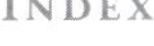

Index

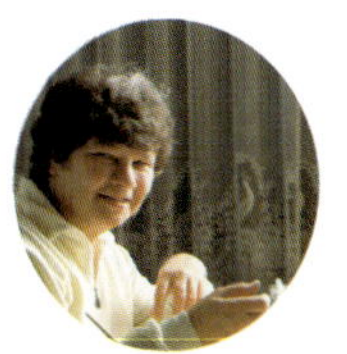

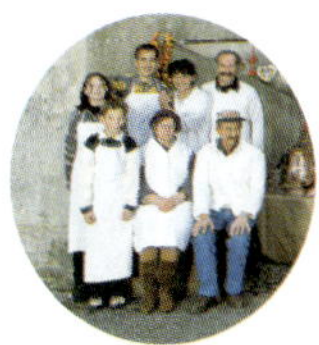

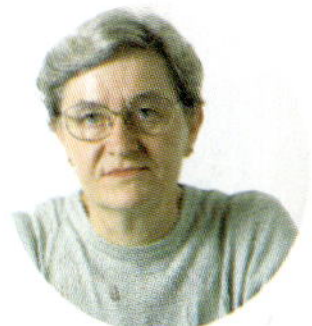

Index

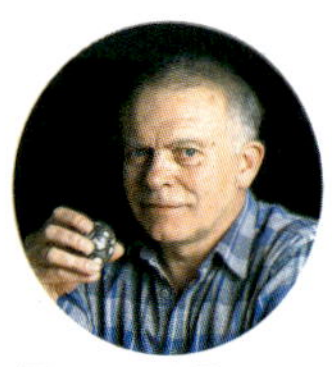

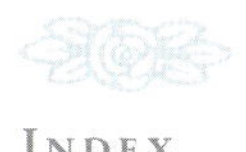

Index

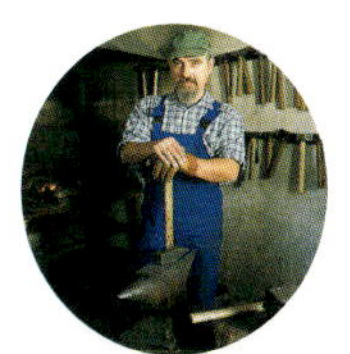

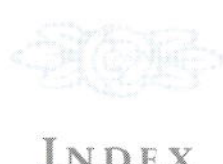

Index

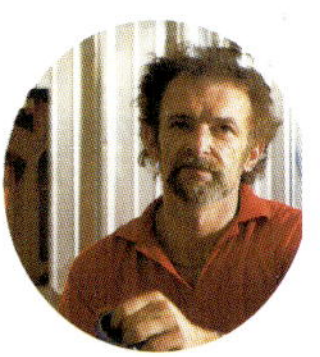

Index

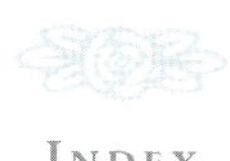

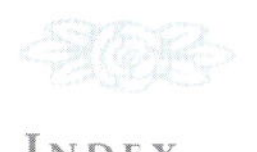

Index

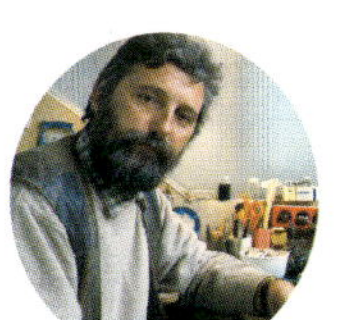

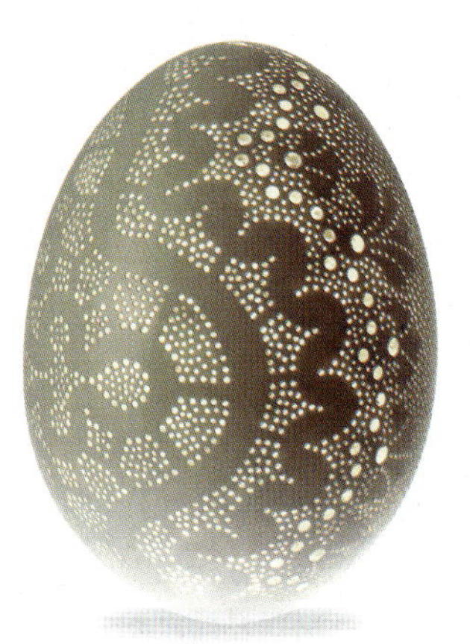